MW00723790

WAS HITLER A RIDDLE?

WAS HITLER A RIDDLE?

Western Democracies and National Socialism

Abraham Ascher

STANFORD UNIVERSITY PRESS
Stanford, California

Stanford University Press
Stanford, California
© 2012 by the Board of Trustees of the
Leland Stanford Junior University

All rights reserved

No part of this book may be reproduced or transmitted in any form or
by any means, electronic or mechanical, including photocopying and
recording, or in any information storage or retrieval system without
the prior written permission of Stanford University Press.

Library of Congress Cataloging-in-Publication Data

Ascher, Abraham, author.
    Was Hitler a riddle? : western democracies and national socialism /
Abraham Ascher.
        pages   cm.
    Includes bibliographical references and index.
    ISBN 978-0-8047-8355-2 (cloth : alk. paper) —
    ISBN 978-0-8047-8356-9 (pbk. : alk. paper)
    1. Hitler, Adolf, 1889–1945—Public opinion.   2. National
socialism—Public opinion.   3. Diplomats—Germany—Attitudes.
4. Germany—Foreign public opinion, Western.   5. Western
countries—Foreign relations—Germany.   6. Germany—Foreign
relations—Western countries.   7. Germany—Foreign relations—1933–
1945.   8. Germany—Politics and government—1933–1945.   I. Title.

DD256.8.A83   2012

943.086092—dc23   2012014297

Printed in the United States of America
on acid-free, archival-quality paper

Typeset at Stanford University Press in 10/13 Galliard

For Anna

Contents

Acknowledgments

In my research for this book, I was fortunate in having had access to the following archives: the National Archives, London, UK; the National Archives, Hyattsville, MD, USA; Churchill Archives, Cambridge, UK; Centre des Archives diplomatiques de Nantes, France. In each of the archives, the staff was at all times helpful in locating documents that were essential for my study and that I could not easily find on my own. I should point out that I focused on archives that contained documents that were widely seen by government officials in London, Paris, and Washington. Personal correspondence between diplomats in Germany and colleagues in the three capitals were of less interest to me because of their limited exposure at the time they were composed. I want to thank Wiley Publishers for permission to quote extensively from my article "Was Hitler a Riddle?," which appeared in *The Journal of the Historical Society*, vol. IX, no. 1 (March 2009): 1–21.

I am grateful to the two outside readers who reviewed the manuscript with great care and made suggestions that improved the study. I also want to thank Guenter Lewy, a close friend for the past sixty years, for his helpful suggestions. Norris Pope, the Director of Scholarly Publications at Stanford University Press, once again gave me excellent advice on the preparation of this book; I especially appreciated his encouragement to write a book-length study after reading my article on Western diplomats in Nazi Germany some years ago. Emma S. Harper and John Feneron, editors at Stanford University Press, could not have been more helpful in handling the many issues that arose during the long process of preparing the manuscript for publication. Janet Mowery's meticulous copyediting of the manuscript significantly improved it and made it more readable.

Finally, I want to thank my wife, Anna S. Ascher, a professional editor, for reading the manuscript and for making many suggestions for its improvement. The remaining shortcomings are of course my responsibility.

WAS HITLER A RIDDLE?

Introduction

On September 27, 1937, just before leaving his post in Berlin for Vienna, the highly regarded journalist William I. Shirer noted with alarm that "there is little understanding of the Third Reich, what it is, what it is up to, where it is going either at home or elsewhere abroad." Shirer granted that the situation in Germany was "complex" and "confusing," but in his view the thrust of Hitler's policies could not be doubted. In *Mein Kampf*, published in two parts in 1925 and 1926, Hitler had "vowed . . . to seek world domination," but not many people in Germany or abroad at all familiar with his ideas took him at his word. Part of the problem was that four years after the Nazi assumption of power there still was "no decent translation" of the work in English or French, which Shirer attributed to Hitler's refusal to permit an accurate rendering of the text because "it would shock many in the West." Neville Chamberlain, a leading figure in the British government who became prime minister in May 1937, about ten months before Germany launched its expansionist program by annexing Austria, had not read *Mein Kampf* and seemed unaware of Hitler's declaration that "Germany will either be a world power, or there will be no Germany." As a result, Chamberlain never understood that Hitler was moved as much by emotion as by rational calculation. Such ignorance of the German leader's intentions and temperament was dangerous, Shirer warned, because the country "is stronger than her enemies realize."[1]

Even statesmen with extensive experience in foreign affairs misunderstood National Socialism and failed to grasp that Hitler posed a menace to world order. Among them, David Lloyd George was the most prominent; for many years a leading member of Parliament devoted to progressive social and political causes, he had served as prime minister from 1916 to 1922. He was known as a friend of Jews, and during World War I he formed a close friendship with Chaim Weizmann, a leading Zionist and lecturer in chemistry at the University of Manchester. In 1917, Lloyd George strongly supported the issuance of the Balfour Declaration, which advocated the "establishment in Palestine of a national home for the Jewish people." Yet after he returned in September 1936 from a short visit to Germany during which he met Hitler, he published an article in the *Daily Press* of November 17, 1936, in which he showered praise on the Führer and his New Order. To be sure, Lloyd George acknowledged that Hitler's methods were "certainly not those of a parliamentary country," but it could not be denied that he and his movement had "made a new Germany." The country was now "full of hope and confidence," the "people are more cheerful," and all this was attributable to Hitler's "magnetic, dynamic personality." The man had accomplished nothing less than a "miracle." Lloyd George also assured his readers that "The idea of a Germany intimidating Europe with a threat that its irresistible army might march across frontiers forms no part of the new vision. . . . The Germans will resist to the death every invader of their own country, but they have no longer the desire themselves to invade any other country." Hitler knew from "personal experience" that war caused dreadful suffering, and hence "The establishment of a German hegemony in Europe which was the aim and dream of the old pre-war militarism, is not even on the horizon of Nazism."[2]

On the other hand, the British journalist Norman Ebbutt, who had spent many years in Germany and was well acquainted with leading officials in the country, including Heinrich Brüning, the chancellor from 1930 to 1932, shared Shirer's concern about Europe's future. On April 21, 1933, he sent a letter to the editor of the *Times of London* warning people in the West not to be misled by Hitler's promise in his speeches to pursue a peaceful foreign policy. The "underlying spirit" of the "new Germany" is "[not] a peaceful one. Germany is inspired by the determination to recover all it has lost and has little hope of doing so by peaceful means. Influential Germans do not see ten years elapsing before the war they regard as natural or inevitable breaks out in Europe. One may hear five or six years mentioned."[3] Ebbutt's warnings did not reach many people. The letter cited here was published, but the editors of the London *Times*, who favored appeasement, did not print many of Ebbutt's other reports from Germany critical of Nazism.

Within the British political class, Winston S. Churchill stood out as the most prominent, perceptive, and persistent Cassandra regarding Nazism.

As early as October 1930, he told Otto Christian Archibald, Prince von Bismarck, a diplomat serving in London, that he had carefully read press reports on political developments in Germany and had concluded that, if Hitler or his followers came to power, they "would seize the first available opportunity to resort to force."[4] Two years later, he argued against proposals for "rapid and comprehensive disarmament" by Britain and other European powers. Sir John Simon, the British foreign minister, believed that this was the only way to avoid war. Churchill, however, warned that "approximation in military strength between Germany and France" would inevitably lead to military conflict. France, with a population only two-thirds the size of Germany's, would be an easy target for its neighbor in central Europe.[5]

And after Hitler assumed power, Churchill delivered a steady stream of well-crafted speeches and published numerous articles urging the British government to rearm and take a strong stand against Hitler's aggressive moves. Invariably penetrating, they all touched on a theme he formulated with special trenchancy on November 5, 1936, in response to a government report on the impossibility of building capital ships that could survive attacks from the air: "There is no greater mistake than to suppose that platitudes, smooth words, and timid policies offer a path to safety. Only by a firm adherence to righteous principles sustained by all the necessary 'instrumentalities,' to use a famous American expression, can the dangers which close so steadily upon us and upon the peace of Europe be warded off and overcome."[6]

Churchill's oratory and premonitions were stirring, but for six years he exerted little influence in Parliament, most of whose members put a premium on keeping Britain out of conflict. Moreover, Churchill was a backbencher; although his colleagues in the Conservative Party and even a fair number of Labourites recognized him as brilliant and a masterful orator, they did not trust his political judgment. Many members of Parliament could not forgive him for having opposed the grant of limited government to India. Nor did his occasional outbursts of vitriolic oratory endear him to his colleagues in the legislature. During one debate, he referred to the "alarming and nauseating" sight of Mohandas Gandhi "striding half-naked up the steps of the Vice-regal palace to parlay on equal terms with the representative of the King-Emperor."[7]

Churchill's opposition in 1936 to the abdication of King Edward VII further isolated him politically. The king's popularity had plunged because he planned to marry a woman who had been twice divorced; neither the

Church of England nor the British public sanctioned such a union. Despite these missteps, on the key issue of the dangers posed by Nazism, Churchill was prophetic. But he was a sullied prophet, and hence his appeal to his countrymen was limited.

Three years after World War II ended, an eminent historian, Sir John Wheeler-Bennett, advanced an argument similar to Shirer's in seeking to account for the failed foreign policies of Great Britain and France in the 1930s. In his scathing criticism of the strategies of the statesmen concerned for having appeased Hitler, Wheeler-Bennett contended that from 1933 to 1939 "all schools of thought in Britain and France" demonstrated a "fundamental ignorance of the German character and a complete inability to comprehend the lengths of evil, dishonesty and deception to which the Nazi mentality could extend. . . . The capacity of the Germans for sheep-like conformity to leadership was not appreciated, nor the fact realized that this new political phenomenon combined all the guile of the old pre-war duplicity of Prussian diplomacy with a new and ruthless deceit of unplumbed depths."[8]

The annoyance of Shirer, Ebbutt, and Wheeler-Bennett with the policymakers of the 1930s and their frustration with the political elite's poor grasp of world affairs are understandable. They wrote at a time when the struggle against Nazism was either unresolved or still fresh in the public consciousness. Newspapers and news magazines carried numerous articles on the Nazi transformation of Germany, but these rarely delved deeply into Hitler's ideology or personality, both critical for understanding the Führer's political success. Moreover, many of the reports by diplomats who had served in Germany were still classified; the information passed on to political leaders was not widely known in the 1930s.

Now that those reports are available, they reveal that the governments in London, Paris, and Washington were well served by their representatives in Germany. Well educated and often fluent in German, the diplomats of the three countries were also diligent; they traveled throughout the country, retained contact with individuals who had been prominent in various political parties, talked frequently with ordinary citizens, and on occasion even discussed public affairs with fairly senior members of the Nazi Party. In the five-year period from 1928 to 1933, the British embassy in Berlin sent the Foreign Office in London no fewer than four hundred reports and telegrams, as well as annual summaries of the staff's findings. The summary for 1932 was especially detailed, running to 718 paragraphs.[9] After Hitler's rise to power, the reports increased in length and number. In addition, the various ambassadors maintained a lively correspondence with officials and friends, in which they frequently touched on political developments in Germany. The French and American embassies in Berlin were no less productive. Moreover, the consulates of the three countries in the major cities of Germany sent extensive reports on local conditions, which in most cases buttressed and deepened the analyses produced in Berlin.

Taken as a whole, the reports and missives drafted by the diplomats of the three leading democracies provided the authorities in London, Paris, and Washington with information and assessments that amounted to an accurate and comprehensive picture of the state of affairs in Germany. The diplomats were not always on the mark in estimating how Nazism would evolve, they occasionally misjudged Hitler's intentions, and at times they were inconsistent in their recommendations on how to respond to Germany's domestic and foreign policies. It could hardly have been otherwise. Hitler and his cohorts created a political movement that was in many ways unprecedented in central Europe, causing much confusion among sophisticated observers of political developments in Germany. It was not uncommon for statesmen to be suspected of deviousness and callousness, but the deceptiveness and ruthlessness of the Nazis reached levels that few thought possible in the twentieth century, and certainly not in a country as enlightened and advanced as Germany.

Most Western diplomats rather quickly overcame their initial bewilderment over the character of Germany's new leadership. Within weeks of the Nazi ascent to power in 1933, they reported on the ways the Nazis were consolidating their position and transforming German society in so much detail and so graphically that senior officials in the three countries had no reason to claim, as they often did, that one could not be sure about the overall policy direction that Hitler was taking or even about the specific policies that his government was implementing. Nevertheless, in the weeks and months immediately after the Nazi accession to power, when the suppression of the opposition and the persecution of Jews proceeded apace, numerous statesmen in the three largest democracies expressed doubts about the durability of these harsh measures. These political leaders were at a loss in trying to make sense of the new regime. In 1934 and 1935, Stanley Baldwin, the British prime minister, described his own puzzlement: "no one knows what the new Germany means—whether she means peace or war."[10] Baldwin was echoing the mood of uncertainty expressed most forcefully by Sir Maurice Hankey, the secretary of the cabinet, in October 1933: "Are we dealing with the Hitler of *Mein Kampf,* lulling his opponents to sleep with fair words in order to gain time to arm his people? . . . Or is it a new Hitler who has discovered the burden of responsible office, and wants to extricate himself, like many an earlier tyrant, from the commitments of his irresponsible days? That is the riddle that has to be solved."[11]

Even years after World War II, Gordon Wright, an insightful historian of modern France, expressed sympathy for statesmen who failed to adopt a firm policy regarding Nazi Germany. In 1960, he wrote that he found it "easy to see how risky and almost irresponsible" it must have "seemed to many" in 1936 to implement a hard line because "clear proof of Hitler's aims was not then available."[12]

The officials as well as large segments of the political class who spoke of Hitler as a riddle were obviously confused by his penchant for contradictory pronouncements. He often vowed to undermine the Treaty of Versailles, whose severe restrictions prevented Germany from regaining its pre-1914 status as a world power, but he almost as frequently declared his opposition to "violence of any kind." He invariably told foreign dignitaries that all problems between nations should be "solved in a reasonable and peaceful manner."[13] In making these comments, Hitler tried to portray himself as a traditional statesman whose only concern was to restore Germany to its rightful place among the nations of the world. It was a deliberate deception that many in the West failed to perceive. On February 3, 1933, the editors of the London *Times*, generally regarded as one of the most sophisticated newspapers in the world, referred to him as a "moderate and decent person." In addition, the editors wrote, "No one doubts Hitler's sincerity. That nearly twelve million Germans voted for him blindly says much for his personal magnetism. . . . But nothing is known so far of his capacity for solid administration and for co-operation with allies or colleagues, which are the real tests for a ruler. And until he proves himself to possess these qualities, it is sheer waste of time to speculate about the future of Germany."[14]

Today, after the horrors of Nazism and World War II, it is difficult to fathom the widespread misunderstanding of Hitler and his movement. But it is much less difficult if we keep in mind the powerful urge to avoid conflict fifteen years after the frightful bloodletting of World War I. Memories of that war were still fresh in the minds of many people in all the belligerents. In some circles, there were also strong feelings of guilt over the imposition of what they considered a harsh and unjust peace treaty on Germany. Even in 1940, months after World War II had begun, Evelyn Wrench, a well-known writer on international affairs and the former editor of *The Spectator*, asserted that "Nazism was the inevitable reaction of the German people to the errors of Versailles."[15]

But there were other reasons for the widespread failure of people in the West to detect the dangers of Nazism. Many among the politically engaged viewed the Führer through ideological blinkers. People on the far left tended to dismiss him as a charlatan, a tool of the capitalists who would be discarded with the collapse of capitalism, which they insisted was imminent. Those on the right tended to believe that Hitler could be controlled by the conservatives in his government, who would soon regain their political preeminence.[16] Many conservatives also viewed the Nazis as an effective counterpoise to Communism.

The diplomats in Germany representing Great Britain, France, and the United States quickly understood the shallowness of these positions. They realized early on that Hitler was a masterful, cunning, and dishonest propagandist, and they insisted that to understand the real thrust of Hitler's policies one would have to do much more than examine his many pronouncements and the decrees he had issued during the first months of his tenure as chancellor. Hitler must also be assessed as a leader: Was he trustworthy? Was he judicious? What was the relationship between his stated goals and his actual aims? In short, the foreign diplomats sought to assess Hitler's character in the broadest possible context.

In this book, special attention is paid to the diplomats' descriptions and assessments of Hitler's personal traits, although his policies and beliefs are by no means given short shrift. After all, by 1933, if not before, he was undoubtedly the preeminent figure in the Nazi Party. Indeed, he had become a cult figure whose judgments and policies were declared by party leaders to be sacrosanct. True, some senior officials were known to differ with him on certain issues and some were even rumored to have challenged his authority, but within a year and a half of his assumption of power Hitler had clearly crushed his potential rivals. His subsequent foreign policy successes, such as the occupation of the Rhineland in 1936 and the annexation of Austria in 1938, further strengthened his personal control. No major political initiatives could be undertaken in Germany without his approval, and much of the time he himself had suggested them. For statesmen who had to respond to his unexpected moves in foreign affairs, a correct evaluation of his state of mind was therefore essential.

Unlike Stalin, Hitler was not a reclusive leader. On the contrary, he enjoyed meeting foreign diplomats and dignitaries, in part because he had confidence in his powers of persuasion, but also because he relished putting on a show for foreigners, whom he generally considered his intellectual inferiors. Whatever the reason, he often met with dignitaries. He had at least twelve such encounters with prominent Britons, including several leading appeasers (Lord Halifax, Nevile Henderson, Lord Londonderry, and Lord Lothian), and with Mackenzie King of Canada.* The latter meetings are interesting not so much for the light they shed on policy issues as for the political insights of the appeasers. The appeasers objected to any firm measures to rein in Hitler, and yet their comments about him were often distinctly unflattering, sometimes not very different from those of diplomats who despised the dictator and urged condemnation of his repressive policies within Germany as well as strong measures to resist his foreign policy moves. Unintentionally, the appeasers occasionally provided information about Nazi leaders that tended to buttress the judgments of their opponents.

I should note here that in the section on British assessments of Nazism I have taken the liberty of defining *diplomat* more broadly than is common. I include in this category several influential "private envoys" who traveled to Germany to meet Hitler and some of his leading subordinates in order to evaluate for themselves the state of affairs in the country. Most of these private envoys did not trust the reports emanating from Berlin and other German cities, and as soon as they returned to Britain they drafted long accounts of their impressions, which they often sent directly to Prime Minister Chamberlain and occasionally to other highly placed officials, so that in a sense they did the work of diplomats. They invariably belonged to the school of appeasement, and their activities are a significant part of the story presented in this book.

The French ambassador, André François-Poncet, saw Hitler more often than any other foreign diplomat, and his reactions to the Führer are both fascinating and puzzling. François-Poncet voiced many sharp and incisive criticisms of Nazi policies and of the dictator. He was especially forceful in pointing out that Hitler was not simply a political leader but a cult figure who commanded the unquestioning devotion of millions of Germans. Yet at times he was surprisingly reticent about Hitler's personality and views. Until 1937, François-Poncet was also one of the most persistent advocates among the Western diplomats of attempts to reach agreements with Hitler.

*I do not discuss the views of outright supporters or advocates of Nazism such as Lord Rothermere and Oswald Mosley because their views had little resonance in senior circles of the British government. Nor do I include detailed considerations of the assessments of people who were ardent pacifists (such as George Lansbury) because they, too, did not seriously influence senior government officials. I include a brief discussion of King's position because he had contact with Prime Minister Neville Chamberlain. On Lansbury, see also below, p. 202.

Even now, after all his official papers have been made public, he is something of an enigma.

American diplomats saw Hitler much less frequently than their English and French colleagues, in large part because William E. Dodd, ambassador from 1933 to 1938, could not bear to be in his presence. Nevertheless, their reports, based on wide reading of the German press and discussions with German citizens from all strata of the population, contain valuable information on the domestic scene in Germany and show an acute understanding of Hitler's conduct of affairs.

Various scholars have challenged the usefulness of the judgments of the diplomats who reported from Germany during the Hitler period. Their principal criticism has been that the dispatches from Germany were not consistent; even those diplomats who early on recognized the dangers of Hitler's foreign policy often hedged their dire predictions of the likely consequences of Nazi behavior. To be sure, the most obdurate critics of Hitler occasionally conceded that they might be wrong in predicting disaster for Europe. The Führer might turn out to be more reasonable and pragmatic than his pronouncements suggested. The leadership of the Nazi Party, the diplomats frequently noted, was divided on major issues, and it was not clear which faction would ultimately prevail. Also, it seemed possible that the German people would not tolerate the extremist policies proposed by the Nazis and would take it upon themselves to overturn the government. These inconsistencies, in the view of some scholars, gave license for statesmen, especially in London and Paris, to adopt a hands-off approach toward Nazi Germany.[17]

The argument is not convincing. Diplomats are trained to be cautious and to express their conclusions undogmatically, and thus to allow for the possibility that their assessments may be faulty. Diplomats in Nazi Germany must have been especially prone to this approach, for they were required to describe and analyze totally unexpected and unprecedented events. In the decades before the Nazis' rise to power, no one thought that Germany, in many respects the most cultivated country in Europe, would be turned into one of the most ruthless dictatorships in history. If the diplomats occasionally faltered in their analyses and forecasts, it was up to their superiors in government to read their dispatches and draw their own conclusions. Although the reports of senior diplomats in Germany during the 1930s were not always consistent, a careful reading of them all indicates quite clearly the direction of their thinking. The diplomats who believed that Nazism was evil and dangerous and should be resisted made this point frequently and forcefully, despite also making occasional concessions to the arguments of those who disagreed with them. Similarly, the appeasers leave no doubt in the reader's mind about the thrust of their arguments, even though they granted that Hitler was not committed to democratic and humane values.

In any case, the primary task of diplomats serving abroad is not to formulate national policy, although they are expected to make recommendations. Their main function is to report as fully as possible on conditions in the countries to which they are assigned, and those who represented the leading Western powers in Germany in the 1930s performed that task remarkably well. They touched on every conceivable aspect of Nazi rule: the ideology of Hitlerism, the primacy attached to racial doctrine, the persecution of political opponents and Jews, the economic policies of the rulers, the Nazis' conflict with the Catholic and Protestant Churches, the reorganization of the country's educational system, the stress on rearmament, and the regime's long-range aims in foreign affairs. Much of the information on the rapid and illegal enlargement of Germany's military forces came from intelligence officers attached to the embassies, and it corroborated the data collected by other intelligence agents. Peter Jackson, a historian of French intelligence, concluded in 1998: "A look at the archival record reveals that French soldiers and statesmen were better informed about the danger of the Nazi menace than has hitherto been assumed."[18] This statement parallels my own findings about the reports of diplomats. Government officials in London, Paris, and Washington had ample information to guide them in devising policies with respect to Germany, but invariably that was not the decisive factor for them. Ideological preconceptions, domestic considerations, and plain poor judgment proved to be more crucial than all of the informative and at times erudite dispatches drafted by conscientious diplomats in Germany.

There are several reasons for my focus on Great Britain, France, and the United States. They were all democracies whose leaders could be expected to be appalled by the destruction of constitutionalism in Germany; and militarily they were the only ones in a position to rein in Hitler. Moreover, they had all fought against Germany in World War I and therefore had a special stake in trying to prevent a recurrence of military conflict. These considerations were not lost on "many" people in Germany who, even as late as December 1938, pinned their "faith" on the "democracies, particularly England, and hope[d] that British rearmament will be carried out with sufficient speed and determination, if not to upset Hitler, at least to deter him from the most dangerous excesses."

But George Ogilvie-Forbes, the British counselor and chargé d'affaires in Berlin, who wrote those words in a report to the foreign minister, Lord Halifax, added that those who hoped that the democracies would act decisively did so "without much conviction."[19]

I begin my study with Great Britain because it was still the predominant world power and most people who followed international affairs—particularly in France—believed that only Britain could take the lead in restraining Nazi Germany. The British political class was clearly aware of this, and their representatives abroad produced an especially large quantity of thoughtful commentary on Nazism. But the French and American diplomats did not lag far behind.

I turn next to a consideration of the French diplomats, whose country had suffered the most during World War I and who therefore had reason to be especially fearful of a Germany bent on expansion. Not surprisingly, the French government appointed as its ambassador to Berlin a man well versed in German culture and politics. François-Poncet was also a man of extraordinary energy and strong opinions, and his dispatches received far more attention in Paris than those of the French consuls in local areas of Germany. More than any other ambassador from major countries, he regularly provided his government with specific recommendations on how to deal with the Nazi regime. He saw himself not simply as an analyst of events but as a formulator and advocate of policies. The section on France is therefore devoted largely to his reports.

Finally, I turn to the American diplomats, whose task was in some ways the most challenging. The United States shared the democratic values of Great Britain and France, but it did not seem to have the same national interests as the other two. The American people widely believed that their country, far removed from Europe and therefore unaffected by developments there, should remain aloof from the unending squabbles of the Continent. In the end, of course, aloofness proved to be impossible, buttressing the argument of the few American political leaders who urged greater involvement in European affairs even in the 1920s and 1930s.

Inevitably, there is overlap in the dispatches of the three foreign contingents. After all, they were reacting to the same events, the Nazi ascent to power and Hitler's transformation of Germany from a democracy to a dictatorship that vested unprecedented power in the hands of the political leadership. I have tried to minimize repetition by focusing wherever possible on the unique character of the reporting of each group of diplomats. Thus, on the Nazi murder on June 30, 1934, of dozens of people suspected of planning to challenge Hitler's authority, I devote more space to the French reporting than to that of the other foreign diplomats because François-Poncet, for reasons that will become evident, dealt with this subject more extensively than his colleagues. I discuss in each section of this study the Nazi campaign against the Jews because it demonstrated early on the barbarism of Hitler's regime. The diplomats of all three countries deplored the persecution of the Jews, but the British and even more so the American officials followed the subject with special care and devoted many dispatches to detailed descriptions of the pain inflicted on that minority. The different emphases on this issue can no doubt be attributed in part to the size and political influence of the Jewish communities in the three countries. On the persistent conflict between the Nazi regime and the Evangelical and Catholic Churches, I have discussed only the reports of the Americans because their dispatches struck me as the most systematic. However, readers should note that all three embassies treated this important subject in considerable detail.

Despite the different emphases of the three groups of diplomats in their assessments of Nazism, it should not be assumed that their approaches contradicted each other in any fundamental way prior to 1937, when the British ambassador swung sharply toward appeasement of Germany. On the contrary, they complemented one another; each group provided as trenchant a picture of National Socialism as one could expect from firsthand accounts. The British tended to focus on the ideology of Nazism and the personality of Hitler. The French stressed specific events, such as the murder of prominent Nazis and conservatives in June 1934 and the steady buildup of Germany's military power, understandably viewed as a serious threat to France, which had been subjected in the nineteenth and early twentieth centuries to three invasions from central Europe. Finally, the Americans devoted many of their assessments to the emergence in Germany of a new form of government, which they characterized as "total" or "totalitarian." Officials from the three democracies often shared information, giving them further insights into the nature of National Socialism. The fact that the diplomats of all three Western countries touched on the same issues demonstrates the degree to which they agreed on the essentials of Nazism. They recognized that their nations faced not only a military threat but also a challenge to their most basic social, political, and moral values.

Although the sources for this study are mainly diplomatic dispatches and other writings by diplomats, this is not a work of diplomatic history of the 1930s in the traditional sense, a subject that has been covered very well by several distinguished historians.[20] Nor have I attempted to write a comprehensive history of National Socialism in power or even a full account of the events that I touch upon. At various points in the book, I consider specific diplomatic negotiations or domestic developments, but I do so only to clarify certain issues. My study is essentially one of perceptions. My aim is to elucidate how the diplomats of the three most important democracies who were stationed in Germany in the 1930s understood the new political and social order that was being established by Hitler and his followers. Did the emissaries convey an accurate picture to their superiors in London, Paris, and Washington of what they observed in Germany? Did they offer a sound and convincing answer to the question that lies at the heart of this study: Was Hitler a riddle, as so many prominent people in the 1930s believed? And if they did provide such an answer, how can we explain the failure of the three governments to take appropriate measures to stem the aggressiveness of Nazism? It is a question that still haunts historians.

CHAPTER ONE

The British Diplomats

When Sir Horace Rumbold arrived in Berlin in August 1928 to begin his tenure as British ambassador, he had every reason to expect a calm and uneventful period of service. True, during its first few years, the Weimar Republic, established in 1919 shortly after Germany's defeat in World War I, experienced almost constant political instability, in large measure the consequence of deep disappointment in the unexpected military defeat, the imposition by the victorious Allies of huge reparations as well as territorial losses in the eastern and western parts of the country, and finally, the economic stagnation followed by hyperinflation. In addition, the Allies had placed stringent restrictions on the size of the country's military, which prevented Germany from regaining its pre-1914 status as a major world power. Several of the most prominent institutions—the army, the civil service, the judiciary, and the educational system—remained in the hands of individuals who despised the new political order. That right-wingers were implacable foes of the "Weimar System," as they called it, became evident in 1920 when some of them attempted to overthrow the constitutional order; for a few days it seemed as though they might succeed. Further evidence of the country's political instability is that during the first nine years of the republic's existence no fewer than nine chancellors (prime ministers) held that office. But by 1928, stability and prosperity seemed to be within reach. Germany's economy had rebounded; the sage foreign minister, Gustav Stresemann, appeared to be on the way to securing significant concessions, financial and territorial, from the Western powers; and the political discourse was much less passionate than it had been in some time. There was reason to be optimistic about the country's future.

In many respects, Rumbold was well prepared for the post in Berlin. Born in 1869 in St. Petersburg to an upper-class family—his father was also a diplomat, as were his ancestors for over three hundred years—Horace had received a first-rate education at Eton, and during his thirty-nine years in the diplomatic corps he mastered seven foreign languages, including German, and had some familiarity with German society and politics, having served at the consulate in Munich in 1909 and at the embassy in Berlin in 1913 and 1914. Rumbold was essentially a political conservative and shared many of the prejudices of the German elite, but he was not a zealot. In Great Britain, he maintained good relations with a number of Labourites and frequently engaged in friendly conversations with people he disagreed with. But, like his father, Horace did not take kindly to people different from those in his social circle. In 1904, he wrote his father that he did not want to meet a friend of his stepbrother because "I hate Jews." On his arrival in Berlin, he was "quite happy" except for one drawback. "The only fly in the ointment," he wrote a friend, "is the number of Jews in the place. One cannot get away from them," a comment that illustrates the depth of his prejudice. Although Berlin counted more Jews than any other German city, they still made up only 4 percent of the population. Rumbold also did not like blacks, and once told the conductor of a train he was taking that he would not "share a compartment with a black gentleman." He tipped the conductor "handsomely" to secure a "compartment to myself." During his two years of service in Madrid (1907–8) he developed a dislike for Spaniards, who, he believed, were "vain, full of pride, untruthful, dirty and inclined to idleness." He also disparaged Persians, Japanese, and the French. Rumbold simply did not like anyone who was not British as he defined the word.[1]

Rumbold's attitude toward Germany and its citizens was mixed, although his negative impressions far outweighed the positive ones. He respected the Germans for their strength of character and resilience, but also considered them to be a belligerent and fickle people solely responsible for the outbreak of hostilities in 1914. In fact, he was convinced that Germans had a natural propensity for brutality, a trait he believed to be alien to Englishmen.[2] Nevertheless, in the early 1930s he did not oppose German expansion in the east to redress grievances generated by what were widely regarded as the harsh conditions imposed by the Treaty of Versailles.[3] All in all, the British government could not have chosen a better person for the post of ambassador in Berlin. He was not viscerally hostile to Germany, and in view of his age, the assignment to Germany was likely to be his last, which would make it easier for him to voice his views candidly, without fear of retribution by senior officials in the Foreign Office who might not appreciate his strong opinions. Certainly some of his most notable dispatches after January 30, 1933, did not mince words.

For the first two years of his stay in Berlin, Rumbold largely ignored Hitler and the Nazi movement. His predecessors had paid some attention to the political upstart as early as 1920, soon after he made his appearance on the political scene, but with few exceptions, their assessments were not strikingly profound. They recognized that Hitler was a central figure in the National Socialist movement and thought of him as a "bulwark against Communism," which had come to power in Russia and was much feared in British political circles. There was one exception to these mundane comments, a perceptive dispatch by the British consul in Munich, Robert T. Smallbones, a name that will appear again in this study. In a short, incisive dispatch of September 28, 1920, Smallbones noted that the leaders of the National Socialist Party, Adolf Hitler and Anton Drexler, were effective organizers committed to three central ideas: anti-Semitism, the use of force in furthering political goals, and the merging of socialism and nationalism. Smallbones surmised that the new party was funded by a circle of industrialists close to Hugo Stinnes, a wealthy entrepreneur with pronounced right-wing views. Astutely, Smallbones predicted that the industrialists would not have to fear Hitler's talk of socialism because the central idea of his movement was nationalism.[4]

Toward the end of 1922, other British diplomats in Germany had collected many details about Hitler, but these did not add up to a coherent evaluation of his potential as a leader. After November 1922, they often referred to him as the "Bavarian Mussolini," an incorrect designation that did not reveal much about the man. None of these assessments was based on personal contact; apparently, throughout the 1920s no British diplomat stationed in Berlin or Munich had made any effort to speak to Hitler.[5] In truth, there was no reason at that time to devote much time or thought to him; he was not expected to rise to the heights of political power.

Only in 1930, when Hitler had demonstrated his ability to gain mass support for his program—in a national election his vote jumped from 2.6 percent to 18.3 percent of the total, and his party secured 107 out of 577 Reichstag representatives—did Rumbold pay serious attention to Nazism, but he showed little understanding of Germany's dire political condition following the catastrophic depression that had hit the country in 1929, or of the nature of Nazism. In 1931, he was certain that the country would not "fail to master its difficulties." After the presidential election of April

1932, in which Hitler received 36.3 percent of the vote, Rumbold reported to Sir John Simon, the British secretary of foreign affairs, that some people believed Hitler had "exhausted his reserves" and would not "go any higher," a judgment the ambassador did not contest.[6] Early in August 1932, when Franz von Papen was trying to cobble together a majority to form a government, Rumbold viewed the Nazis as a political party that could be expected to act pragmatically, and he went so far as to refer to Hitler as a "visionary, but quite a decent sort of man."[7] Papen's aim was to "draw the teeth of the [Nazi] movement by saddling the National Socialists with a certain amount of responsibility." The Nazis would then have to "come into the open and no longer shelter themselves behind a nebulous programme." Rumbold thought that Hitler and his supporters were in a tight spot and would have to make some hard decisions. "It would appear that they have shot their bolt and have exhausted the reservoir from which they drew many of their adherents, and yet have failed to obtain an absolute majority in the Reichstag. Their storm troops will soon begin to ask themselves what their marchings and their 'Alarmbereitschaft' (being on the alert) are leading to. In other words, the time is fast approaching when Hitler will be expected to deliver the goods. He cannot indefinitely play the role of a revivalist preacher and yet even if he consents to the inclusion of one or two members of his party in the Government he will be unable to fulfil his promises to the electorate."[8] In December 1932, a month before Hitler's appointment as chancellor, Rumbold spoke of Nazism as similar to other political movements and described Hitler's camp as one of the "three great parties of the Left."[9]

Rumbold clung to his view of the Nazis' poor chances of gaining power until the very moment that Hitler received the call to assume the office of chancellor. On January 16, 1933, the ambassador informed Secretary Simon that the Nazis were in serious financial straits and implied that this would hinder their political work. Erwin Planck, who served in the important post of secretary of state under the last two chancellors before Hitler, had told Rumbold that the Nazis were so desperate that several of them had appeared at a recent funeral and "had not scrupled to rattle their money-boxes in the immediate neighbourhood of the grave, thereby disgusting all the persons present."[10]

Yet there is evidence to suggest that by this time Rumbold had some inkling that many of the Nazi leaders were unscrupulous and dangerous. In June 1932, he had referred to Joseph Goebbels, one of the more repulsive leaders of the Nazi movement, in the following words: "He may be classed as a vulgar, unscrupulous and irresponsible demagogue and his success is in direct relation to the ignorance and lack of critical faculty of his audience."[11] At the same time, in his missives to the foreign secretary, Rumbold stressed the Nazi penchant for violence, although he also noted that the Communists were responsible for even more violence. But he emphasized that the attacks against Jews in various parts of Prussia outside Berlin were the work of Hitler's followers. In East Prussia, a stronghold of the Nazis, they had perpetrated some of the "most disgraceful outrages." "The windows of shops owned by Jews were smashed and their contents looted." The Nazis also firebombed the offices of the "democratic newspapers." During the first ten days of August 1932, shootings, stabbings, and arson by means of "high explosives" had occurred "in almost every part of Germany."[12]

By this time, some officials in London had begun to view developments in Germany with alarm. On November 26, 1931, the Foreign Office submitted a "Report to Cabinet" that now reads like a prophecy in calling attention to the enormous impact on world history of a Nazi ascent to power. The section on Germany, if not the whole document, was almost certainly drafted by Sir Robert Vansittart, the permanent undersecretary of the Foreign Office, who had a special interest in that country, which he believed was intrinsically drawn to militarism. He became the most vigorous spokesman among foreign policy professionals for a firm stand to keep Nazi Germany in check. The first sentence of the German section warned, "People in this country seem to be unaware of the extent to which the future of 'civilisation' depends on what happens in Germany in the course of the next six months and of the grave doubt as to whether the upshot will be peace or war, recovery or collapse."[13]

One of the more interesting reports on conditions in Germany in the immediate pre-Nazi period was drafted by Malcolm Grahame Christie, who had a second career as a diplomat after a successful stint in the Royal Flying Corps in World War I, during which he attained the rank of group-captain. After his discharge, he became an intelligence officer in the Foreign Office and served as air attaché in Berlin from 1927 until 1930. For reasons of health, he retired in 1930 but continued to visit Germany and other central European countries to gather information for reports he then submitted to the Foreign Office. He was fluent in German and had cultivated valuable contacts in industry, finance, diplomacy, and the Nazi Party itself. After 1934, he wrote reports for Vansittart.

In his report of May 20, 1932, which Christie called his "impressions," he clearly grasped the mood in Germany that had enabled the sudden growth of the Nazi Party, although he also showed a lack of understanding of the inner workings of the movement. He noted that Hitler had succeeded in gaining the support of a "heterogeneous swarm of malcontents" who were disgruntled and had been demoralized by the misfortunes that had befallen Germany. The people were "rudderless," and "in a bewildered fashion" they seek "to find scapegoats" for their "troubles and leadership" to guide them out of their predicament. Many people had concluded that "Adolf Hitler will satisfy and fulfil both these cravings." Christie warned that the German people were deluding themselves, for Hitler was neither a statesman nor an idealist. "I can only see a rather vain and vacillating demagogue, one whose original healthy ideals have become befogged in the intoxication of super-ability to sway the masses: where many detect a prima donna I can easily discover a soubrette." The Nazi leader was a "vastly ambitious opportun-ist" who knew how to organize a mass movement. He was also skilled at finding helpless scapegoats, the Jews and the Marxists, and at rousing the passions of the masses against them, as well as against the injustices of the peace treaty. If Hitler succeeded in attaining power, Christie predicted, he would never become a "great statesman"; in fact, Christie did not think that he would remain in power for very long because—and here he grossly misjudged Hitler's views and role in the movement—the Nazi leader was "for all intents and purposes a Constitutional Monarch within the Party," which was controlled by a "small camarilla." Christie also thought that Hit-ler would adopt a "wait and see" strategy rather than initiate a putsch to secure power. But he warned that the "growing impoverishment of the masses" and their "gullibility" could sway many to vote for Hitler and thus bring him to power. Still, he was confident that since Hitler would not evolve into a "strong statesman" he would soon be "swept aside." Christie was uncertain about who would succeed him. He did not think that the Communists would take over. More likely, the masses would "rally round a 'volkstümlich'" ("national" or "popular") person such as Dr. Otto Strasser, also a Nazi, who was more radical on economic and social issues but more restrained on racial matters.[14]

Of course, in 1932 no one could predict Germany's political future. Even a man as perspicacious and rational as Horace Rumbold was so baffled that he considered it important to report on certain occult prognostications. On February 17, 1932, he sent a "confidential" message to Secretary Simon that contained the following information: "Incidentally, I know for a fact that Hitler recently consulted a fortune-teller and was informed that he had no future."[15]

Conditions were so fluid and precarious that very many people were unable to make reasoned decisions about their country's future. The "golden years of the republic," which began in 1924 and were marked by economic recovery and relative political stability, ended with the devastating depression of 1929. Early in 1933, close to 7.5 million people, about one-third of the workforce, were unemployed. In addition, the country was now "full of private armies" and political violence was a regular occurrence, mostly involving street fights between Nazis and Communists. During the last two weeks of June 1932, seventeen people lost their lives in politically motivated clashes, and in July the number rose to eighty-six. Hundreds of citizens were wounded. The government did little to stem the violence, and to many Germans it seemed that the country was undergoing a breakdown of authority and that it faced a slide into anarchy.[16]

There were other signs of the republic's fragility. In the elections to the Reichstag on July 31, 1932, the National Socialists became the largest party in the legislature, having captured 230 out of 608 seats and 37.2 percent of the vote. The Nationalists were supported by 6.1 percent, which meant that 43.3 percent now favored right-wing parties hostile to the republic. The moderate and liberal parties were almost wiped out, and the Social Democrats, the one major party still committed to democracy, received only 21.6 percent of the vote. The Communists, who rejected "bourgeois democracy," gained 14.3 percent of the vote, which indicated that only about 43 percent of the electorate supported the constitutional order established in 1919. In a new election in November 1932 the Nazis declined to 33.1 percent, but the Nationalists' support rose to 8.3 percent, which gave the right wing a total of 41.4 percent, still not a majority.

Their strength, however, was sufficient to persuade the aged President Paul von Hindenburg—then eighty-five-years old and no longer fully in control of his faculties—to succumb to the endless intrigues of his advisers in favor of Hitler's appointment as chancellor. Hindenburg was not enamored of Hitler, whom he considered to be an uncultivated upstart, a "Bohemian corporal" who could not resist delivering long monologues. But the reigning assumption in the Presidential Palace was that in a coalition government consisting of nine conservatives and three National Socialists, the former would be able to rein in the latter. Better to tame the Nazis by bringing them into the political system than to let them cause national havoc as an opposition movement without any responsibility for their actions.[17]

Christie and some other British diplomats knew that the Weimar political system was no longer functioning, that intriguers in the Presidential

Palace were making the most important decisions for Germany. But none of them fully grasped the sources and extent of the power wielded by Hitler within the National Socialist Party, or his fanaticism, which is why very few within the diplomatic corps or among political commentators foresaw that once he came to power he would be able to crush the opposition with astonishing speed and fundamentally reorder German society within a matter of months. Christie and a few of his colleagues suspected that Hitler would not honor the rule of law and that he would adopt radical policies, but they did not envision an upheaval that would turn Germany upside down.

A brief survey of the principal changes that Hitler and his party introduced in the period from March to May 1933 will suffice to indicate the radicalism and scope of Nazi policies as well as the speed with which they were enforced. On March 23, the Reichstag passed the Enabling Act, which authorized the cabinet to enact laws for four years without any participation by the legislature. As the dominant figure in the cabinet, Hitler was now in effect the dictator of Germany, and he used his power freely. He directed Hermann Göring, a man not known to respect the civil rights of citizens, to take control of the Prussian police. Göring immediately proceeded to purge the force of unreliable elements. He also ordered them to collaborate with the SA and the SS* in putting down the political left, "if necessary by resort to the unconditional use of weapons." Göring made a point of promising to protect policemen if they were charged with the excessive use of force. In fact, the police were told that when they were in doubt about how to deal with Communists, they should not hesitate to use their weapons; otherwise they would be subject to "disciplinary punishment."

The Gauleiters—who served as provincial or regional governors—were given increasing power to run local affairs. The Communist and Social Democratic Parties were outlawed, and many of their members, as well as others considered opponents of the regime, were incarcerated in the

---

*The SA (Sturmabteilung), also known as Brownshirts, was established in 1921 to protect Nazi meetings, but they were most active in street battles against leftists; they also intimidated voters during elections and frequently attacked Jews. By 1932, SA membership had risen to 400,000 and to perhaps 2.5 million in 1933. The SS (Schutzstaffel or Protections Squad, also known as Blackshirts for their uniforms) was founded by Hitler in 1925, to whom its members always remained answerable and whose protection was their initial task. The SS was an elite group within the Nazi movement that insisted on the most rigorous standards of racial purity before accepting anyone into its ranks. By 1933, it had grown to 50,000 and by 1939 to about 250,000. It was headed by the notorious Heinrich Himmler and supervised the enforcement of Nazi racial policies; administered the concentration camps; and played a major role in the murder of Jews, Gypsies, and many others the Nazis considered undesirable for one reason or another. The Gestapo was one of its subdivisions.

seventy concentration camps established in various localities. Trade unions were dissolved and absorbed by the Nazi Labor Front. In mid-March the government unleashed a press campaign against Jews in the legal and medical professions, a predecessor to the decree of April 11, which stipulated that except for veterans and their relatives, Jews were to be excluded from the practice of the law. At about the same time, the various physicians' associations were placed under Nazi control and Jews were removed from all committees. Soon thereafter, the government ordered hospitals not to grant access to Jewish doctors. Another decree, known as the Law for the Reestablishment of the Professional Civil Service, stipulated that all "non-Aryans"—defined as anyone with one non-Aryan grandparent—were to vacate their government positions immediately. The law exempted only those who had entered the civil service before World War I, were veterans of that war, or whose sons had died in the conflict. Early in May, the law was extended to non-Aryan judges and teachers at gymnasiums (high schools) and universities. It has been estimated that about two thousand people with the academic training required for civil service employment and seven hundred teachers at the secondary and university levels lost their jobs.[18]

The most dramatic and in some ways the most frightening anti-Jewish action in the early period of Nazi rule was the boycott of April 1. The idea of a boycott of Jewish businesses was not new. During the late 1920s a movement had sprung up among right-wing circles that called for such action for the specific purpose of eliminating Jewish businesses. Then, immediately after the elections of March 5, 1933, in which the Nazis substantially increased their Reichstag representation, the campaign was revived, setting April 1 as the date for the nationwide boycott. The ostensible reason for the action was that Jews abroad were conducting an anti-German campaign by accusing the new government of atrocities against them. Hitler himself denounced the "atrocity campaign" and issued the following warning: "Jewry must realize that a Jewish war against Germany would have a severe effect on Jewry itself in Germany."

Overall, the boycott was not a great success, although Nazis stationed outside Jewish stores did their best to persuade Germans not to enter. The Nazis generally obeyed orders to eschew violence and confined themselves to parading with placards that featured the words "Germans, don't buy from Jews." A sizable number of people throughout the country ignored the appeals and did their shopping as usual. Recognizing the limited popularity of the boycott, the Nazis called it off during the night of April 1 without, however, issuing an official statement to that effect. Nevertheless, it would be a mistake to minimize the boycott's significance. For one thing, a fair number of Christian businessmen dismissed their Jewish employees for fear that they would otherwise lose customers. More important, April 1 marked a turning point for German Jews, as it was now beyond any doubt that the government had made anti-Jewish policies an essential part of its program. For the Nazi leadership, the boycott was a success because, as Avraham Barkai noted, "It set the stage for tightening the screw of economic discrimination and the ousting of the Jews from the economy."[19]

RUMBOLD'S REAPPRAISAL OF NAZISM

Rumbold followed these developments with growing alarm, prompting him to reappraise his views of Hitler, his ideology, and the entire Nazi movement. He now adopted a far sharper and more critical tone in speaking of the Nazis. In the first few days after Hitler's rise to power, he still put credence in the encouraging remarks of Konstantin Freiherr von Neurath, the foreign minister. On February 4, 1933, Rumbold informed Foreign Secretary Simon that Neurath's impressions of Hitler after several cabinet meetings "were not unfavorable." The new chancellor had been "reasonable" at those meetings and on several issues had actually voted against his two Nazi colleagues. He had also asked Neurath and Johann Ludwig Graf Schwerin von Krosigk (the minister of finance) for advice on some matters.[20] But three days later, the ambassador indicated to Simon that he doubted Vice Chancellor Papen's claim that he had succeeded in persuading Hitler "to drop his claim to exclusive power" and to "cease aping Mussolini." According to Papen, Hitler had agreed that he would act as the leader of "a political party [that was] like any other." Rumbold thought that Papen was deluding himself into believing that he could "harness" the Nazi movement "to the Chariot of the Right." In fact, considerable evidence already suggested that Hitler intended to run the country on his own without much concern for the desires of other parties. He had dismissed many officials in the Prussian civil service and replaced them with loyal Nazis. Also, the government had resorted to "unscrupulous propaganda methods."[21]

Only a few days later, Rumbold described a mass meeting in the Sportspalast in Berlin, held on February 10. In a speech greeted with "immense enthusiasm," Hitler denounced the Versailles Treaty, the Jews, and especially the Jewish press; called for the destruction of Marxism; and vowed to restore national unity. His most ominous statement touched on his own political future if the Nazis did not receive a majority in the upcoming elections on March 5 for a new Reichstag. "If the German people abandon us in this hour," he declared, "then—Heaven forgive us—we will follow the road which we feel to be necessary in order that Germany may not perish." One day after the meeting, Alfred Hugenberg, a right-wing politician who served as the minister of commerce in Hitler's government, made a similar statement about retaining power regardless of the election returns.[22] On February 22, Rumbold reported that it was widely believed that the elections of March 5 would be the last and that "the doom of popular representation has now been sealed."[23]

Rumbold was especially troubled by the growing lawlessness throughout the country, for which he blamed the speeches of Nazi leaders, which in most civilized countries would be "regarded as deliberate incitements to violence." Recently, the government had also put its stamp of approval on political murder by staging an elaborate state funeral for the "Nazi gangster" Hans Eberhard Maikowski, who had murdered a Communist in December 1931 and was then himself killed in a street fight with Communists on January 30, 1933.[24]

Despite his antipathy toward Jews, Rumbold was appalled by Nazi actions against them. He looked down on Jews and wanted to avoid all contact with them, but he did not favor their persecution—his prejudice might be called "benign anti-Semitism." The Nazi government's assault, legal as well as physical, on the Jewish community, was quite another matter. He pointed out that in recent weeks there had been "kidnappings, floggings and other visitations," and most of these attacks had been carried out by men "who wore the Nazi uniform." Many of the incidents were not even reported in the press, and victims often remained silent "because they knew that they have no means of obtaining legal redress." Rumbold considered it necessary to dwell on this aspect of the new government's conduct because "foreign opinion does not appear to have fully grasped the fact that the National Socialist programme is intensely anti-Jewish." He stressed that the measures against the Jews were not "directed against the Hebrew faith" but were designed to achieve certain racial goals. For Hitler, the Jews were "parasites of alien race" and he considered it necessary to purify the "German blood . . . from this contamination." Rumbold predicted at this early stage of Nazi rule that the authorities were likely to intensify this persecution, for "it is certainly Hitler's intention to degrade and, if possible, expel the Jewish community from Germany ultimately."[25]

The ambassador followed all these events with great care, but he also went to the trouble of attentively reading *Mein Kampf*, a book whose principles, he concluded, accurately reflected Hitler's policies and ultimate goals. On April 21, he indicated, in a confidential letter to Secretary Simon, that he was now pessimistic about Germany's future. He had been secretly shown a letter by Dr. Fritz Klein, the editor of the *Deutsche Allgemeine Zeitung*, one of the few newspapers that still maintained "a semblance of independence." Klein maintained close contact with Papen and was generally regarded as an astute observer of the political scene. He thought that Nazism might evolve into a "more moderate," though "certainly . . . rather radical," movement that might be "supportable." But he considered it "more probable" that the movement "will become more and more extreme until it becomes unbearable," which could happen "in a few months."[26]

Rumbold was now prepared to draft his most famous dispatch, perhaps the most famous and most widely read in the history of the British Foreign Office. Sent to London on April 26, 1933, only three months after Hitler became chancellor, the dispatch ran to five and a half long pages (about four thousand words) and reads like an analytical assessment of the Nazi regime that one might expect from a mature, insightful historian after the collapse of the Nazi state, when the relevant sources were available. The report was recognized at the time as a masterpiece and within the Foreign Office came to be known as the *"Mein Kampf* dispatch." James Ramsay MacDonald, the prime minister, read it and circulated it to the cabinet, which included Neville Chamberlain, who was then chancellor of the exchequer.

Rumbold began by pointing out that in their first three months in office the Nazis had not come up with a "constructive" economic policy but had instead concentrated on achieving "unchallenged supremacy" and on establishing "a regime of brute force" with ultimate authority in Hitler's hands. "The Nazi leader has only to express a wish to have it fulfilled by his followers." Rumbold conceded that the president and the Reichswehr (Armed Forces) might still have some restraining influence on the government, but he predicted, accurately it turned out, that once the president died—which happened in August 1934— the Reichswehr would abandon its reservations and throw in its lot with the Führer. It therefore seemed advisable to Rumbold to devote an entire dispatch to Hitler "and the uses to which he may put his unlimited opportunities during the next four years."

The foci of the dispatch are Hitler's fanaticism, his commitment to militarism, his intention to expand into Russia and the Baltic states "by force of arms," and his cleverness in lulling Germany's adversaries "into such a state of coma that they will allow themselves to be engaged one by one." Rumbold urged Hitler's neighbors "to be vigilant" and warned that they were deluding themselves if they believed that they did not have to act quickly to rein in Germany. The ambassador ended his dispatch with a general comment about an especially dangerous aspect of Nazism that, in his view, explained Hitler's "prestige and popularity. . . . Someone has aptly said that nationalism is the illegitimate offspring of patriotism by inferiority complex. Germany has been suffering from such a complex for over a decade. Hitlerism has eradicated it, but only at the cost of burdening Europe with a new outbreak of nationalism."[27]

Rumbold also deserves credit for realizing early in 1933 that the Nazis' racial doctrines stood at the core not only of their anti-Semitism but also of their entire conception of politics, and especially their views on foreign policy. It was actually an "extremely simple" conception, essentially a crude restatement of the doctrines of Social Darwinism. Hitler "starts with the assertion that man is a fighting animal; therefore the nation is, he concludes, a fighting unit, being a community of fighters. Any living organism which ceases to fight for its existence is, he asserts, doomed to extinction. A country or a race which ceases to fight is equally doomed. The fighting capacity of a race depends on its purity. Hence the necessity of ridding it of foreign impurities. . . . Pacifism [especially widespread among Jews] is the deadliest sin, for pacifism means the surrender of the race in the fight for existence. . . . Only brute force can ensure the survival of the race. . . . The race must fight: a race that rests must rust and perish. The German race, had it been united in time, would now be master of the globe. . . . To restore the German nation again 'it is necessary to convince the people that the recovery of freedom by force of arms is a possibility.'"[28]

Rumbold warned that it would be foolhardy to expect Hitler to moderate his program. He could no more do that than Lenin or Mussolini could renounce his doctrine. Hitler regarded his proposals, which most people in the West considered to be "fantastic," as the "granite pillars on which his policy is supported. He asserts again and again that they cannot be altered or modified." To hope for a return to "sanity" by the Nazis, Rumbold feared, would be "misleading." "Hitler's own record goes to show that he is a man of extraordinary obstinacy. His success in fighting difficulty after difficulty during the fourteen years of his political struggle is a proof of his indomitable character. He boasts of his obstinacy."[29]

Rumbold's evaluation of Hitler was confirmed during his one meeting with the chancellor, held on May 11, 1933, only fifteen days after he had sent the long dispatch to London. The interview lasted only one hour, but time enough for the ambassador to size up the man's character. Both men were frank, but they nevertheless parted, in the ambassador's words, "on perfectly good terms." Baron Neurath, the German foreign minister from 1933 to 1938, attended the meeting but kept quiet or said very little, his customary behavior in Hitler's presence.

The Führer made several dubious claims, and Rumbold duly noted them without comment, which he no doubt considered unnecessary since they were so far-fetched. Hitler insisted that the recent revolution in Germany that had brought him to power was unique because it had been accomplished with a "minimum of violence and bloodshed. He maintained that not even a pane of glass had been broken," a blatant falsity since it was well known that before and after the Nazis joined the government a considerable amount of street violence had broken out in Berlin and many other localities. To drive home his point and to put the British ambassador on the defensive, Hitler declared that in 1921 there had been much more violence in Ireland. So far, Hitler had remained calm, but when Rumbold brought up the treatment of the Jews, the Führer, as was his wont whenever this subject was raised, worked himself "into a state of great excitement: 'I will never agree,' he shouted as if he were addressing an open-air meeting, 'to the existence of two kinds of law for German nationals. There is an immense amount of unemployment in Germany, and I have, for instance, to turn away youths of pure German stock from the high schools. There are not enough posts for pure-bred Germans, and the Jews must suffer with the rest. If the Jews engineer a boycott from abroad, I will take care that this hits the Jews in Germany.' These were remarks delivered with great ferocity." In fact, Hitler was so agitated that Rumbold forbore from making a point he had carefully prepared ahead of the interview, that Hitler had introduced "two standards of treatment of German nationals, inasmuch as those of Jewish race were being discriminated against."[30]

Rumbold dwelled on the Jewish question in this dispatch and elsewhere not only because he considered the persecution of the Jews deplorable, but also because many people refused to believe—as some do even today—that racism was a cornerstone of his political creed. Hitler's prejudices seemed to be too outlandish. Moreover, Rumbold wanted to stress that the anti-Jewish policies were Hitler's personal responsibility, not that of "wilder men" in the party whom Hitler could not control. "Anybody who has had the opportunity," the ambassador continued, "of listening to his remarks on the subject of the Jews could not have failed, like myself, to realize that he is a fanatic on the subject." So certain were "convinced Nazis about any of their principal tenets" that it was pointless to raise objections to them.[31] It was this fanaticism, coupled with the Führer's "extraordinary obstinacy" and ruthlessness, that led Rumbold to write to Sir Clive Wigram, the private secretary to the sovereign, on June 28, 1933: "Many of us here feel as if we were living in a lunatic asylum" and consider it necessary to warn the Foreign Office against the hope that Hitler or his entourage would "return to sanity." The Nazi leaders, he insisted, would not waver in pursuing their goals, and if they proclaimed their commitment to international peace, they would do so only because they wished to "calm the fears of foreign leaders." Rumbold warned his superiors in London that the rulers of Germany were "very cunning people" and that it would be dangerous to underestimate them.[32]

On June 30, 1933, just before leaving his post, Rumbold sent what he described as a "summing up of the situation here" to Foreign Secretary Simon. Here he sought to be "fair" to National Socialism by recognizing "the good points in the Hitler ideology": the stress on comradeship and devotion to the state, the attempt to restore "the self-respect of the citizen and, through him, of the State itself." The ambassador also admired the Nazis' stated intention to end class warfare and to "ennoble" labor. But Rumbold warned that the Nazis would go to extremes in furthering these worthy ideas. He pointed out that Goebbels and other Nazi leaders believed that their ideals would not be adopted by other countries, which had been "corrupted by democracy and by association with the Jews." Thus, Germany had no choice but to assume the role of moral leader of Europe. Finally, Rumbold seemed to back away somewhat from his predictions about Germany's future aggressive moves. He was not at all sure, he now said, that Hitler or his ministers "have any clear idea of the course which events will take, nor have I met anyone who is prepared to venture an opinion."

But in the rest of this message, Rumbold was even more critical of the Nazi leaders than he had been in the "*Mein Kampf* dispatch" of April 26. Outside Germany, he said, only Hitler was seen as an extremist who might be slightly unhinged, but in fact many men in his inner circle were "not normal people" either, and within the Nazi movement as a whole the "strain of hooliganism still survives." The three most important people in the Nazi Party—Hitler, Göring, and Goebbels—were "notoriously pathological cases," the first two because of "wounds and hardships" endured during World War I, and the third because of "a physical defect and neglect in childhood. His club-foot is a constant source of bitterness to him, and his friends attribute his peculiarly venomous tongue to a 'vanity complex' arising out of it." As for the leaders just below these three, there were none of "real worth." They were brutal, even sadistic, and would not hesitate to "adopt the most ruthless methods and outlandish ideas." Rumbold emphasized that he was not just voicing his own conclusions; he had talked to almost all his colleagues in the diplomatic corps and was "struck by the unanimity of their views on the present situation. They are bewildered by the whirlwind development of Hitler's internal policy, and view the future with great uneasiness and apprehension."[33]

SIR ERIC PHIPPS ON NAZISM

Sir Eric Phipps, who succeeded to the ambassadorship in the summer of 1933, was also an experienced diplomat, having served for some thirty-four years in four different countries. He was the brother-in-law of Vansittart, who recommended him for the post, knowing that Phipps generally agreed with him that Germany posed a threat to Britain.[34] Although the new ambassador's most recent post had been Vienna, where interest in German politics was strong, he apparently did not know much about the history of Germany or its politics and was not particularly interested in the country. He had hoped to be assigned to Paris, and when he was posted to Berlin instead he indicated that while he was not fond of Germans, he was "[not] totally hostile to the new regime."[35] He nurtured a certain admiration for the idealism in National Socialism and thought that Hitler might even be serious in his desire for peace.[36]

In fact, in November 1933, after painting a picture of Hitler that was far from flattering, Phipps confessed to being puzzled by the German leader. Was he "the man of *Mein Kampf* or the more restrained man of the election in November 1933, who emphasized his peaceful intentions"? True, Hitler had not changed his attitudes on the Jews or on Germany's right to annex Austria, and he had not toned down his hatred of France, all central themes in his partly autobiographical book. But Phipps believed it was "too simple" to assume that the Führer still clung to all the views he had expressed ten years earlier while in prison. If he had not changed his views, then the only course of action for the West would be a preventive war, an option rejected by Phipps. Instead, he proposed that an attempt be made to "bind him" to an international agreement "bearing his signature freely and proudly given. . . . By some odd kink in his mental make-up he might even feel impelled to honour it." At the very least, such an agreement, which would have to be acceptable to Britain, France, and Italy, "might calm all Germany for a while," and the result might be years of peace. In the meantime, Hitler "might grow old" and "there'll be no problems and present ones will not be so pressing."[37]

According to Phipps's diary, published in 2008, he continued to be baffled by what he saw in Germany well into 1934. Early in July of that year, he noted that he could not fathom the behavior of Nazi leaders. He concluded that "one thing only is *certain* and that is the *general* uncertainty. The actors are too unstable, the factors too numerous and too shifting to allow a prophecy for more than a few weeks, which should bring a lull. To indulge in a guessing game on a rainy day in a country house might be amusing. To attempt any reasoned prognostication of the future course of events in Germany would be the height of unreason."[38] The diary was compiled in 1940, three years after Phipps left his post in Berlin. It is not known whether he informed the Foreign Office that he was that confused by the Nazis' conduct of affairs. He was not always consistent in his policy recommendations, but the burden of his message to London tended to be sharply critical of the Nazi regime.

Certainly he was as unsparing in his assessments of Hitler's character and policies as his predecessor in Berlin. If his dispatches over the next few years lacked the historical depth, political insight, and sense of outrage of Rumbold's analyses, they were nevertheless of high quality and colorful; and they demonstrated an understanding of Hitler's psychological make-up that was shrewd as well as penetrating. His portrait of Hitler the man, sprinkled with humorous asides, still stands up as thoroughly convincing. Given Hitler's growing power and the cult of Hitlerism, which was evolving rapidly in Germany, such a portrait of his psychology was potentially very useful to the officials in London who shaped Britain's foreign policy.

In his first meeting with the chancellor, on October 24, 1933, Phipps was taken aback by Hitler's unexpected and passionate outburst on his willingness to die for his people rather than "sign away their honour" by failing to press for an end to foreign intervention in German affairs. "I could see him," Phipps wrote, poking fun at Hitler, "as he spoke, advancing, unarmed and Mahdi like,* clutching his swastika flag, to meet death from a French machine gun. A trace of healthy, human fear of death would have

---

*According to an ancient prophecy, the Mahdi (Guided One) referred to here was to be the redeemer of Islam who would transform the world into a perfect Islamic society before the "Day of Resurrection."

reassured me more. Once or twice I felt inclined to smile at Herr Hitler's shouting crescendo, but the seriousness, not to say tragedy, of the situation prevented that inclination from developing. It is disquieting to feel such power in the hands of so unbalanced a being. I fancy it is to the emotion of Germany's dictator rather than to his reason that we must suddenly appeal on any issue."[39]

This was not the only exchange during that first meeting with Hitler that Phipps found bizarre. Phipps was also shocked by the Führer's response to his question about the substantial increase in the size of Germany's military forces in violation of the Treaty of Versailles. The ambassador pointed in particular to the SA and SS, well-armed Nazi military groups that had frequently used their weapons to silence political opponents. This increase in the military was taking place, Phipps stressed, at a time when Britain was reducing its forces to what many believed to be "a dangerous minimum." Hitler dismissed Phipps's query as groundless and then assured the ambassador that the "SA and SS might be compared to the Salvation Army." Phipps acknowledged that "here I regret to say that I laughed," not a very diplomatic gesture. Perhaps because he realized that he was not being taken seriously, Hitler agreed to procedures designed to demilitarize the SS and SA, but there is no evidence that they were implemented.[40]

About a year later, in November 1934, Phipps again saw Hitler, this time at the urging of the Foreign Office, which was deeply troubled by the rapid rearmament of Germany, especially the creation of a military air force and the "militaristic trend of German education and training." Phipps had been instructed to impress upon the Führer that the British government and people viewed these developments with utmost seriousness. Although the Nazis claimed that the rearmament was for defensive purposes only, "the fact remains," Phipps noted, "that the psychological reaction on others is to inspire suspicion of an offensive purpose." On hearing this, Hitler flew into a rage, warning his guest that "Germany cannot consent any longer to allow other States to wipe their boots on her." He also declared that he knew "for certain" that Russia and France had formed a military alliance, and when Phipps denied this, Hitler simply ignored him. As for the warlike German textbooks, the Nazi leader urged the ambassador to "read the French, Italian and Czech text-books." It was the first time that Phipps had had a personal interview with Hitler since the Night of the Long Knives in June 1934.* The Führer was clearly in a foul mood, which "[did not] increase his charm or attractiveness. Whilst I spoke he eyed me hungrily

---

*On the Night of the Long Knives, see below, pp. 35–36, 113–16.

like a tiger. I derived the distinct impression," Phipps reported, "that had my nationality and status been different, I should have formed part of his evening meal."[41]

In what appears to have been Phipps's last extensive interview with Hitler, on December 13, 1935, the Führer again behaved in an aberrant manner. He referred to the Russians as "noxious microbes who should be politically isolated," while conceding that he himself had sanctioned commercial dealings with the Soviet Union. As in the past, Phipps brought up the question of German rearmament, and once again Hitler lost his composure. Every so often, he would mutter sentences such as "Germany is a very great country and always will be. She was great in a military sense under the Hohenzollerns and is great now. Prussia was also great as a military Power under Frederick the Great." He referred to Russia with "supreme contempt" and boasted that the country was no match for Germany, militarily or technologically. "At times he ground the floor with his heel, as though crushing a worm." Phipps warned his superiors at the Foreign Office that it would be folly for Western countries to make any concessions to the Germans. Returning the colonies Germany had lost in 1918 "would not only act as a stimulating *hors d'oeuvre* to the German gormandizer, it would enormously increase Hitler's prestige and power. Such a reward for present iniquity would be positively dangerous; and how then could we ever show our approval of some possible emergence of any future German virtue?" The only appropriate policy for Great Britain was to rearm as quickly as possible. "It is only force that Nazism admires; generosity spells weakness in its eyes, and is therefore despicable."[42]

Still, in an addendum to the report on his interview with Hitler, written six days later, Phipps offered a slight modification to his position on Germany's threat to world peace. He now argued that although the international situation was perilous, it was not yet desperate. Germany was not ready for war, and the country faced serious financial and social problems, which might yet force the Nazi leadership to change course and turn away from its aggressive policies. Under no circumstances should the West offer to help Germany recover economically.[43] These mildly hopeful words did not seem to carry much conviction.

Hitler was not the only prominent Nazi whose behavior in public was so eccentric that it troubled Phipps and should have disturbed the Foreign Office. He was also taken aback at the behavior of Göring, who was widely considered to be the second most powerful man in the Nazi movement, as Phipps made clear in his dispatch of June 10, 1934. That day the ambassador, together with his American, Italian, and French colleagues as well as several senior officials in the German government, attended a social function at Göring's "new bison enclosure" some forty miles from Berlin. When all the guests had arrived, Göring "opened the proceedings by a lecture delivered to us on the outskirts of the bison enclosure in a stentorian voice with the aid of a microphone. He celebrated the beauties of the primeval German forest, in which roamed the primeval German animals, and announced his intention of reconstituting such a forest, ensuring to the animals the necessary forest peacefulness and to the German citizen the possibility of glancing at primitive German animals in German surroundings."

Then the forty guests were treated to a series of other events: a drive to a new "shooting-box" that had just been completed for the host and an "excellent and purely Germanic collation." Phipps was especially unnerved, and amused, by the "concluding scene in this strange comedy," which took place "at a lovely and very beautiful spot some 500 yards distant, overlooking the lake, where a mausoleum has been erected by General Göring, to contain, as he told us in his final and semi-funeral oration, the remains of the Swedish wife [who had died of tuberculosis in 1931] and his own (no mention was made of Fräulein Sonnemann [an actress, his "secretary" and mistress]). Under an oak tree General Göring planted himself, harpoon in hand, and celebrated to his guests, drawn up in a semi-circle round him, the Germanic and idyllic beauties of these Germanic surroundings. The mausoleum was placed between two German oak trees and flanked by six Druidical (but Germanic) sarsen [pagan] stones reminiscent of the Stonehenge, which itself must be Germanic though we do not know it. The stones are to have various appropriate marks engraved upon them, including the swastika, but no sign of the Cross. The only blot in an otherwise perfect, and consequently Germanic, picture was the tombstone itself, which is made of Swedish marble; but this could not be avoided, as General Göring explained to me apologetically, for it was the original tombstone on his wife's grave in Sweden. 'She will rest here in this beautiful spot, [Göring said] where only swans and other birds will come; she will rest in German earth and Swedish stone. The vault will serve for all eternity, as the walls are 1 metre 80 centimetres thick.'"

Phipps ended his report on the outing with some insightful comments on what it all signified. "The whole proceedings were so strange as at times to convey a feeling of unreality; but they opened, as it were, a window on to Nazi mentality, and as such were not perhaps quite useless." Visitors could observe the "almost pathetic naiveté" of Göring, "who showed us his toys like a big, fat, spoilt child." The things he had paraded before his guests were "all mere toys to satisfy his varying moods" and everything in his bison enclosure was, as he proudly proclaimed, "Germanic." "And then I remembered there were other toys, less innocent, though winged, and these might someday be launched on their murderous mission in the same childlike spirit and with the same childlike glee."[44] This last sentence was eerily prophetic.

The dramatic events of June 30, 1934, now known as the Night of the Long Knives, reinforced Phipps's forebodings about the Nazi regime. That day Hitler's henchmen murdered at least seventy-seven senior officials in the National Socialist Party and several former political leaders such as General Kurt von Schleicher, a right-winger who had briefly served as chancellor in 1932. The leader of the "conspiracy" quelled by Hitler was said to have been Ernst Röhm, who headed the SA, or Brownshirts, whom he was eager to integrate into the regular army. If Röhm had succeeded, the army and its leadership would have been markedly weakened.

Consequently, the minister of war, General Werner von Blomberg, the commander in chief of the armed forces and a lackey of Hitler, was only too eager to be rid of Röhm. He saw to it that the Reichswehr supplied the SS, which played a key role in the massacre, with weapons and the means of transportation.

Röhm had been a close comrade of Hitler ever since the early 1920s, but he did not hide his sense of superiority to the Führer, who had served as a mere corporal in World War I. Hitler, on the other hand, feared that incorporation of the SA into the army would alarm France long before Germany was strong enough to keep the French at bay. In addition, Hitler feared that Röhm wanted to take over the reins of the Nazi Party.

Phipps immediately understood that with this mass murder Hitler had "killed several birds with one stone." He had rooted out disaffection in his ranks, pleased many Germans who could not abide "moral perverts"—Röhm was a homosexual—and disposed of several people who "knew too much about past events, especially the Reichstag fire." And, of course, he put the army, crucial for Hitler's future foreign policy moves, in his debt. Phipps speculated that fruitful consequences might result from this action. The Nazis might now turn to "more and more normal methods of government." But he considered it more likely that the consequences of this "act of barbarism" would be further government violence. In murdering some of his "oldest and closest associates," Hitler had set a "dangerous precedent" that did not augur well for Germany's political future. In fact, at about this time Phipps saw Hitler on a Berlin street, and he was stunned by how pale the Führer looked. "Something must have changed—the man struck me at our first meeting, as I reported at the time, as an 'unbalanced being.' His last week-end only has made him still less normal." The country was now governed by a "less than ever balanced Führer who is himself flanked by two such lieutenants as Göring and Goebbels." Phipps concluded that in a country ruled by "unstable" men it was impossible to foresee future events beyond a few weeks. "To attempt any reasoned prognostication on the future course of events in Germany would be the height of Unreason."[45]

THE PERSECUTION OF THE JEWS

The reports that emanated from British diplomats during Phipps's ambassadorship provided mounting evidence of the Nazi leadership's brutality toward its Jewish minority of about 525,000. It has been suggested that after the initial round of anti-Semitic measures in the first months of 1933, the regime pulled back somewhat and moderated its persecution of Jews.[46] There is truth to this view, especially if the anti-Jewish legislation and violence from May 1933 to 1938 is compared with the massive attacks on Jews on Kristallnacht, the night of November 9 to 10 of the latter year. But, as the British diplomats noted and as historians have confirmed, the persecution of Jews had not been abandoned, although there were regional differences in how they were treated. To draw attention to this point was important, not only because it enhanced the picture of Nazi conduct, but also because it served as a warning to British authorities in London: they would make a serious mistake to assume that the Nazis were abandoning their commitment to violence in pursuit of their goals. In alerting the Foreign Office to the violence directed against Jews, the British diplomats were also intimating that it was wrong to draw a distinction between the treatment by a government of its own citizens and its foreign policy. Insensitivity at home was more than likely to be matched by insensitivity to the interests of foreign nations.

In May 1935, Phipps, who shared Rumbold's anti-Jewish prejudice, reported on a "recrudescence" of the anti-Semitic campaign, which took different forms in different parts of the country. Because many of the incidents were restricted to local areas they were not widely, if at all, mentioned in the Western press. The harshest attacks took place in Franconia, where Julius Streicher, the leading purveyor of anti-Semitism, was in charge, and where he conducted a campaign against Jews "fortunately unparalleled in the rest of the country." Other "bad districts" were Breslau and Pomerania. In general, conditions for Jews were the most difficult in the countryside and, after that, in small towns. Phipps was convinced that the "semi-pathological fanatics" in the Nazi Party would eventually succeed in reducing the Jews to a "racial minority devoid of even the most elementary rights." He also did not doubt that Hitler favored Streicher's anti-Semitic campaign. Local officials would shut down Jewish shops; prevent Jews from patronizing restaurants, bathhouses, and boarding houses; and urge "Aryans" not to use Jewish doctors. Phipps found it difficult "not to sympathize with the fate of the patriotic, decent, and industrious element amongst the Jewish population."[47] A few of the anti-Jewish measures at this time were so repellent that they deserve to be recounted in some detail.

In Breslau a Jewish manager at a large textile business spotted a beautiful young woman who had just started to work at the firm and commented in jest to one of his subordinates that "she was definitely worth almost committing *Rassenschande*," that is, "racial defilement," by making love to her. The subordinate or someone else who heard the remark immediately informed the senior manager and within short order the Jewish manager was sent to prison, where he remained for two weeks. He secured his release only by dint of his close connections with important Breslau citizens.[48]

On August 8, 1935, the consul general in Munich, D. St. Clair Gainer, one of Britain's most perceptive consular officials, sent a report to the embassy in Berlin on an occurrence he found troubling in the small Bavarian resort town of Bad Toelz, which was then forwarded to London. Early in August, the district council of Bad Toelz, acting with the approval of the Bavarian Political Police, closed the fashionable Park Hotel "on the ground that the guests were principally Jewish." The officials also announced that in the future no "cure cards" would be issued to non-Aryans, and the local branch of the Nazi Party warned all Jews to leave the district within twenty-four hours. These actions were taken, according to the official announcement, because the local population was "shocked" to discover that so many Jews stayed at the Park Hotel. Officials also noted that "serious disturbances" had broken out in protest against the large number of Jews who visited the area. Actually, it was the local Nazis who had launched a campaign in front of the hotel with placards that carried the following slogans: "Death to the Jews!" and "We want no Jews!" Local Nazis also marched through the main street with banners that denounced Jews as "Germany's curse" and "monsters," and called on the local population "to throw the Jews out of our city." Then, on August 4 the Nazi demonstrators smashed all the windows of the Park Hotel's dining room. At that point, the local authorities decided on the "first mass expulsion of Jews which has yet taken place in Germany." The press proudly announced that the area was now free of Jews, and the Bavarian minister of the interior, Gauleiter Adolf Wagner, congratulated Bad Toelz; he expressed the hope that the "whole of the Bavarian Oberland would follow this example."[49]

A few days after these events in Bavaria, D. C. Newton, a senior diplomat at the British embassy, sent a report to Sir Samuel Hoare, the foreign minister, on a speech that Streicher had delivered at the Sportspalast. It had lasted for almost three hours and included "a series of incredibly indecent stories," which struck Newton as so extraordinarily bizarre that he thought they deserved to be publicized. Streicher's aim was to warn against the dangers of intermarriage between Jews and non-Jews, and he made a special point of including in the first category people who had been converted from Judaism to Christianity. Conversion, he insisted, was a delusion. "Water could be poured over a Jew in buckets, but it would not make him anything but a Jew." He also denounced priests who refused to officiate at the marriage of two Aryans if one was a Catholic and the other a Protestant but who did not object to the marriage of an Aryan woman to a baptized Jew. To buttress his assertion that the latter kind of union was unacceptable, Streicher "told a story which appeared to move him greatly, of the misery of a German mother who had married a Catholic Jew and who discovered that her new-born child was clearly stamped with the mark of the Jewish beast. The creature that looked up at her from its cot was not a happy, laughing Nordic child, but a hook-nosed, dark-eyed Jewish monster."[50]

Toward the end of 1935, by which time the notorious Nuremberg Laws had been enacted,[51] Phipps began to pass on to the Foreign Office dire predictions about the fate of the Jews after hearing from Newton that a member of Alfred Rosenberg's staff had told a British lecturer that "animals killed off cripples and that National-Socialism would do the same. It looks as though this policy were now being applied to the Jews with typical German thoroughness and ruthlessness."*[52] At about the same time, Newton reported that he had been told by the journalist Norman Ebbutt that in his view "the [Nazi] party were determined to make life so impossible for the Jews that they might be reduced to starvation." Newton then gave his own

---

*Rosenberg, an early supporter of Hitler, was one of the leading ideologues of Nazism. He published a tract on the "immorality" of the Talmud as early as 1919. During the 1920s, he was an adviser to Hitler on foreign affairs, and after 1933 he played an important role in the dissemination of Nazi doctrines.

assessment: "Wherever the party extremists are allowed to have their way, and in this respect Herr Hitler must be included amongst them, it seems likely [that such a policy will be] put into practice, if not in one way then in another."[53] Late in 1936, Phipps reported that Acting Gauleiter Karl Holz, a deputy to Streicher, had raised the hope that all Jews would disappear. In a speech in Herzbruck on October 27, he declared, "We have not built up the Third Reich for decayed professors or for monks and nuns and Hallelujah singers. If all the Jews were one night struck dead throughout the world, this would be one of the most sacred days of celebration in the whole history of the world."[54] Even before this speech had been delivered, Newton had included (in late August 1936) in a dispatch to Anthony Eden the observation that "Even if no further persecution is in store, and this is doubtful, the present situation is such that there is no doubt that to the rising generation of Jews, emigration offers the only hope of a free and useful life."[55]

SAVIOR OF JEWS

Sympathy for the plight of the Jews was widespread among British officials in Germany, but one man who was not a diplomat but connected with the British embassy took it upon himself to help Jews escape. It is an extraordinary story and deserves retelling, even though it departs slightly from the main theme of this book. Francis Edward Foley, born in 1884, was well acquainted with Germany and German culture long before he began his tour of duty in Berlin in the early 1930s. When World War I broke out, he was in Hamburg as a student of philosophy; eager to avoid arrest and to return to his home country, he resorted to various ruses. He donned the uniform of a Prussian army officer and made his way to Emden, where a priest and several fishermen helped him reach Holland, which was not involved in the conflict. Soon after returning to England, he joined the army, received a commission as second lieutenant, and was sent to the western front, where he engaged in some fierce battles and was seriously wounded. When he recovered, he joined a unit that supervised a network of spies in France, Belgium, and Holland.

For the rest of his life, Foley worked as a spy, and during the Nazi era he headed the British Secret Intelligence Service (MI6) in Berlin. His primary task was to track Soviet spies and agitators; officials in London appointed him as the passport control officer to serve as cover. He took the post seriously; he wrote several reports on the plight of the Jews and, more important, he "bent the rules" by granting visas to Jews that enabled them to escape to Britain or Palestine. In November 1938, when the Nazis rounded up Jews to be sent to concentration camps, he allowed several of them, including Rabbi Leo Baeck, the leader of the Jewish community, to hide in his home. He also took some great risks in securing the release of Jews from concentration camps and then arming them with forged passports so that they could leave the country. It has been estimated that he saved thousands of lives, and in 1999 the Holocaust Museum in Israel (Yad Vashem) anointed him "Righteous Among the Nations."[56]

Foley's motivations can be gleaned from a confidential report he sent to the "The Chancery," his superiors in London, on May 7, 1935, entitled "The Situation of Jews in Germany." The Foreign Office and the cabinet were thus not the only government agencies that received reliable information on the conduct of the Nazis.

Foley was appalled that the lull in the anti-Semitic campaign initiated early in 1933 had come to an end. It had been assumed that the "revolution in so far as it affected the Jewish question might be considered as completed." With the "recrudescence of anti-Semitism" early in 1935, it was evident that the "Party has not departed from its original intentions and that the ultimate aim remains the disappearance of the Jews from Germany or, failing that, their relegation to a position of powerlessness and inferiority in Germany." The new campaign consisted of a wide range of government decrees designed to exclude Jews from economic activities and was marked by "the increasing virulence of speeches of leading members of the Party." Foley listed many of these decrees, and he focused on the so-called Aryan paragraph, which had a long history dating back to the nineteenth century. Various student organizations as well as social and political organizations resorted to it to exclude Jews. In April 1933, the Nazis invoked the paragraph to dismiss Jews from the civil service and prohibit them from practicing certain professions, such as the law and to a significant extent medicine. Foley gave graphic examples of how the new decrees affected not just professionals but also ordinary Jews. On the street where he lived, the windows of a Jewish butcher's shop were smashed to pieces at least twelve times. "After about eight times the insurance company appealed to the presumably Aryan window smashers to cease their activities, as they were destroying not Jewish property but German property. The bandits have refused to be enlightened. The police seem to be uninterested. The window breaking continues." Foley indicated that this sort of vandalism was "far more" widespread in the provinces.

In concluding his report, Foley warned that the position of the Jews was "desperate." Earning their livelihood had become increasingly difficult, and government regulations restricting access to their assets hampered their efforts to emigrate.[57] In his capacity as passport control officer, he had first-hand knowledge of their desperation. Within two months of the Nazi rise to power, his office had been "overwhelmed with applications from Jews eager to proceed to Palestine, to England, to anywhere in the British Empire." The applicants did not complain of having been molested, "but they suffer under the moral persecution—*seelicher Druck*—of the present system." Foley reminded the Chancery that he had not received any instructions on how to deal with the applications for entrance into England, but he reasoned that Jews should be encouraged to emigrate to Palestine rather than to any other place. He feared that the settlement elsewhere of large numbers of refugees would give rise to widespread anti-Semitism. He hoped that the British government would "find ways and means of increasing the yearly quota" for settlement in Palestine. "The persecution," he informed his superiors on January 17, 1936, "is as relentless as ever though perhaps more subtle in method."[58] For his part, Foley concentrated on finding ingenious ways of skirting the laws of both Germany and Britain to enable many German Jews to emigrate to Palestine or the United Kingdom.[59]

GERMAN REARMAMENT

As disturbing as these reports on Nazi domestic policies may have been to the government in London, they paled in comparison with the fears inspired by the assessments of German rearmament. From the moment the Nazis assumed power, officials in London repeatedly asked their emissaries for information on Hitler's aims in building up Germany's military forces. The Treaty of Versailles had imposed strict limitations on the size of the German army; it was not to be larger than 100,000, a figure settled upon after considerable discussion among the Allies.[60] In addition, Germany was not permitted to conscript men into the army, a provision designed to prevent the creation of a large reserve military force. It was known that even during the 1920s the German government had ignored the limitations, but the violations did not at first seem to pose a serious threat. However, Hitler's frequent assertions, in *Mein Kampf* as well as in his speeches, that Germany must recover its great-power status frightened Western governments and Germany's eastern neighbors.

In 1959, Burton H. Klein published a book with the controversial thesis that when World War II began in 1939, the Nazi leadership had not yet put the country on a full war footing.[61] That assessment seems to be true, but it is also true that the process of remilitarization began in 1933 and progressed at a rapid pace, which suggested that the country was preparing for conflict at some future date. The British diplomats in Germany certainly feared as much, and in closely following the rearmament program, sent a stream of messages on the subject to London. The first concern, as already noted, was the growth of the SS and SA, paramilitary groups that, it was feared, could easily be turned into regular army units in a time of conflict. Hitler denied that either one of the services could be considered as in any way strengthening the country militarily, but no British diplomat believed him. They noted that these organizations alone increased Germany's military establishment by about 880,000 men.[62] In September 1933, Colonel Andrew Thorne, the military attaché to the British embassy in Berlin, prepared a report that concluded that the "so-called semi-military associations," as he called the SS and SA, should definitely be considered as "part and parcel of the German defence forces and . . . their leaders are possessed of the determination and facilities to make them fit for their roles." Thorne emphasized that the men in the two organizations received vigorous training and that they were known for their toughness, dedication, and experience derived from military service in World War I. In "keenness and discipline, if not yet in training," the Nazi units were already superior to the British Territorial Army.[63]

But that was only part of the story. In July 1934, Thorne reported that Germany intended to increase the Reichswehr to 300,000, triple the number permitted under the Treaty of Versailles, and to boost substantially the supply of officers needed to supervise the growth and leadership of the new army. The German government had promised to allow foreign military attachés to visit military training camps, but suddenly the visits were "indefinitely postponed with very unconvincing explanations." For six months, foreign observers could not obtain any information on the progress of rearmament.[64]

The most alarming step in German rearmament was announced on March 15, 1935, in a Proclamation to the German People: the government would immediately establish compulsory military service, clearly another violation of the Treaty of Versailles. According to Consul General Gainer in Munich, the announcement was greeted with many parades and demonstrations. Gainer thought that the enthusiasm was not necessarily a sign of approval for conscription itself but, rather, an expression of relief that

"Germany has at last shaken off the remaining shackles fastened on her by an unjust treaty." And he was convinced that the "enthusiasm is genuine and sincere."[65]

It was also at about this time that Phipps was invited by Goebbels to attend a showing of the film *Triumph of the Will*, produced by the talented and chauvinistic Leni Riefenstahl. Aside from its glorification of Hitler, the film was "alarming" to Phipps because it showed "to what extent the idea of robot militarism has now possessed itself of the German nation, and particularly the German youth." Phipps urged that "no educated person [in Great Britain] should fail to see the film" because it will bring home "to the British public the true state of affairs in Germany."[66] Early in November, Phipps told Foreign Minister Hoare that on a drive along any road in Germany one could see indisputable evidence of the vast investment in the military. "There are few towns of any importance where barracks or military schools are not being built, some of them still far from completion." "Enormous aerodromes" were also being constructed. It was hard to avoid the conclusion that Germany was already "living in a state of war. . . . Everything is subordinated to the needs of the defence forces." It seemed clear that Germany planned a major expansion either into Africa or in eastern Europe.[67]

This dispatch was circulated among the cabinet members, and several ministers, whose signatures are illegible, made comments on the document. One referred to the warning at the end of the dispatch and stated, "This is very important. . . . This is undoubtedly what the French govt. have so much in mind." Another noted that one could not get a clearer warning about the looming danger. "There is nothing new in it. Sir E. Phipps and the F.O. [Foreign Office] have both been saying this for years, which have unfortunately passed without any preparations for defence on our part. The overlong period is now tardily over; but there is not a week to lose in our measures."[68]

The British government and the British people were especially alarmed by reports that Germany was building a vast air force. They feared, correctly it turned out, that German bombers would wreak havoc on their major cities, especially London. Some military experts predicted in 1937 that six hundred thousand people would be killed and 1.2 million injured during the first sixty days of an air campaign.[69] This gloomy prediction was not a revelation. Two years earlier, Group Captain F. P. Dow, the air attaché in Berlin, had succeeded in securing an interview with General Göring, who was in charge of expanding the air force, and Dow asked what kind of increase in the production of bombers was anticipated. He requested specific data, comparable to the data regularly published in the British "Air Force List." The interview had already lasted an hour and a half, and Dow had learned nothing of consequence. After contemplating Dow's query, Göring spoke with "some heat, and said that I can have no details so long as every German aeroplane is spoken of in Parliament as a 'flying devil.'" Then he added, "I hate Parliament." On that provocative note the interview ended.[70]

Late in November 1935, the vice-consul in Breslau, R. F. Bashford, sent some information to London that strongly hinted at Germany's plans for territorial expansion. He reported that for some time railway officials and military authorities had been pressing senior employees and officers to study Polish. In a smaller town like Frankfurt-on-the-Oder, railway officials traveled to Breslau two or three times a week to take lessons. One professor at the technical high school in the Charlottenburg neighborhood of Berlin complained that he was so busy teaching Polish to military officers, for whom the program was compulsory, that he could take on additional students only late in the evening.[71]

THE RHINELAND CRISIS

Germany's march into the Rhineland in March 1936 almost certainly marked the last occasion when the West could have inflicted a serious defeat on Hitler without risking a military conflict, as Churchill contended in *The Gathering Storm*.[72] The peace settlement of 1919 had provided for the demilitarization of the left bank of the Rhine and a stretch of land fifty kilometers wide on the right bank. This restriction, later confirmed by treaties, was generally considered the most effective preventive measure against another European war. Both France and the Low Countries counted on it to preclude an attack. It is therefore all the more surprising that France took no action when the Germans moved their troops without formal warning on March 7. There is evidence that the French government considered a counteraction, but the British authorities made it clear that they would not support such a move. "England," the British Foreign Office told the American chargé d'affaires, "would make every endeavor to prevent the imposition of military and/or economic sanctions against Germany."[73] Exactly why Whitehall refused to back a French military action remains a complicated issue; the most convincing explanation is the inability of British leaders to take firm measures against Germany, a subject discussed at some length below. However, what can be said with certainty is that the British government was fully aware of the threat posed by massive German rearmament.

It is now also clear that in 1936 Hitler could have been dealt a severe blow without risking massive bloodshed. The German "forward troops" were under orders to withdraw if a confrontation with French forces seemed likely. Hitler himself is reported to have said to several associates, "Had the French then marched into the Rhineland, we would have had to withdraw again with our tails between our legs (mit Schimpf und Schade). The military force at our disposal would not have sufficed even for limited resistance." He also acknowledged that had the withdrawal taken place, "it would have become the greatest political defeat for me."[74]

Phipps did not report very extensively on the remilitarization of the Rhineland, although he did find it dangerous. Immediately after learning that troops would be dispatched into the region, he told Neurath that he considered it the "gravest event that had occurred since I took up my appointment here."[75] On March 13, he sent a ciphered message on information he had received from a "private" source to the effect that there was "the greatest uneasiness in high military and business circles" about what he called "this coup." Even if Germany avoided war over the Rhineland, "she risks intensifying the suspicions and hatred of all European countries." Army officers believed that the country took an "unnecessary risk merely to enhance the prestige of the Nazi party and provide a favourable election program." Phipps ended his report with a warning that the disgruntlement in Germany should not be interpreted to mean that the army would refuse to "fight to the bitter end if hostilities break out."[76]

Eager to avoid war, the ambassador supported the British government's decision not to confront Germany militarily in the Rhineland. But two and a half years later, at the time of the crisis over German demands on Czechoslovakia, he acknowledged that in the spring of 1936 the West had missed its last opportunity to take effective preventive action to restrain Hitler.[77]

In 1936, however, he did not think that the Nazis could be stopped so easily. He disputed the argument, voiced in Parliament and in the British press, that if the League of Nations had succeeded in halting Mussolini's advance into Abyssinia, Germany would not have moved into the Rhineland. The ambassador did not believe that "heavily armed and successful treaty-breakers" such as Germany, Japan, and Italy could be so easily discouraged from their aggressive actions. "Nothing could be further from the truth," he wrote in a dispatch to Eden on May 12, 1936. "It must not be imagined that

Herr Hitler and his friends are building up the most formidable military machine in the world to-day merely to relegate it to the scrap-heap when threatened with sanctions, even if the hitherto despised Italian nation had yielded to their pressure. On the contrary, this country would rally like one man to the clarion call of the 'Führer' and again astonish the world by its fortitude and resolution in resistance." Phipps feared that Austria was next on the list of Hitler's moves to enhance Germany's power. The annexation of Austria, he warned, "would be a far greater blow to civilization than even the inclusion of Abyssinia in the new Roman Empire."[78]

WAS PHIPPS AN APPEASER?

Some historians have argued that despite these warnings about Hitler and Göring, Phipps cannot be said to have been a consistent anti-appeaser during his four years in Germany. Too often, these historians argue, he urged the West to make every effort to defang Hitler by persuading him to enter into treaties and agreements that would rule out changes in national borders by means of force.[79] This interpretation misses the complexity of Phipps's views and career. It was only after he arrived in Paris in April 1937 to begin service as British ambassador that he underwent a change of heart. He increasingly turned to appeasement of Nazi Germany, and by 1938 he was one of the most fervent advocates of that approach within the foreign policy establishment. At one point, in September 1938, he went so far as to declare that he was "against war at any price."[80] Phipps explained his shift as a response to his realization that the French government would not take a stand against Germany. It is also conceivable that Phipps, who eagerly sought the approval of the cabinet, adopted views that he knew would find favor with Chamberlain, who assumed the office of prime minister in May 1937 and quickly made clear that he was committed to reaching agreements with Hitler on all outstanding issues. Vansittart, who had welcomed Phipps's reports from Berlin and frequently quoted them in his analyses of international developments that he wrote for the cabinet, now sharply criticized his brother-in-law. At the Foreign Office the ambassador's reputation plunged.[81] Phipps's final change of mind in August 1939, when he abandoned appeasement for the "war party" that called for immediate military action to stop Hitler, did nothing to restore his standing as a perceptive diplomat.[82]

A careful reading of Phipps's dispatches, however, as well as some of the entries in his diary, indicates that during his four years in Germany, the period when Hitler could have been humbled and stopped in his tracks without bloodshed, he served his country well. At that time, he placed much more emphasis on the dangers of Nazism than on the feasibility of reaching agreements with Hitler. As a seasoned diplomat, he tended to avoid the appearance of rigidity.

From his earliest days in Berlin, Phipps argued against any weakening of Britain's military posture. In December 1933, he expressed alarm at newspaper accounts in Germany that pacifism was a growing movement in Great Britain. The German ambassador to London had reported that during a local election in Fulham in October 1933, the Labour candidate who favored rearmament was dubbed a warmonger, and as a result had lost the election. Phipps warned that if the Führer, who attached great significance to these reports, believed that large sectors of the British public held pacifist views and were prepared to accept peace at any price, he and his subordinates would "open their mouths wider than ever."[83] Two years later, when it appeared that Hitler had abandoned his frequent disavowal of interest in regaining the colonies in Africa, Phipps cautioned against giving in to Germany's demands. A return of even some colonies "would, I have always felt, only constitute an hors d'oeuvre for a really square Teutonic meal later on." Moreover, Phipps warned that Germany would inevitably establish "air and submarine bases" in the colonies, posing a threat to English interests. He had been told by Minister of Economics Hjalmar Schacht that Germany would send Nazi extremists to "future German colonies," and Phipps feared that these "gentry would not be very agreeable neighbors, nor would they be likely to be overly squeamish in their treatment of the unfortunate natives." Any concessions to Germany on the colonial question, Phipps warned in summing up his position, would "merely whet the German appetite, increase German prestige and strength and ultimately . . . render more probable an Anglo-German conflict."[84]

Repeatedly Phipps made the point that Hitler held ultimate power within the Nazi movement and that his authority could not be challenged. Today such a view may seem to be so obvious as to be dismissed as trite. But for a few years after the Nazis took over, numerous reports and rumors circulated about sharp divisions between moderates and radicals that were likely to lead to serious conflicts within the movement. For example, early in 1934 Consul General Gainer, stationed in Munich, contended that "the danger of . . . a split is now a real one."[85] To be sure, over the years there had been differences within the Nazi Party, and in 1932 a split seemed possible, but in the end only one leader, Gregor Strasser, "broke off from Hitler." By February 1934, Phipps rejected these analyses and insisted that a split was highly unlikely. Hitler was so superior to his colleagues, and the devotion to him of the "vast majority of the nation inside and outside the party" was so pronounced, that no one could challenge his authority. A sizable sector of the working class was opposed to the new order, but "they are too cowed to undertake anything against it." Four months later, Phipps was even more convinced that he was right. Hitler, he now pointed out, "was a cunning man with streaks of genius. No other such has emerged in present-day Germany." Both major factions in the Nazi Party believed that he was on their side, but Hitler had been careful not to identify fully with either one of them. Most important of all, "for countless Germans he still stands supreme on a lofty, lonely eminence. In his hands he holds their happiness, and him they still worship like the God they now neglect."[86] Since Phipps had stressed the Führer's psychological instability in several dispatches from Berlin, it is hard to believe that his change of heart after a few months in the new post in Paris was based on a reasoned reevaluation of his critical views of Nazism. His last major dispatch from Berlin, discussed below, certainly contained nothing to suggest that he was reconsidering his position on Hitlerism.

During the five years that Rumbold and Phipps served as ambassadors in Nazi Germany, remarkably little division of opinion could be found within the British diplomatic corps in Berlin and other German cities with regard to the new regime. Some may have been more forceful than others in deploring the policies of Hitler and his party, but the archives contained only one dispatch that could be construed as taking a benign view of Hitler. Curiously, it was written by Consul General Smallbones in Frankfurt, the same man who in 1920 had drafted a highly critical evaluation of National Socialism. In March 1937, he underwent a volte-face. It seems to have originated during his attendance at a speech by Hitler at the Festhalle in Frankfurt. The speech did not break any new ground, but Smallbones was impressed by the change that "has come over" the Führer since he last saw him some years earlier. "His bearing and his very features seem to have become more refined and more gentlemanly. The truculence has gone from his eyes and he smiles and nods benignly. His hands which used to look squat and grasping have turned white and emaciated. He used to hold on to the table before him with an iron grip but now the fingers hardly look for support and they flutter gently in the air to explain, as it were, a point; gone is the continual thumping of the table and, while the old fire has not left him, the most violent gesture is a smart slap of the clenched right hand into the open palm of the left," Smallbones could not help conjecturing "that these outward manifestations denote a spiritual change and that the man of 'Mein Kampf' has become the convinced advocate of an era of peace for at least twenty-five years."[87] It is difficult to account for this curious and unconvincing portrait of Hitler by a seasoned diplomat who had spent some fifteen years in Germany. Perhaps Smallbones's change of mind should be viewed as a preview to the shift in governing circles in Great Britain to outright appeasement, the subject of the next section of this chapter.

Be that as it may, Phipps, who was to leave Berlin in the late spring of 1937 for Paris, which had been his first choice in 1933, did not share Smallbones's conversion. By this time, Phipps's views, as well as his caustic remarks about Göring, had somehow become known to several political leaders, and as a result his relations with them had deteriorated to such an extent that his departure from Germany was virtually inevitable.[88]

In one of his last dispatches from Berlin, dated April 13, 1937, he reiterated many of the points he had made throughout his residence in Germany. He placed his arguments within the framework of a broad analysis of Germany's goals and capabilities. The dispatch is reminiscent of Rumbold's "*Mein Kampf* dispatch" in that it sought to paint a comprehensive picture of Germany's present situation. It was not as elegant and penetrating as the analysis of his predecessor, but it revealed a solid understanding of Nazism and deserved careful attention in London.

As was his practice, Phipps acknowledged that his conclusions about Germany's warlike intentions might be mistaken. The country might avoid military adventures "in the near future," and it was conceivable that despite the "vulgar demonstrations of hostility" that frequently appeared in the press, the Nazi leaders, "without friends to encourage them, as Austria did in 1914, . . . may, I do not say they will, refrain from the final gamble of war."[89] The rest of the eight-page dispatch, however, carried quite a different message. Phipps now accepted the argument that Italy's success in its war against Abyssinia in 1936 and the failure of the League of Nations to intervene to stop the aggression inevitably gave confidence to the warmongers in a country where "might is worshipped. . . . The German began to ask himself whether it was necessary to conciliate a Power [Great Britain] without whose favors Italy seemed to be doing very well." Britain's weakness encouraged average Germans to question the necessity for their country to pursue an Anglo-German understanding. Some Nazi extremists had also concluded that Great Britain was so weak that it was pointless even to attempt to reach agreement with it. On the contrary, a show of force by Germany could be very effective. The extremists believed that "it would be only necessary to drop a couple of bombs on London to bring His Majesty's Government to reason in regard to the colonial question."[90]

Phipps was convinced that Hitler saw no reason to abandon his three principal goals: the annexation of Austria and other territories with large German populations, most notably parts of Czechoslovakia; expansion in eastern Europe; and recovery of colonies lost at the end of World War I. But even after Germany had achieved these goals, the appetite of Nazi leaders would probably not be satiated. "To-day Germany is strong, the achievements of the last four years are stupendous and there seems no reason to set a limit to German ambitions." In the course of a private conversation with the British military attaché, an officer of the German General Staff had recently offered his opinion that Germany could only begin to form a real colonial empire after consolidating its position in Europe; this meant possession of the Netherlands and access to the Adriatic at Trieste, both of which, he declared, were "formerly Germanic." In military circles, such grand schemes of expansion were not rare.[91]

Moreover, many Germans were disgruntled over what they perceived to be their country's place in the world, which may have resulted from its late appearance on the historical scene. Germany, these people believed, had not received its "fair share of the good things in this world. To make matters worse, . . . [the Nazis] have embarked on an experiment in autarchy and in new-fangled political ideas which subordinate business to party considerations, with the result that a primitive, credulous and docile people, [has] almost implicit faith in their present leaders . . . . [Germany had a brief period of democratic rule in the 1920s.] Unfortunately for humanity, this country is again in the hands of an arbitrary authority. Indeed, the imperial regime was liberal and democratic compared to the regime to-day. Is there any remedy for the present state of affairs? Is there anything that any outside agency can do to improve the situation, to ward off the risk of an ultimate explosion?" Phipps's answer was that the Germans could be deterred from their dangerous course if they "feel the chill air of isolation blowing about their ears." European countries should collaborate and, together with the United States, pursue the following course: They should categorically refuse to pander to German threats and there should be no "slackening of our rearmament." Finally, Western countries should retain the "closest" friendship with France. Phipps placed special emphasis on involving the United States in the effort to isolate Germany.[92]

LONDON'S RESPONSE
TO THE DIPLOMATIC REPORTS

Phipps's recommendations were sensible, but by 1937 the political leadership in Great Britain had taken a turn that made their implementation impossible. In point of fact, the odds that London would take action in response to the warnings of its diplomats in Germany had always been remote. London's inaction did not stem from the failure of senior officials to be moved by the accounts of Nazi brutalities and the warnings that Hitler and many of his supporters were fanatics unlikely to be restrained in their quest to establish Germany as the preeminent power in Europe. Rather, the government's tepid response to Hitler's conduct of affairs must be attributed to a policy of reconciliation pursued together with France after 1924, but more fundamentally to the disarray that characterized British politics after the onset of the Great Depression in 1929. Among the most important factors responsible for the disarray were the ideological predispositions of the country's elite, the political ineptness of many government leaders, and, perhaps most important, the widespread hostility among the population at large to any policy that might lead to military conflict.

When Germany turned to Nazism, Ramsay MacDonald was the prime minister. He had been a leading pacifist in 1914, and when the Labour Party, which he had helped to found in the late nineteenth century, supported the war effort, he stepped down as chairman of the party's representatives in Parliament. He certainly deplored Nazism and at times thought that war with Germany could not be avoided. In fact, he became "exasperated" with those who endlessly called for disarmament—he called them "the pure sentimentalists"—and yet he could not fully shed his own long-held pacifist convictions. As his biographer noted, "even when he had become convinced intellectually that force might have to be answered by force, his emotions rebelled against the idea."[93] In truth, it is not clear whether MacDonald's views on world affairs mattered at all because he did not exercise much influence in the national government that was formed under his leadership in 1931 to combat the depression. He still considered himself a Labourite even though he had defied the party's wishes in forming a unity government with the Conservatives, who held 470 seats in Parliament as against only 13 by the prime minister's newly created National Labour Party. Even if he had been inclined to play a significant role in the government, he was politically too weak to do so.

But it also became increasingly evident that MacDonald was slowly slipping into senility. Under the circumstances, Stanley Baldwin, who had twice led a Conservative government during the 1920s and now held the position of Lord President of the (Privy) Council, became the de facto prime minister, and in 1935, after MacDonald's resignation, he again assumed that office. By all accounts, Baldwin was an intelligent man and a shrewd politician with an excessive yearning for public affection. He was not the kind of leader who would inaugurate a foreign policy that did not enjoy wide support among the British electorate.

His views on foreign affairs were rather complicated, so much so that he could not pursue a firm policy. Baldwin did not admire Fascism or Nazism, but, like most Tories, he considered Communism an even greater evil that must be confronted by Western democracies. In 1936, he indicated that he would not find it regrettable if the "Bolshies and Nazis" fought each other. Despite his disapproval of Nazism, he could not decide—as noted in the introduction—whether Hitler was committed to peace or intended to go to war to conquer territories in eastern Europe. His recent biographer, Philip Williamson, considered Baldwin's uncertainty understandable because it "was difficult to obtain accurate and agreed estimates of the scale and speed of German production," a judgment that is not consistent with the reports provided by British diplomats and military experts posted in Germany, as this study makes clear. It would be more plausible to conclude that Baldwin's puzzlement about Nazism flowed from his deeply held convictions. He believed that universal disarmament was desirable and feasible and—as he privately noted—that the Treaty of Versailles was "iniquitous." Nevertheless, late in 1933 he accepted the cabinet's view that a modest degree of rearmament was called for. But naïveté remained the hallmark of his foreign policy. He never gave up his belief that agreement with Hitler on international issues might be achieved. In the winter of 1933–34 he seriously contemplated visiting Hitler to iron out differences. However, Sir John Simon, the foreign secretary, and Anthony Eden, the undersecretary of foreign affairs, persuaded him to abandon the plan on the grounds that such a trip to Germany would strengthen the Führer at home and dismay friendly governments in Europe, which already harbored doubts about Britain's commitment to resisting Germany's aggressiveness. Even after Germany's march into the Rhineland early in 1936, Baldwin thought that Hitler might now be content and that he would jettison any further plans of expansion. Once again, Baldwin thought of visiting Hitler, and once again members of his cabinet persuaded him that it was a bad idea.[94]

The three foreign ministers during the ambassadorships of Rumbold and Phipps in Berlin—Simon, Samuel Hoare, and Eden—were not much bolder or more perceptive than their prime ministers; they also did not fully grasp the danger signals for Britain in the reports emanating from Germany. Although none of them was in any way sympathetic to Nazism, they chose not to pursue a consistent policy of resistance to Hitler's frequent violations of the Treaty of Versailles. Hoare clearly understood the cruelty of the Nazi regime and helped organize the Kindertransport, which brought Jewish children out of countries dominated by the Nazis. And Eden later changed course and acquired the reputation of a stalwart opponent of appeasement.[95]

In office from 1931 until early 1935, Simon played an important role in shaping Britain's response to the demand by Germany to be accepted as a leading world power and permitted to build up its military forces. Unfortunately, Simon occupied a position for which he was almost totally unsuited. The son of a reverend of modest means, he demonstrated rare gifts for study as a teenager and was accepted as a law student at Oxford University; he was also a dedicated worker and by the tender age of thirty had achieved recognition as an outstanding lawyer. Simon could analyze complex issues with remarkable speed and he won numerous cases for his clients, for which he earned large fees. But he had higher ambitions, and in 1905, when he was only thirty-two, he ran for Parliament, winning a seat as a Liberal. Within five years, he was appointed solicitor-general, the youngest man in eighty years to attain that position.

Simon seemed destined for a successful career at the highest levels of government, but two fatal flaws in his personality stood in the way, and in the end he did not achieve an enviable place in history books. For one thing, he was thoroughly unpleasant and almost completely bereft of friends who would stand by him in times of crisis. As his sympathetic biographer put it, Simon was "cold, insincere, and almost dehumanized." Rumor had it that he perceived his personal shortcomings and that every night he knelt by his bedside and prayed: "Oh Lord, make me a good fellow."[96] His second flaw, which became evident once he held high political office, was indecisiveness.

Prior to the appointment of Simon as foreign secretary, little is known about his views on foreign policy except that he had a strong aversion to military conflict. In 1914, when H. H. Asquith's government declared war on Germany, Simon drafted a letter of resignation as solicitor-general, but he was persuaded by party officials not to submit it to the prime minister.

Two years later, however, he resigned from his new position as home secretary in protest against the government's decision to introduce conscription into the army. Simon contended that it was "wrong to compel a man to be a soldier."[97] To demonstrate that he was nevertheless a patriot, he then voluntarily served for a short time as an officer on Commander Hugh Trenchard's staff in the Royal Flying Corps.*

It was not until 1931 that Simon returned to a senior government post, secretary for foreign affairs, and then the second flaw in his character became most evident. By that time, he had acknowledged that his opposition to conscription had been a mistake, but other than that he retained many of his earlier views and, more to the point, showed himself to be indecisive; he could not make up his mind on the most pressing issues, and once he reached a decision, he often failed to stick to it for very long. Eden, who served as undersecretary for foreign affairs during three years of Simon's tenure as secretary, complained about his superior's "methods" of reaching decisions. He was too slow in making up his mind on critical matters and he failed to "stand up" for his department "in the highest councils of government."[98] Simon, Eden noted in his memoirs, "could master a brief quicker than any man, but this is only part of the business in foreign affairs. His colleagues used to complain that he was more apt to turn to them for a policy than to champion his own."[99]

It is difficult to find contemporaries or historians with a kind word about Simon's stewardship of the Foreign Office, but some of the criticisms seem misguided. Rumbold, for example, referred to him as a "congenital pacifist," and many academics and politicians have claimed that he was one of the most "prominent appeasers," second only to Chamberlain in importance.[100] An examination of Simon's reaction to Rumbold's *Mein Kampf* dispatch and of Simon's other writings on how to cope with Nazism reveals that his views were rather complicated and that he cannot be dismissed simply as an appeaser. True, Simon lacked deep knowledge of German politics, he had not paid much attention to National Socialism before Hitler's appointment as chancellor, and his recommendations on how to respond to Hitler's foreign policy moves were often too timid to have had any effect on the Führer. Yet at a critical moment in 1933, Simon showed real insight into the dangers that a National Socialist Germany represented for all of Europe.

*Hugh Montague Trenchard was a professional soldier who served as commander of the Royal Flying Corps in France from 1915 to 1917 and played a central role in establishing the Royal Air Force.

On May 16, 1933, he distributed a detailed memorandum he had written on Rumbold's famous dispatch, which he had previously sent to all cabinet members. On the same day, he also passed on to the cabinet an "Enclosure" written by Major-General A. C. Temperley, Britain's military representative at the disarmament conference in Geneva, whose views were very much in harmony with those of Rumbold. It is evident that Simon distributed Temperley's report because he endorsed it.

The most striking feature of Simon's memorandum and the enclosure is that in addition to accepting the ambassador's assessments of Hitlerism, they put forward proposals for firm measures against Nazi Germany that were less qualified than those of Rumbold. Simon appeared to be more convinced than the ambassador that Hitler had embarked on a path bound to lead to military conflict. The difference between them may have been one of emphasis, but it was nevertheless noteworthy.

Simon began his analysis of Rumbold's document by stressing the ambassador's description of Germany's vast program of remilitarization, which started with young boys aged twelve. "Thus the spirit of the moment is definitely disquieting," Simon wrote, "and the Government of Germany, for the first time since the war, are giving State sanction and encouragement to any attitude of mind, as well as to various forms of military training which can end in only one way." Simon conceded that Hitler's regime might collapse or that a peaceful resolution of outstanding differences might be achieved, but he focused on the possibility, which he considered most likely, that Hitler would succeed in realizing his program and that a European war would break out "in four or five years' time." Simon quoted the German foreign minister, Neurath, and the vice chancellor, Papen, to the effect that Germany would not shrink from resorting to force to attain its goals. "Germans must explain," Papen had declared, "why they have removed the word 'pacifism' from their vocabulary, and prove that the anti-pacifist campaign is not synonymous with warlike intentions." This sort of "organized Nazi propaganda," Simon stressed, was now standard fare in Germany. He warned that German leaders had their eyes set on the annexation of Danzig, Austria, and the Saar region. Moreover, the foreign minister found it "difficult . . . to continue to assume that the German Government still intend to achieve equality of status by legal methods and in stages to be settled by international agreement."

In response to this threat, the British government "should consider all possible contingencies." Western countries should turn to the League of Nations for help in containing German aggressiveness, but if that failed,

Britain, France, and the United States should issue a warning to Hitler not to embark on a "policy of open defiance." Simon was not optimistic that such an appeal would prove effective.

The enclosure by Temperley that Simon appended to his discussion of Rumbold's dispatch bluntly characterized the transformation that Germany had undergone during the three and a half months of Hitler's rule. Temperley referred to the "orgy of military parades," the ceaseless propaganda by the Nazis and by "Hitler himself," and the brutality of the regime. "Hitler has been swiftly consolidating his position. On the political side, he has imprisoned a sufficient number of his political opponents to get the Reichstag to vote its own temporary extinction. He has successfully abolished the rights of all German States and put Nazi Commissioners in charge. In Prussia Göring has been installed as commissioner, the appointment carrying with it the all-important control of the police. He is Hitler's chief lieutenant and is spoken of as the most violent, the most stupid and most reckless of his entourage. . . . The whole country has been Hitlerised."

Temperley considered it a fatal mistake for the British government to ignore the political changes in Germany. He warned that the "warlike spirit is being openly roused to a fever heat against the Poles as the first objective, with France as the ultimate enemy." The arguments in favor of universal disarmament struck him as sheer folly, since Hitler would never abide by any such arrangement. He advised his colleagues in the government to heed the advice "of the old Ironsides' motto of 'Trust in God and keep your powder dry.'" Temperley proposed that France, the United States, and Britain issue a "stern warning to Germany that there can be no disarmament, no equality of status and relaxation of the Treaty of Versailles unless a complete reversion of present military preparations and tendencies takes place in Germany." Temperley acknowledged that such a stand by the three powers would "provoke a crisis and [that] the danger of war will be brought appreciably nearer." This prospect did not faze him, because, as he put it, "Germany knows that she cannot fight at present and we must call her bluff. She is powerless before the French army and our fleet. Hitler, for all his bombast, must give way." Temperley predicted that if his advice was not taken, Germany would continue its present policies, making war "inevitable" in five years under conditions far more favorable to Germany because by then it would have built up a powerful military force. The enclosure ended with the following argument in favor of a hard-line policy: "There is a mad dog abroad once more, and we must resolutely combine either to secure its destruction or at least its confinement until the disease has run its course."[101] A few weeks after sending these recommendations to the cabinet, Simon thanked Rumbold for pointing out the "abnormality of the Nazi regime" and predicted that the ambassador's warnings would be of "great and permanent value to His Majesty's Govt. in determining their policy towards Germany."[102]

The distribution of Simon's memorandum and the enclosure demonstrates, first and foremost, that leading politicians in Britain, including the prime minister and Chamberlain, the future leader of the government, had been informed early on of the dangers of Nazism to all of Europe. Equally important, the two documents pointed to a path that could be taken to impose restraints on Hitler without unbearable bloodletting.

It is also worth noting that Rumbold's *Mein Kampf* dispatch, which inspired Simon's recommendations to the cabinet, quickly acquired a fairly wide readership within the political class in Britain and the British Empire. The dispatch was sent to King George V and the representatives of the British dominions, and it was widely distributed within the Foreign Office. According to Sir Orme Sargent, a senior official in that department, the dispatch came to be known among its employees as "the Bible of our knowledge about Hitler." Somehow it reached Harold Laski, a political theorist and prominent member of the Labour Party, who was so impressed by it that he asked Rumbold for permission to send it to William E. Dodd, the new U.S. ambassador to Berlin.[103]

At the senior level of the Foreign Service, sentiment for a firm policy toward Germany was in the ascendant. In addition to Temperley, Vansittart argued passionately that Germany should be warned that it could expect a revision of the Treaty of Versailles only if it abandoned the policy of remilitarization. Vansittart was relentless in his warnings to the government that it was courting disaster in not responding forcefully to Germany's aggressive moves. He produced one of his more trenchant analyses of the dangers posed by Nazism early in April 1934 in an eight-thousand-word report that Foreign Minister Simon called a "formidable judgment on Germany's intentions" and that he passed on to the cabinet. Although Vansittart tended to weaken his case by insisting that Hitlerism was basically a continuation of long-standing German militaristic traditions dating back to the Hohenzollerns—he called it a "continuity of the German spirit"—he correctly warned that "Germany was making unmistakable preparations for war in all its phases." He supported his argument with frequent quotations from the dispatches of Rumbold and to a lesser extent from other British diplomats in Germany.[104]

A leading spokesman on the other side, Ralph Wigram, head of the Central European Section, proposed that Britain, France, and the United States make Hitler aware of their strong opposition to Germany's rearmament but at the same time commit themselves to supporting the elevation of Germany to the status of a European great power. As Ian Kershaw aptly noted, the "problem with this approach was that the 'carrot' was not tempting, and the 'stick' was not threatening."[105]

The political leadership, however, tended to favor a cautious approach to Germany out of fear that any criticism of the Nazis would only make matters worse. Even Rumbold, who in early April 1933 had sent a report to London on the mistreatment of the Jews, urged the government not to make it public to avoid offending the new rulers, who "may be in power in Germany for a long period." He had been told by a prominent German that "we Germans will not tolerate any outside interference." In Great Britain, Jewish organizations pressured the government to make known its concern about the measures against Jews, and the issue was brought to the floor of Parliament. Prime Minister Baldwin poured cold water on the initiative with the following statement: "It is a matter of discretion. We are quite willing to leave it where it is." No official criticism was issued.[106]

The most potent opposition to a firm stand against Hitler came from below. A vocal peace movement that had emerged in Britain by the early 1930s quickly gained wide support for its opposition to increases in the military budget and moves by the government to hem in Germany with threats of military action.

An Anglican priest, popularly known as Dick Sheppard—his full name was Hugh Richard Lawrie Sheppard—founded the largest and most effective pacifist organization in 1934, the Peace Pledge Union, which mobilized people from all walks of life in support of unqualified opposition to war under all circumstances. Sheppard had not always been a pacifist; in 1899, when he was nineteen, he volunteered to fight for his country in the Boer War, and only an accident that injured one of his legs and left him with a limp for the rest of his life forced him to abandon his plan to join the army. At the outbreak of war in 1914, he assumed the post of chaplain in a military hospital in France, and it was there that he turned to pacifism. "War is awful, more awful than I supposed possible," he wrote to his family. On his return to Britain, he spared no effort in seeking converts. According to one scholar, he quickly became "one of the best known and best loved men in Britain." He devoted his life not only to pacifism but also to charitable work among the poor.[107]

Although the Peace Pledge Union's central concern was the avoidance of war, it often resorted to controversial political arguments to bolster its case for pacifism. For example, it expressed sympathy for the plight of Germany after it lost the war in 1918, in particular its loss of territory in Europe and Africa. One of the Union's pamphlets urged Britain "to win German friendship by surrendering African territories taken from Germany at the end of World War I." This is not to suggest that the pacifists looked with favor on Nazi ideology, but in their eagerness to prevent a military clash with Germany, they at times went so far as to overlook the most distasteful aspects of Nazism, such as the persecution of the Jews. They also took at face value the frequent pronouncements by Hitler that he was determined to avoid war.[108]

Sheppard's plan for the organization of a peace movement was simple and amazingly successful. On October 16, 1934, he placed a "peace letter" in three daily newspapers asking readers who agreed with his views to send him a postcard indicating their support. He received so many cards—eighty thousand in one year—that he moved to a more ambitious plan, to conduct what might be called a referendum on the kind of foreign policy the government should adopt. During an eight-month period, from November 1934 through June 1935, close to 11.2 million citizens of Great Britain and Northern Ireland (roughly 40 percent of the eligible voters) took part in the National Peace Ballot. Although controversy surrounded the wording of the questions on the ballot, the results revealed that an overwhelming majority of the participants (over 90 percent) favored "all-round reduction of armaments by international agreement" and that about 87 percent of the signatories favored "economic and non-military measures" against nations committing aggression. When asked whether they favored military action if that became necessary, slightly over 50 percent voted in the affirmative, but the pacifists, zealous in their pursuit of their goals, ignored this particular result and vigorously campaigned for the adoption of their policy, avoidance of war under all circumstances.[109]

To what extent Foreign Minister Simon was influenced by this widespread rejection of a forceful foreign policy is not known. But it is known that despite the fiery language of his memorandum of May 17 and his endorsement of Temperley's even stronger denunciation of Nazism, he favored negotiations with Hitler in the hope of signing an "air-Pact" with Germany to outlaw, in the event of war, the bombing of areas outside the battle zones and the conclusion of agreements that would place limitations on the size of the navies of both Germany and Britain. Eden believed that

Simon's change of policy was the result of his confusion over "what to do next" with regard to Germany, and he may well have been right.[110] In a report to the cabinet on July 14, 1933, Simon admitted as much. During a discussion of Germany's disregard of the disarmament clauses in the Treaty of Versailles he confessed that "I have not found it easy to reach a view of my own as to what should be done." Interestingly, he thought that "public opinion" in Britain was then "so roused by Germany's internal policy that it will not tolerate the idea of German rearmament." Of course, he made this statement before the peace movement had been fully mobilized. And he himself tended to play down the immediate danger of Nazism by predicting confidently that Germany would not be "ready to take violent action for years to come."[111]

In February 1934, Eden, the second in command at the Foreign Office, left for Germany to meet with the Führer and his senior lieutenants to find out whether some agreement could be reached on outstanding issues. Although there were no major breakthroughs, Eden's impressions of the dictator were far more favorable than those of Rumbold and Phipps. Remarkably protean, Hitler cast off the angry persona that had rattled the ambassadors and in Eden's presence adopted the demeanor of a reasonable statesman. The ploy worked. The Führer struck the undersecretary as "much more than a demagogue. He knew what he was speaking about and, as the long interviews proceeded, showed himself complete master of his subject." He was at all times "restrained and friendly." To his wife, Eden confided, "Dare I confess it? I rather liked him." And in a letter to Prime Minister Baldwin, he wrote: "Poor Man . . . he was badly gassed by us and was blind in consequence for three months."[112] Eden's discussions with Hitler focused on what were by now the usual topics: the withdrawal of Germany from the League of Nations, its insistence on maintaining the paramilitary organizations (the SS and SA), and the government's program of rearmament in general. Eden was pleased that the Führer had made one concession: he promised that if agreements were reached on other issues, he would see to it that in the future the SS and the SA would not be permitted to carry arms or receive training from army officers. Eden had not yet learned that Hitler's promises were meaningless.[113]

Thirteen months later, in March 1935, Eden accompanied Simon on a visit to Hitler, and this time Eden's reaction to the dictator was distinctly negative, leading him to conclude that the "future looked ominous." In his diary, he noted that the results of the discussions were "bad . . . whole tone and temper very different to a year ago, rearmed and rearming with the old Prussian spirit very much in evidence. Russia is now the bogey." His unfavorable view of Hitler was shared by André François-Poncet, the French ambassador. At a dinner party in Berlin, Eden remarked that it was now seventeen years to the day since the last major offensive by the German army in World War I began. Hitler's interest was piqued and he began a discussion with Eden about that crucial battle; it turned out that both Eden and Hitler had fought in it. After dinner, François-Poncet, who had heard this conversation, approached Eden and asked him whether it was true that "you were opposite Hitler." When Eden responded yes, the Frenchman exclaimed: "Et vous l'avez manqué? Vous devriez être fusillé." [And you missed him? You should be shot.][114]

The substantive discussions with Hitler on current issues stretched over two days and led nowhere. One of the Führer's comments was as far-fetched—or as Eden put it, as "ridiculous"—as those he had occasionally made to Rumbold and Phipps, who had duly reported them to the Foreign Office. The topic under discussion was the paramilitary groups. Hitler "poo-poohed their significance" and claimed that foreign countries maintained similar institutions where youths were trained to use rifles; he specifically mentioned Eton, the school Eden had attended. Eden "laughed" and pointed out that the Officers' Training Corps "were not taken so seriously. For many boys they were the occasion for smoking on field days." The British diplomat appealed to Neurath for some statement of support, but "he was silent." And Hitler simply "shook his head, completely unconvinced." Eden further protested the Führer's claim that the English public schools were designed to produce paramilitary organizations and that therefore Germany should be permitted to have similar programs. But "my protests were disregarded as patriotic deception." Eden confessed that his optimism of a year earlier had been misplaced. Hitler's unyielding demands for the enlargement of the German military forces made "an agreement impossible."[115]

Simon, too, left Germany pessimistic about Europe's future. He feared that the situation was "pretty hopeless." Europe might still take steps to calm the waters, but he believed that even this "may not prevent an ultimate explosion"; it could only "delay it."[116]

By this time, the failure of British political leaders to rein in Hitler was clearly not the result of ignorance of the Führer's political agenda; rather, the leaders—as well as the people at large—were gripped by a stultifying lack of political will, which in turn resulted in part from a misunderstanding of the balance of power in Europe. When Rumbold and Phipps

Above: Sir Horace Rumbold, British ambassador to Berlin from 1928 to 1933, leaving President Hindenburg's headquarters. *Below:* François-Poncet conferring with Sir Eric Phipps (left), British ambassador to Berlin from 1933 to 1937, at a social event. Photos courtesy Associated Press.

Sir Nevile Henderson, British ambassador to Berlin from 1937 to 1939, conferring
with Hitler in 1937. Courtesy AKG London.

sent their dispatches warning of the dangers that Nazi Germany posed to Europe—from 1933 to 1936—Germany had not yet established itself as a strong military power. A central point of Rumbold's and Phipps's missives was that Britain and other European powers should stop Germany before the country could fully implement its program of rearmament, before Hitler's regime acquired the military and economic wherewithal to resist pressure from abroad. Put differently, during the first three years of Hitler's rule, the ambassadors based their recommendations on the conviction that Germany was too weak to withstand economic and military pressure from Britain, which almost certainly could have relied on the support of France. But the leaders in Great Britain made no effort to educate the public on the dangers of Hitlerism and the feasibility of restraining the Führer without military conflict. In fact, they vigorously opposed Churchill's many warnings. It is difficult to avoid the conclusion that had the men who governed Britain drawn the right lessons from all the reports about Hitler's character, program, fanaticism, and ruthlessness, they probably would have taken steps that could have prevented the catastrophe of 1939.

THE APPEASERS IN CONTROL

With the appointment of Chamberlain as prime minister in late May 1937, British policy toward Germany came under the influence of outspoken appeasers. Disregarding Rumbold's and Phipps's assessments of Hitler as a serious threat to international peace, Chamberlain and his supporters argued that the Führer's appetite for aggrandizement could be stilled and war avoided by making concessions to him on such issues as the annexation of territories in Europe inhabited mainly by German speakers and by returning to Germany at least some of the colonies it had lost after World War I. All that Hitler was expected to offer in return was a promise to honor the principle of "mutual understanding" and to avoid the use of force in pursuit of his goals.

This definition of appeasement, although not inaccurate, is incomplete, for the movement consisted of three different strains. Chamberlain was the leading spokesman of the largest, which might be called "realist appeasement." Subscribers to this strain did not necessarily oppose recourse to war as a matter of principle. Rather, they believed that Britain and France were too weak to stop Hitler and should therefore be prepared to make far-reaching concessions to avoid military conflict, a goal that was uppermost in their minds. Chamberlain had vivid recollections of the horrors of World War I, especially the loss of his favorite nephew, and to avoid another round of bloodletting he was willing to go far to meet Hitler's demands. There is no evidence that the prime minister was in any way sympathetic to Nazism or to its brutal treatment of opponents, real or assumed.

The second group of appeasers was made up of pacifists, those who opposed war under any circumstances. This group received its strongest and broadest support from young people, and especially from students at elite universities. The pacifists also did not admire the ideology of National Socialism or the Nazi form of government.

The third group might be called, for lack of a better term, ideological appeasers, for its adherents admired some or all of the major aspects of National Socialism and regarded the Nazis as the most ardent opponents of Bolshevism, in fact as the only political force that could defeat that scourge and thus protect the West from a great evil. The British Union of Fascists, a party that favored appeasement without reservation, advocated the establishment in Britain of a new social and political order following the Nazi model.

One common thread in the thinking of all three groups was the conviction that Germany had been treated unfairly at the end of World War I and that Nazi demands that the Treaty of Versailles be altered were not unreasonable. This study focuses on the first group of appeasers because they were the ones most directly responsible for government policy during the period that Chamberlain was prime minister.[117]

Remarkably, the change in Britain's foreign policy under Chamberlain was not based on a reassessment by foreign diplomats in Germany of Hitler's character or his conduct of affairs. On the contrary, the portrait of the Führer and his senior subordinates fashioned by most of the diplomats continued to be highly unflattering, its central features not much different from the assessments formulated by Rumbold and Phipps. For example, in mid-October 1938, F. M. Shepherd, the consul in Bremen, reported that "the opinion that the Führer is not quite normal, which for some time past has been held by local medical circles, is now shared by quite a number of the general public."[118]

Even the new ambassador to Berlin, Nevile Henderson, who assumed office in May 1937 and soon emerged as a leading proponent of appeasement in government circles, found much to criticize in Hitler's demeanor and political stance. If statesmen and officials in London chose to depict Hitler as a riddle, it was not because they lacked evidence to the contrary or because new evidence about him had come to light but, rather, because they did not wish to confront him.

To the surprise of many in the Foreign Office, once Henderson took up residence in Berlin he turned out to hold views he apparently had kept to himself. His major sponsor for the Berlin post was none other than the passionate anti-German Vansittart, who favored Henderson because in his previous position as ambassador to Yugoslavia he had demonstrated exceptional gifts in handling an authoritarian ruler, King Alexander. Henderson would go on hunting trips with the king and on these outings persuaded his host to adopt policies favored by the British government. Vansittart believed that Henderson might be similarly successful with Hitler. In his autobiography, written twenty years later, Vansittart could not resist ridiculing the selection process: "Nevile Henderson . . . made such a hit with the dictator by his skill in shooting that he was ultimately picked for Berlin. All know the consequences."[119] Eden, the foreign minister, approved Henderson's appointment without having met him or studied his credentials in depth, much to his later regret.[120] Henderson subsequently maintained that he had told Eden that "he would probably incur the appellation of pro-German," but no known evidence supports this claim. Chamberlain knew Henderson, and apparently during a meeting in April 1937—before Chamberlain became prime minister—the two men agreed on Britain's future policy toward Germany.[121]

Aside from the achievements in Yugoslavia, there seemed to be no compelling reason for Henderson's appointment to what was considered in the 1930s to be the most important diplomatic post. He had entered the Foreign Service in 1905 at the age of twenty-three and before his assignment to Belgrade had held various positions in Constantinople, Egypt, France, and Argentina and distinguished himself in none of them. He was not very pleasant, and one of his biographers, who was generally well disposed toward him, characterized him as a "stormy petrel" who tended to be "argumentative, indiscreet and on occasions self-righteous." He was also a man with many prejudices. He disliked Slavs and Jews and referred to Jews and Communists as warmongers. On one occasion he suggested to the German ambassador in London that the treatment of Jews in Germany should "be regularized in orderly and systematic manner." And he shocked many of his colleagues when he claimed that at a meeting in April 1937, Chamberlain, then still chancellor of the exchequer, had given him license "to commit calculated indiscretions."[122] No evidence has been found to substantiate this claim. Henderson had convinced himself that he was destined to make his mark in world affairs and that he was therefore entitled to act on his own. After he left his post in Berlin, he wrote that he had been "specially selected" by Providence to help prevent an outbreak of hostilities.[123]

To put it gently, Henderson had a memory lapse. He himself was surprised when, after only two years in Buenos Aires, he was sent to Berlin. His German was rusty and his knowledge of German affairs not very deep. Rumbold, who had been his superior in Constantinople, gave him a "qualified endorsement" but did not think he was a "strong man" and considered him "prone to be oversympathetic to the government to which he was accredited," a serious flaw in a diplomat.[124]

In his reminiscences about his years in Berlin, Henderson wrote that despite his aversion to the "detestable aspects" of Nazism, he went to Berlin determined "to see the good side of the Nazi regime as well as the bad, and to explain as objectively as I could its aspirations and viewpoint to His Majesty's Government."[125] He also contended that "It was just as much my duty honourably to try to co-operate with the Nazi Government to the best of my ability as it would be for a foreign ambassador in London to work with a Conservative Government, if it happened to be in power, rather than with the Liberal or Labour opposition, even though his own sympathies might possibly be rather with the policy or ideologies of the latter."[126] Henderson's drawing of a parallel between Nazism and the three major British political parties reveals either his ignorance or his indifference to right-wing extremism. In any case, once Henderson settled down in Berlin, it did not take him long to demonstrate eagerness to report on the positive aspects of National Socialism. Prime Minister Mackenzie King of Canada reported that the Führer had told him in June 1937 that although the new British envoy had been in Germany only a few weeks, "they all liked him and felt he had a good understanding of German problems."[127] Critics of appeasement referred to him as "our Nazi ambassador to Berlin."[128]

Henderson, for his part, very quickly thought of himself as an ambassador with special ties to the British prime minister, as a sort of personal agent of Chamberlain. He and the prime minister seemed to see eye to eye on how to conduct relations with Germany and hence the ambassador did not consider it necessary to act merely as a subordinate to the Foreign Office. He also corresponded frequently with Sir Horace Wilson, a civil servant of long standing who became so trusted an adviser to Chamberlain that he was assigned an office at 10 Downing Street. The prime minister also entrusted Wilson with some important missions; in 1938 he was sent to Hitler to deliver a message and was permitted to negotiate with the Führer.

Often, when Henderson ran into difficulties with the Foreign Office, he would appeal to Wilson for support.[129]

Wilson's rise to this influential position reveals much about the quality of political leadership in Britain in the years from 1937 to 1940. Wilson had moved up the ladder in the civil service in good measure because of his servility to his superiors. He knew how the bureaucracy worked, but his familiarity with foreign affairs was meager at best. "Like his chief [Chamberlain], he spoke no foreign language, had rarely been outside England, and had no experience in foreign affairs." He admitted as much, but did not think that it was a handicap. "Foreigners are people, just like trade unionists," he said. "Chamberlain was a practical man, I was a practical man. What more did we need?" A fervent supporter of the prime minister's foreign policy, he denigrated his opponents as the "Churchill—Eden—Jewish clique."[130]

Henderson arrived in Berlin in mid-March 1937 and within a few weeks was embroiled in his first conflict with the Foreign Office. On June 1, he delivered a short address to the Deutsch-Englische Gesellschaft (German-English Society) in which he vowed to do his utmost to improve relations between Germany and Great Britain. That was a reasonable theme for the occasion, and if he had confined himself to that subject no one would have objected. But he chose to touch on other, highly controversial matters: he discussed two misunderstandings, one prevalent in Britain and the other in Germany. In his own country, few people understood National Socialism. If they did, "they would lay less stress on Nazi dictatorship and much more emphasis on the great social experiment which is being tried out in Germany. Not only would they criticize less, but they might learn some useful lessons. It is regrettable to see how much concentration is applied to some trees which appear misshapen in English eyes and how little appreciation there is of the great forest as a whole." The Germans, on the other hand, were convinced that "Great Britain is attempting to hem Germany in on every side." He assured his listeners that, on the contrary, the British admired German efficiency and culture and had no intention of placing any restriction on the country. The English wanted only peace. And he was certain that all controversies between the two could be settled if both sides showed good will. He ended with the following startling words: "Gentlemen, I ask you to rise and drink with me the health of the *Reichskanzler* [that is, Hitler] and of the German nation."[131] In Britain, this speech and especially the toast came under heavy criticism, but Henderson always claimed that he had done nothing wrong since he was free to be "indiscreet."[132]

The foreign secretary was not satisfied with that explanation. Two days after Henderson delivered the speech, Eden sent him a letter marked "Personal" asking him to avoid such comments. Eden appreciated the ambassador's motives but warned, "As a rule I think it is undesirable—often dangerous for Ambassadors to make anything beyond formal speeches owing to the danger of misrepresentation." He urged Henderson to refrain in the future from any reference to German internal affairs. It might be, Eden suggested, that Britons did not fully understand the domestic situation in Germany, but "the régime as such [was] profoundly distasteful to the majority of people in this country." Henderson's comments in Germany had already provoked a hostile reaction in Parliament and the press, and Eden feared that, as a result, the "very purpose you had in view in making the speech," namely, an improvement in relations between Britain and Germany, would be undermined.[133]

In his reply to Eden, also marked "Personal," Henderson expressed the hope that he would not have to make any more speeches "for a long time" and ended his letter on the same note. Other than that, he defended his speech by declaring that he would have neglected his duty had he not "ventured to be a little indiscreet." Three hundred "leading party men" had attended the affair and he wanted to win "the confidence of these people," even if that led to some hostile questions in Parliament. He had sensed that in Berlin there was a "very dangerous state of mind" not only among Nazis but "among just about *all* Germans," who were convinced that Great Britain is "putting the spoke in . . . the evolution of the German wheel. As Goering said to me, 'if Germany wants to pick a flower, England says *verboten*.'" Unless the German people could be convinced that their fears were unjustified, "we are back once more on the fatal slope which led headlong to 1914." Henderson, for one, "absolutely" refused to "accept such a disastrous view of despair." All he wanted to convey to his audience was that Great Britain did not oppose "the *peaceful* evolution of Germany." For that reason he had referred to the "internal regime, which is one of the points the Nazis are sorest about."[134]

If Henderson felt chastised, he did not show it by giving up his attempts to placate the Nazis. Shortly after delivering his controversial speech, he told Ambassador François-Poncet that he planned to attend "Party Day," the annual Nazi rally in Nuremberg scheduled for September. It seemed to him "a pointless irritation to the Germans" to boycott the affair. In previous years, the British, French, and American ambassadors had declined Nazi invitations to these gala affairs, and Vansittart was disturbed by Henderson's decision to abandon this policy, all the more since he had reached it without even consulting the Foreign Office. Vansittart warned Henderson that criticism in England would be harsh, "you would be suspected of giving countenance or indeed eulogy (as alleged by one Member of Parliament) to the Nazi system," and the Foreign Office would be accused of having "Fascist leanings." Vansittart also suggested to the foreign secretary that "reconsideration would be necessary."[135] Henderson yielded grudgingly and told Vansittart that he "didn't love the Nazi system any more than you do." But he told Eden that he and every other "competent observer" were certain that even if Hitler left office "the country . . . would probably go on just the same, if not even on more exaggerated lines." In politics, he continued, one had to be "empirical to a certain degree," and since Nazism could not be wished away, what was the point of being discourteous to Hitler and unnecessarily irritating him?[136] In the end, the Foreign Office, for reasons unknown, changed its mind and allowed him to attend the meetings at Nuremberg.

Henderson found the two-day gala on September 10 and 11 very impressive. The 140,000 people who attended the various meetings and activities responded enthusiastically to the events and the long marches of uniformed Nazis, as did all the honored guests who were also invited to the formal dinner hosted by party leaders. Diplomats were well treated by the German authorities, who supplied private telephones to all the foreigners and billeted them in well-appointed railway compartments. The diplomats were further indulged with appetizing food and an enjoyable movie. Henderson did not doubt that "we are here witnessing in Germany the rebirth, the reorganisation and the unification of the German nation. One may criticize and disapprove, one may thoroughly dislike the threatened consummation and be apprehensive of its potentialities. But let us make no mistake. A machine is being built up in Germany, which in the course of this generation, if it succeeds unchecked, as there is no reason to believe that it will not, will be extraordinarily formidable. All this was achieved in less than 5 years. Germany is now so strong it can no longer be attacked with impunity, and soon the country will be prepared for aggressive action." Yet Henderson was convinced that Germany was not at all interested in undertaking an "adventure." In fact, he was inclined to believe that "we are perhaps entering upon a quieter phase of Nazism, of which the first indication has been the greater tranquility of the 1937 meeting [at Nuremberg]." Hitler, it seemed to the ambassador, was prepared to pursue policies marked by "reasonableness." He and his subordinates were especially interested in reaching an "Anglo-German understanding." Henderson's final observation on the Nuremberg festivities touched on the "adulation, amounting almost to idolisation of Hitler himself." He was pleasantly surprised that, "so far, I see no very visible sign of this worship going to his head. But he will have to be superhuman to resist it."[137]

A far different assessment of the Nuremberg meetings was made by Consul-General Gainer in Munich, who had served in the same position during the Rumbold and Phipps eras. As protocol required, Gainer sent his impressions after he had returned to his post to Ambassador Henderson as well as to London. Gainer observed, "There is one word which National Socialists are fond of saying is not included in their vocabulary and that word is 'compromise,' but until that word is reintroduced, even though it should be somewhat Germanised, there is little hope for a peaceful future for the world." Gainer admired "many aspects of the social work" that the Nazis were introducing, but in his view it was nullified by their disregard of "human liberty, which boded ill for the rest of the world. A nation that toward its own people, even from the highest motives, will not recognize this absolute value, cannot either be expected to recognize it in its dealings with other nations. It has once been said that the only logical attitude for a Church to adopt is: 'Believe or be damned'; this seems to me to be also the attitude of the modern German State in its relations not only with its own citizens, but also with foreign nations."[138] It is not known how Henderson reacted to Gainer's report, but it is safe to assume that he was not pleased to learn that a British diplomat who ranked below him did not share his views.

In the meantime, Henderson had been involved in yet another misstep that irritated Eden no end. On June 22, 1937, Eden reported to Henderson, again in a letter marked "Personal," that the Austrian ambassador to Berlin was "rather disturbed" because Henderson had asserted that he could not understand why Austria wished to remain independent. After all, its citizens were just as German as those of Germany. Henderson also told his Austrian colleague that England wanted, above all, to maintain peace and that "matters would be simplified if Germany and Austria formed one State." Eden could not believe that Henderson had made these statements because they ran counter to Britain's publicly stated policy. He suspected that there had been some misunderstanding and therefore wrote to Henderson "in a private and friendly manner." In his reply, Henderson both denied and confirmed that he had made the quoted remarks to the Austrian ambassador. He thought it "far-fetched" for his Austrian colleague to maintain that he had claimed not to understand Austria's desire to be independent. His real position, he told Eden, was that although he would not welcome Austria's joining Germany to form one state, it would be "extremely unwise to shut one's eyes to the possibility" that it would happen. Henderson, it seems, was trying to wiggle out of an awkward and embarrassing hole he had dug for himself.[139]

Despite his various expressions of sympathy for Nazism during his early months as ambassador—and he made quite a few during the two years he served in Berlin—Henderson's assessment of Hitler's character and conduct of political affairs at times could hardly be distinguished from that of his two predecessors. Thus, in a report of March 5, 1938, to Lord Halifax, who had been appointed foreign minister a couple of weeks earlier, Henderson acknowledged that his recent interview with Hitler "left me with a feeling of profound disappointment" because he could not obtain answers to the questions the Foreign Office had asked him to raise: Was Hitler prepared to further world peace by announcing that he would not force the issue with regard to his claims on Austria and Czechoslovakia? Would he enter into disarmament agreements, especially ones that would focus on the abolition of bombers? Would he be interested in acquiring colonies in the Congo Basin?[140]

Instead of responding to these questions, Hitler had claimed that "nothing threatened security as much as the intrigues of . . . [the English] press," which was leading a campaign of "international incitement" directed, above all, against him. He regarded himself as "one of the warmest friends of England," but his advances had consistently been "ill-requited." Henderson expressed sympathy for Hitler's annoyance and conceded that probably no one had been attacked as "heavily" in British newspapers as the Führer, and it was therefore "comprehensible that he would now have withdrawn into isolation which appears to him more dignified than making advances to someone who did not want him and who always repulsed him." Hitler was certain that "if it had wished to do so, the British government could have influenced the press in another direction" by issuing a prohibition on attacks against him. He then declared that he had no intention of interfering in the relationship between England and Ireland, and, similarly, under no circumstances would he allow "third parties to interfere with Germany's relations with Germans in foreign countries," a reference to Austria and Czechoslovakia.

After recounting the exchanges with Hitler that took place during a two-hour meeting, Henderson concluded with surprising comments about the Führer. He noted that he could not find a "common basis for reasonable discussion. Hitler's sense of values is so abnormal that argument seems powerless. The ordinary rules of the game seem to have no meaning for him and some of the statements which he makes and which, to give him his due, I am sure he believes to be true, leave one aghast." Henderson was stunned to hear Hitler claim, with "the utmost emphasis and conviction," that despite the trial of Pastor Martin Niemöller (for publicly criticizing the repressive measures of the Nazis), "nowhere in the world was religion freer than in Germany!" Henderson concluded that "His capacity for self-deception and his incapacity to see any point which does not meet his own case are fantastic, and no perversion of the truth seems too great for him to accept as the gospel of Hitler and of Germany." It was likely, the ambassador suggested, that Hitler's self-confidence, his ability to sweep aside all doubts and any inferiority complex, accounted for his extraordinary influence over the German people. No one like that had ever been the leader of Germany, and Henderson could not think of any dictator "past or present" to whom Hitler could be compared.

A few months later, in mid-September 1938, Henderson suggested that the Führer might actually be somewhat deranged: "driven by megalomania inspired by military force which he has built up . . . , he may have crossed the border-line of insanity."[141] At about the same time, Henderson complained that he could not speak with "certitude" about the international crisis over Germany's designs on Czechoslovakia because "everything depends on the psychology of one abnormal individual." He had recently talked briefly with Hitler at the Nuremberg Party Day and had noticed that, "even while addressing his Hitler Youth," the Führer was so nervous that he could not relax. "His abnormality seemed to me greater than ever."[142]

Astonishingly, Henderson's assessment of Hitler's psychological makeup did not prevent the ambassador from finding much to admire in his leadership, and he warned against discounting the positive features of his rule. The Führer had "sublime faith in his own mission and that of Germany in the world," and there could be no doubt that "he is a constructive genius, a builder and not a mere demagogue." Like several other diplomats, Henderson admired the Nazi program "Strength through Joy" (*Kraft durch Freude*), and he lavished praise on Hitler for his commitment to doing "the right thing—for Germany—at the right moment" and for knowing how to "get . . . away with it." To be sure, Hitler was prepared to go to great lengths to "secure fair and honourable treatment for the Austro- and Sudeten Germans," even if it meant waging war, but Henderson assured the Foreign Office that the chancellor "hates war as much as anyone." In fact,

Henderson was convinced—on March 5, 1938, eight days before Hitler marched into Austria—that the Führer was not thinking of "*Anschluss* or of annexation" because that would "merely add to his present difficulties rather than simplify them."[143]

The avoidance of war was uppermost in shaping Henderson's views on Nazism, but in articulating them the ambassador revealed sympathy for the racist views of Hitler's movement. On January 26, 1938, he wrote Eden that a war between Germany and Britain "would . . . be absolutely disastrous—I could not imagine and would be unwilling to survive the defeat of the British Empire. At the same time, I would view with dismay another defeat of Germany, which would merely serve the purpose of inferior races."[144]

It is hard to explain why Henderson sent such mixed messages to London. He may have feared that an unqualified defense of Hitler would raise eyebrows at the Foreign Office, where Chamberlain's appeasement policy was viewed with much skepticism. As it was, many in the government suspected him of being sympathetic to Nazism. Or perhaps he occupied a post for which he was simply unqualified, which might explain behavior that was notably inconsistent or perhaps simply irrational.

As ambassador to Berlin, Henderson was, of course, the key arbiter of the contents of the dispatches to London, and he was careful to put his stamp on the information that left his office. In addition, he exerted considerable influence at the highest circles of the British government, much more than most envoys. When he was in London, he often attended cabinet meetings devoted to foreign policy matters, and senior officials paid careful attention to his advice.

But it turned out that his influence at the embassy did not match either his expectations or his hopes. When he was away from his Berlin office, the staff at times sent messages to London that represented its views, not those of the ambassador. In 1938, Henderson was diagnosed with cancer, and from October until February 1939 he stayed in London for treatment. During that long absence, the embassy was run by Sir George Ogilvie-Forbes, a forty-seven-year-old descendant of an upper-class Scottish family. Ogilvie was highly gifted and quickly acquired a reputation as an excellent diplomat. A protégé of Vansittart, Ogilvie held views of Germany and Nazism that differed sharply from Henderson's. Henderson had done his best to ignore him, but during the ambassador's long absence, Ogilvie came into his own.[145] The tone and substance of the dispatches sent to the Foreign Office changed dramatically.

Ogilvie was not a hothead and certainly did not favor a rush to war against Germany. In fact, he thought that the Treaty of Versailles was unjust and that Germany had a legitimate moral claim to the area where Sudeten Germans lived, and he did not advocate military action against Hitler to protect Czechoslovakia. But he harbored no illusions about the nature of National Socialism, which prompted him to send a stream of dispatches to London on the brutality of Hitlerism and the dangers it represented for Europe. In one of his first reports to Halifax during Henderson's absence (dated December 6, 1938), Ogilvie harked back to the warnings of Ambassador Rumbold. He quoted at length from chapter 14 of *Mein Kampf,* in which Hitler spoke of the need for Germany, if it was to regain its position as a world power, to seize territory in the east from Russia and from Russia's "vassal border states." Hitler, Ogilvie pointed out, had already removed two major obstacles created by the peace treaties: Germany had engaged in a large-scale rearmament program and had reoccupied a fair portion of the lands severed from it after 1918. Ogilvie then warned that it was generally believed in political circles in Berlin "that Herr Hitler is about to embark on the third stage of his programme, namely, expansion beyond the boundaries of the territories inhabited by Germans. How exactly this is to be achieved is the subject of much speculation. One thing is certain: Nazi aims are on a grandiose scale, and there is no limit to their ultimate ambitions." Political circles also speculated at length that in 1939 Germany might seek to establish "an independent Russian Ukraine under German tutelage." The Nazis would try to achieve this goal peacefully but were prepared to resort to force. Neither France nor Great Britain was expected to come to Russia's defense.

Once the eastern advance had been completed, it seemed likely that Germany would seek to achieve hegemony in the Balkans and would also establish an "outlet in the Mediterranean via Italy" to prevent the imposition of a blockade. According to Ogilvie, another school of thought predicted that Hitler would move against the West before advancing in the east. The goal would be to "liquidate" France and England before they implemented their rearmament programs. A senior German official had told Ogilvie that Hitler was still pondering his possibilities, but "it is indeed the profound conviction of almost every thinking German that the tiger [Hitler] will jump soon." Hitler, Ogilvie also learned, was sorry that he had not taken a "stronger line" in Munich, when he acceded to Chamberlain's wishes and refrained from a military attack on Czechoslovakia.* Hitler was now "abusing his moderate counselors for their pusillanimity" in urging restraint. It was widely known that the Führer had "dubbed all his generals as cowards."

*On the Munich agreement, see below, pp. 80, 89, 90, 131–32.

When Field Marshal Göring asked him if he also deserved that censure, he received the following reply: "Yes, naturally."[146]

Ogilvie also demonstrated his independence from Henderson in writing about the persecution of the Jews. Henderson occasionally and briefly touched on the subject, and despite his anti-Semitic prejudices, at times he expressed disapproval of the government's anti-Jewish campaign. But he seemed to believe that nothing could be done to stop it because hatred of the Jews was so central to the thinking of Hitler and his supporters. On June 21, 1938, when the Nazis greatly intensified the oppression of the Jews, most notably in incorporated Austria, Henderson had predicted that the "regime of the Ghetto will soon be a reality. . . . Anti-semitism is an integral part of the National Socialist doctrine and as such it will be pursued regardless of its disadvantages and of the inconvenience of other countries."[147] Ogilvie, however, attached much greater significance to the anti-Semitic outbursts and was much more appalled by them, as were Gainer in Vienna and Smallbones in Frankfurt am Main. Ogilvie was moved to devote several long dispatches to Nazi anti-Semitism, in large part because he was repelled by it, but also because he considered it to be "symptomatic of [Hitler's] frame of mind"; he wanted to drive home the point that Hitler himself was "personally conducting" the campaign against the Jews. To Ogilvie, the virulent anti-Semitism in Germany was "not a national but a world problem, which, if neglected, contains the seeds of terrible vengeance."[148] He also noted that the "best elements" in Germany were distressed by it, but that the "National Socialist machine has the people relentlessly in its grip." Indeed, it was widely assumed in Berlin political circles that nothing could be done to stop Hitler's aggressive moves, at home or abroad.[149]

Late in January 1939, in one of his broad surveys of developments in Germany during the preceding year, Ogilvie warned that the "extermination" of German Jewry "can only be a matter of time."[150] Ogilvie was so moved by the plight of the Jews that he proposed to the German government that the "atonement fine" of one billion marks that it had imposed on the Jewish community for having caused the death of the diplomat Ernst Eduard vom Rath and the subsequent destruction of property during Kristallnacht be used to pay for Jewish emigration.* Needless to say, the government ignored his suggestion.[151]

Unlike Henderson, Ogilvie was thoroughly pessimistic about Europe's future. Several times he returned to the theme of Hitler's displeasure with the Munich agreements. The Führer was especially disappointed that the

---

*On Rath and Kristallnacht, see below, pp. 190–94.

agreements had not slowed down British rearmament, on which he had counted to enable Germany to achieve undisputed military supremacy in Europe. He was also annoyed at the West for continuing to criticize his treatment of the Jews. Ogilvie singled out the speech made by Hitler on January 31, 1939, which is now widely considered to have been a clear warning that he had in mind the most serious action against the Jews. "In attacking the Jews bitterly on familiar grounds, Herr Hitler referred to the shameful spectacle of the whole democratic world oozing sympathy for the Jews, but hard-hearted when it came to practical help. In a passage which met with loud applause he declared that if international financial Jewry plunged the world into war, the result would be not bolshevism but the annihilation of the Jewish race in Europe."[152] In Ogilvie's view, it was impossible not to despair about the near future even if one could not be certain of Hitler's next moves. But "what is certain is that the military and civilian resources of the country are being prepared for an emergency."[153]

Despite his pessimism, on one occasion, on January 3, 1939, Ogilvie suggested that even if war broke out in Europe, Britain might be able to avoid entanglement in the conflict, and he urged his government to take the necessary steps to that end. Britain must come to terms with the simple truth that it was unable to guarantee the status quo in central and eastern Europe and that it should therefore make every effort to "cultivate good relations with Field Marshal Göring and the moderate Nazis with a view to their exercising a restraining influence on the extremists, such as Ribbentrop, Goebbels,* and Himmler, who at the present have the ear of Hitler." But in the same dispatch to Halifax in which he expressed these opinions, Ogilvie warned that Göring was so "devotedly loyal to his chief, that I see no indication whatever of his leading a movement against the Führer." Moreover, Göring supported the measures against the Jews, which hardly accords with the depiction of him as a moderate.[154] A substantial portion of this dispatch clashes to such an extent with the views in the overwhelming majority of Ogilvie's reports from Berlin that one is hard put to know what to make of it. Was he not thinking straight when he wrote it? Or was he engaging in some appeasement of his own, not of Hitler but of Ambassador Henderson, who was expected to return to his post when his medical treatment was completed?

But if that was Ogilvie's intention, he failed completely. On his return to Berlin on February 13, 1939, Henderson lost no time in calling a meet-

---

*Elsewhere in the dispatch, Ogilvie referred to Goebbels as "that vile and dissolute demagogue."

ing of the embassy staff to rebuke them for having adopted a negative tone in their dispatches. He informed the assembled group that henceforth all dispatches would have to conform with the ambassador's views. Five days after his return to his post, Henderson wrote to London that "Herr Hitler does not contemplate any adventures at the moment and . . . all stories and rumours to the contrary are completely without foundation."[155]

Three weeks later, on March 6, 1939, Henderson sent a huge dispatch to Halifax clearly designed to counteract the reports sent to London during his absence. Because of "unforeseen circumstances" he had been unable to contribute to the annual report of the embassy and now felt it was "incumbent" on him to submit a "personal record of the events of the past year." Henderson was known for wordiness, but this time he outdid himself: his account ran to twenty-four typewritten pages (about twenty thousand words) and it contained some of his more bizarre opinions. He criticized the newspapers in Europe and America for being too eager to belittle and humiliate Hitler and Nazi Germany. "If a free press is allowed to run riot without guidance from higher authority," he warned, "the damage which it may do is unlimited. Even war may be one of the consequences." The "upshot" of the press campaign in the West was to drive Hitler to side with the extremists in the Nazi movement and to threaten force against Czechoslovakia should its government refuse to yield to his demands. Similarly, the press campaign also encouraged the Czech government to stiffen its resistance to Germany's demands.[156]

Henderson had nothing but praise for the way Chamberlain had handled the Czech crisis, and he was certain that Hitler was "undoubtedly touched (his sentimentality is a characteristic which we have failed hitherto to exploit), and I was given to understand that his first reaction was to save the elder man [Chamberlain] fatigue of the journey by going himself to London or at least half-way there. His second [reaction] was to invite Mrs. Chamberlain to accompany her husband." Still, Henderson granted that the "humiliation of the Czechs [in Munich] was a tragedy," but they had largely brought it onto themselves because they had refused to make concessions.[157]

In an epilogue to the dispatch, Henderson discussed the "November pogrom of the Jews" (Kristallnacht), which he denounced as a reversion "to the barbarism of the Middle Ages" and a "disgusting exhibition" that appalled many Germans. He explained the violence, which had followed the assassination of a German diplomat in Paris, in two ways, one of them quite fanciful. First, the pogrom gave the Nazis an opportunity to "plunder the Jews," which is true. Henderson found this reason unacceptable, but another reason might "have been comprehensible . . . within limits. The German authorities were undoubtedly seriously alarmed lest another Jew, emboldened by the success of Grynszpan [the diplomat's assassin], should follow his example and murder either Hitler or one of themselves."[158]

Three days after sending the long dispatch to London, Henderson composed another one in which his assessment of Hitler ran counter to some of his own earlier ones. He raised the question whether Hitler was likely to behave rationally in the new Czech crisis, which was coming to a head. He answered his own question by declaring that although the Führer was a demagogue, he was not mad "or even verging on madness; therefore I am of the opinion that he is not thinking in terms of war." On the other hand, if Western democracies interfered "excessively" in "Germany's special sphere of interest," Hitler might follow the advice of the minority in the Nazi movement that believed that "force and force alone can ensure to Germany her legitimate rights and her due place under the sun." To avoid war, Henderson urged his own government to help Germany as much as possible to fulfill its legitimate demands. Such help, he assured London, would be cheaper than rearmament. To win support for his position, he again stressed the decent proclivities of Hitler, who, he claimed, would appreciate Britain's help. "I have little faith in the gratitude of nations, though I believe that Hitler is personally not lacking in that rare quality." He also assured London that if an agreement was reached on Czechoslovakia, Hitler could be trusted to honor it. "Personally, I would not go further than to say that, as an individual, he would be as likely to keep it as any other foreign statesman—under certain conditions probably more so. Strange though it may sound, he prides himself on keeping his word. One might quote numerous instances of his having broken it, the concordat, [for example]. . . . He himself would argue that in those instances it was the action of others which drove him to do so."[159]

After Hitler marched into Czechoslovakia on March 15, Henderson expressed outrage and declared that "Nazism has definitely crossed the Rubicon of purity of race," which had not been done when Hitler annexed Austria and the Sudetenland, both inhabited by German speakers. The seizure of lands controlled by Czech speakers "cannot be justified on any grounds."[160] Six weeks later, Henderson reversed course again and claimed that Hitler still wanted "good relations" with Britain, but only if London recognized German interests and abandoned the "policy of encirclement" of Germany. Danzig would have to be returned to Germany, which would make possible the "untrammeled railway and motor connexion between East Prussia and the rest of the Reich." Still, the ambassador firmly believed that Hitler did not want war at this time, although he might risk it "if his offer to Poland is uncompromisingly rejected." After all, Danzig was "practically wholly a German city," a surprising statement by Henderson since by this time he had concluded that Hitler also had his eye on lands where Germans did not predominate.[161]

More such conflicting opinions on Hitler and Nazism by Henderson could be cited, but the ones mentioned here suffice to demonstrate that he was a committed appeaser with an extraordinary penchant for inconsistency. Diplomats are almost by nature cautious and often issue ambiguous statements on major diplomatic events; this makes it possible for them to change their positions in response to political pressures. But Henderson regularly made statements that were not just vague but contradictory; indeed, it could be said that he made contradiction into a fine art, puzzling many readers of his dispatches.

By late March 1939, the authorities in London had apparently reached the decision to remove Henderson from Berlin, but it was awkward to dismiss an ambassador who occupied so important a post without finding another assignment for him. Senior officials considered appointing him as ambassador to the United States, certainly a prestigious post. But the American government was not receptive to the suggestion because many in Washington believed that Henderson "would start here as 'the man who sold Czechoslovakia down the river.'"[162] Henderson remained the ambassador to Germany, but early in April he was "granted a short period of leave" at the end of which the Foreign Office decided not to send him back "at least for the time being," in part, apparently, to protest Germany's march into Czechoslovakia. When, in the spring of 1939, Henderson considered a trip to Canada, O. E. Sargent, the deputy-undersecretary at the Foreign Office, expressed the hope that the ambassador would not give any lectures there or in the United States. If he did plan to lecture, he was to give the Foreign Office a copy of his speeches beforehand. In December 1939, when Henderson planned a visit to the United States, the foreign secretary, Halifax, requested that Henderson, who was still on active duty as ambassador, be advised to hold his tongue.[163] Chamberlain's government had by now concluded that Henderson could not be trusted to speak sensibly about Germany.

OCCASIONAL EMISSARIES TO HITLER

In addition to the diplomats in Germany, some British emissaries as well as Prime Minister King of Canada reported on Nazism to the government in London. They were all prominent and influential citizens, they were all given interviews by Hitler, and they all supported a conciliatory policy toward Germany.* Only one of them actually occupied an official position when he met Hitler, but they all deserve a hearing, not because their analyses of Nazism were perspicacious but, rather, because their views carried weight in government circles and among many people eager to avoid another military conflict. Prime Minister Chamberlain distrusted the Foreign Office, which he believed was totally hostile to his policies, and was therefore especially interested in the reports of these emissaries.[164] Within the government, Chamberlain—as already noted—relied heavily on the advice of Sir Horace Wilson. Hardly a day passed without a discussion of current developments by the two.[165] The emissaries often sent their assessments of Hitler and Nazi Germany to Wilson, who saw to it that their views reached the highest authorities in Britain.

Lord President of the Council Halifax was the most prominent Englishman outside the diplomatic corps to visit ranking Nazis in Germany. A leading proponent of appeasement, Halifax would become foreign secretary in February 1938, replacing Eden, who had grown increasingly critical of Chamberlain's policies toward Mussolini and Hitler. The promo-

---

*It could be argued that Lord Londonderry should be included in this discussion of emissaries to Hitler who favored appeasement. After giving the matter some thought, I decided against it. It is true, as Ian Kershaw showed in his interesting book *Making Friends with Hitler*, that after 1935 Londonderry became a prominent advocate of friendly relations with Nazi Germany and advocated a policy of appeasement, but his career and his politics took such strange turns that his influence in government circles was minimal. From 1931 to 1935, he was the secretary of state for air, and at first he supported the government's policy of disarmament, but after Hitler's ascent to power he argued strongly for an increase in funds for the Royal Air Force. He was so passionate on the subject that opponents dubbed him a warmonger. After he was relieved from his position in the government in 1935, he thought he would be able to restore his reputation by engaging in diplomacy aimed at promoting good relations between Britain and Nazi Germany. He traveled to Germany, where he met Hitler, Göring, and Himmler as well as other Nazi leaders. On his return to Britain he became a passionate advocate of appeasement even though he did not share Hitler's views on many issues, most notably his anti-Semitism. But his standing among political leaders had declined sharply; Winston Churchill, his cousin, had a low opinion of his abilities, and he was not the only one with that opinion. In 1940, when Londonderry sought to return to government service, he had "long been a spent political force" and no one in a position of authority took him seriously. See Kershaw, *Making Friends*, p. 324.

tion raised eyebrows in London since Halifax lacked foreign policy experience. Even his sympathetic biographer conceded that he was not qualified "by knowledge or inclination" to serve as foreign secretary. He had never shown much interest in European affairs and admitted that he had not read Hitler's *Mein Kampf*, and it soon became clear that he did not understand Rumbold's warning about Nazi Germany's expansionist ambitions. Aware of his limitations, he accepted the appointment as foreign secretary only because the prime minister had offered it to him, and he thought it "his duty to accept." Once in that office, he was very slow to make up his mind on issues, but when he had made a decision he did not change his mind easily. On the other hand, he was a "man of high moral courage who did not shirk unpleasant duties." And he was deeply loyal to his friends and superiors. After he changed his mind about Nazism and had grave doubts about the wisdom of appeasement, he urged Chamberlain to reconstitute the government and pursue new policies, but the prime minister refused. Nevertheless, Halifax remained loyal "to his chief" and did not make his reservations public.[166]

In November 1937, three months before he replaced Eden at the Foreign Office, Halifax accepted an invitation from Göring to attend a hunting expedition, and during his stay in Germany he paid a visit to Hitler. He spent three hours with the Führer—the need for a translator slowed the conversation—and when it was over the lord president found it difficult to sum up the drift of the discussion because the meeting did not follow "a very orderly course" and no subject was covered in depth. Except for occasional outbursts over Russia, Hitler was "on the whole very quiet and restrained." Nevertheless, Halifax now understood Hitler's phenomenal success as a public speaker. "The play of emotion—sardonic humor, scorn, something almost wistful—is very rapid." At the same time, Hitler "struck me as very sincere, and believing all he said." Hitler insisted, as he did so often in his pronouncements, that he wanted good relations with Britain, and the only concession he wished for was a return of German colonies. But this was not a matter of great concern to him, and he would not go to war with Britain to secure them.

Halifax was pleased to have made contact with Hitler, and although his overall assessment of the German leader was positive, he did point to basic differences over values between himself and his host. He did not think that they stemmed simply from differences of outlook "between a totalitarian and a democratic state." They were, rather, the consequence of divergent historical experiences. Hitler had attained power "after a hard struggle with present-day realities," whereas Britain was still living comfortably "in a world of its own making, a make-believe land of strange, if respectable, illusions." The British subscribed to such "shibboleths" as "collective security," "general settlement," "disarmament," and "non-aggression pacts," none of which made sense to Hitler and therefore could not provide him with guidance in seeking to solve "Europe's difficulties." Instead of accepting the "shibboleths," Hitler preferred to deal with specific problems in isolation.[167] Halifax expressed no opinion on Hitler's approach to foreign affairs, and his silence suggests that he either was not altogether unsympathetic to it or did not quite know what to make of it.

By contrast, two other politicians who visited Hitler, Lord Lothian and Prime Minister King, sent reports to the British government that amounted to unqualified support for Chamberlain's appeasement policy. Anyone reading them today cannot avoid being taken aback by the superficiality and gullibility of the authors. To these two men, the Führer's character did not appear to be at all strange or puzzling. They were convinced that he was a moderate statesman without any proclivities for violence, a leader concerned only with restoring Germany's position as a respected power. Hitler, in short, seemed to them to be someone with whom it would be easy to negotiate and to find solutions to outstanding problems. How they could have reached conclusions so at odds with most of those we have examined so far is in itself a riddle, which can perhaps be explained only by the cliché that people often find what they wish to find. It is noteworthy, however, that one of these apologists for appeasement soon completely changed his mind and became a prominent supporter of the war effort against Germany. The other, the Canadian prime minister, took longer to abandon appeasement, but once war broke out, he supported Britain, more, it seems, out of a sense of loyalty to the nation and Chamberlain than the conviction that Nazism was a threat to the West.

King led a fascinating double life. On the one hand, he was an extraordinarily efficient and somewhat ruthless politician who between 1921 and 1948 served as prime minister for a total of twenty-one years. In 1999, historians ranked him as the greatest political leader in Canada's history. But his private life, which became known only after his death in 1950 when the diary he had kept since 1893 was published, was rather idiosyncratic. It turned out that he had regularly visited prostitutes and out of guilt tried to rehabilitate them after having enjoyed their company. He ended his attempts at rehabilitation in 1895 as a young man of twenty-one, but not the visits. At the same time, King was a deeply religious person with a strong mystical streak. In 1932, at the age of fifty-eight, he became a devotee of spiritualism. That year, he faced a general election and was deeply worried about his chances, as is indicated by the following entry in his diary about several members of his family and a successful politician, none of whom was still alive: "I believe dear mother and father and Max and Bell are near and about me and Sir Wilfrid as well. Their spirits will guide and protect me."* During the campaign, he also consulted a fortune-teller.[168]

King decided on a trip to Germany in the late spring of 1937 because he believed he could contribute to preventing an outbreak of hostilities. Hitler agreed to meet him on June 19, 1937, and the Canadian was so pleased with the encounter that he made sure to inform Prime Minister Chamberlain about it. In a note written shortly afterward, King "confess[ed] that the impression gained by this interview was a very favourable one." He was much relieved by the "very positive manner in which [Hitler] spoke of the determination of himself and his colleagues not to permit any resort to war." King indicated that he understood that Hitler had to cope with "big problems" in his country and he was convinced that the Führer was "a man of deep sincerity and a genuine patriot." Hitler's demeanor during the meeting also impressed the prime minister. He was never excited, he spoke "with great calmness, moderation, and logically in a convincing manner." The three other leading officials he met—Göring, Rudolf Hess, and Neurath—made an equally favorable impression on him.[169] We know that Hitler and several of his subordinates were adept at putting on a good show when the need arose, but we also know that King wanted to be impressed, and given his amazingly limited understanding of foreign affairs he could easily be won over. Within two years, King's ignorance—and naïveté—would become embarrassingly evident.

In a longer report to Chamberlain on the German visit, dated June 29, King again stressed Hitler's warmth; the chancellor was so eager to talk to him that he had postponed several other appointments and extended their meeting from the scheduled half hour to one and a half hours, which clearly flattered the Canadian. Hitler not only was emphatic about maintaining peace in Europe; he also stressed his desire to "improve the conditions of the working classes and those in humble circumstances." All these endeavors, King told Hitler, "appealed very strongly to me." King was also persuaded by Hitler's explanation of Germany's foreign policy, whose alleged purpose was merely to enable the country to avoid "indefinite subjec-

---

*The reference is to Sir Wilfrid Lourier, the first Francophone prime minister of Canada; he is widely regarded as one of Canada's leading statesmen. He died in 1919.

tion." The Führer assured his guest "in a most positive and emphatic way" that Germany "would not initiate a military conflict" because a war would destroy all his achievements and "would mean the desolation of Europe." To further reassure King that he was a decent man and a democrat, Hitler declared, "I am not like Stalin. I cannot shoot my generals and Ministers when they will not do my will. I am dependent for my power on the people who are behind me. Without the people I am nothing."[170] Toward the end of the interview, King strongly praised Chamberlain, who, he used to fear, would be rigid on "certain policies." But he could now assure Hitler that the British prime minister, whom he had seen recently, had a solid understanding of foreign affairs, and King predicted that relations between Germany and Britain were bound to improve. "Hitler said he was pleased to know this." In the course of the conversation, King also made it clear to Hitler that if any country within the British Empire believed its freedom was endangered, the entire empire would unite to defend freedom, a clear warning that in the event of war Britain would not stand alone.[171]

In early July 1939, by which time war in Europe seemed inevitable, King renewed contact with Hitler in an attempt to prevent an outbreak of hostilities. He wrote a letter to the Führer in which he referred to their meeting two years earlier, which, he believed, had "established a basis of confidence" that might be "helpful" in this time of crisis. King also reminded Hitler that he had expressed strong admiration for the Führer's achievements and especially for his determination to maintain peace. King now urged him to act on that commitment. "You will, I know," King almost pleaded, "accept this letter in the spirit in which it is written—an expression of the faith I have in the purpose you have at heart, and of the friendship with yourself which you have been so kind as to permit me to share." Hitler replied that he remembered the meeting with the prime minister "with pleasure," but then he completely ignored the issue raised by King. However, as a gesture of friendship—and clearly in an effort to pry Canada loose from Britain—Hitler invited several Canadian students and army officers on a three-week excursion to Germany, during which they would be introduced to various circles of Germans and would travel to different parts of the country. The purpose of the visit, Hitler said, would be to "convey to [the Canadians] an impressive picture of Greater Germany's newly-won strength and its will to peaceable constructive work." Amazingly, King was moved by the invitation and told the German ambassador to Canada "of the warm appreciation of the contents of the letter." King regarded Hitler's response "as an evidence of the confidence which I felt had been established between Hitler and myself at the time of our meeting, and the sincere desire mutually shared that every endeavour should be made towards mutual understanding."

King then negotiated with the German ambassador to Canada about the exact number of Canadians to be sent to Germany. The prime minister had thought of four or five, but Hitler insisted on twelve, all of whom would be the "personal guests" of the Führer, who would pay all expenses. King acknowledged that various interpretations, not all of them flattering, could be placed on Hitler's offer, but he "personally believed it to be sincere in its intent." King was so pleased with the project that he sent a copy of his letter to the Führer to Chamberlain with a request for his opinion. Chamberlain's response could not be found and it is reasonable to assume that the outbreak of war on September 1 brought the negotiations to an end.[172]

～

Lord Lothian (Philip Kerr, 1882–1940) was the most interesting of all the appeasers who met Hitler and talked with him at length. Born into the Scottish aristocracy, Lothian benefited from many social and economic advantages that enabled him to move easily into a life of public service. Soon after completing his studies at Oxford he went to South Africa, where he worked in the British administration for four and a half years. He proved to be an able and charming civil servant with a gift for clear writing on political issues. A convinced imperialist, he began to publish articles on imperial politics and became editor of the new journal *Round Table*, which focused on that subject, after his return to Great Britain in 1910. Over the next twenty years, he wrote some eighty-four articles for the journal, in which he expressed his political philosophy: he regarded the state as the "noblest of human fabrications" and was convinced that the British Empire was a force for good, although he feared that it was likely to face a crisis in the near future. His reputation in political circles soared, and in 1916, Prime Minister David Lloyd George appointed him as his private secretary; by the time he left government service in 1921, Lothian had played a part in virtually all the major foreign policy decisions reached by the British government, including the peace treaty negotiated with Germany in 1919. By now, Lothian, in the words of his biographer, was a "public figure." He knew everyone who was prominent in British politics and he was frequently invited to lecture on political issues.[173] When he expressed himself on issues that touched on the country's foreign policy, he was taken seriously by the highest circles of British society. Lord Halifax in particular relied upon him as a close adviser.

In the years immediately following the conclusion of the peace treaty, Lothian believed that the harsh conditions imposed on Germany were not unreasonable; some minor features that were unjust or not workable could in time be easily corrected. But by 1923 he began to change his mind and eventually concluded that Germany had been "sinned against." He soon became "obsessed" with this notion, which is the key to understanding his attitude toward Nazism in the 1930s. Although he strongly advocated disarmament and put a high premium on the avoidance of another war, he thought that Hitler's demands for basic changes in the restrictions imposed on Germany were justified.[174]

In January 1935, Lothian went to Germany on a business trip in his capacity as general secretary of the Rhodes Society, and during meetings with various dignitaries, including Ambassador-at-Large Joachim von Ribbentrop, he indicated interest in meeting some "representative Nazis" to learn their views on future developments in Europe. The meeting with Ribbentrop had been arranged by an English scholar, Dr. T. P. Conwell-Evans, who was then lecturing on Anglo-German diplomatic history at the University of Königsberg. A staunch admirer of the "new Germany," Conwell-Evans was only too eager to bring Lothian to the attention of leading Nazis, including Hitler, who granted Lothian two interviews.

The first one took place on January 19, 1935, and lasted two and a half hours. Conwell-Evans acted as interpreter, and both Ribbentrop and Hess were present, but, as was usual at such gatherings, they said very little. Basically, the proceedings consisted of a monologue by Hitler, in which he repeated his commitment to peace and offered an outline of a peace plan "for at least ten years." In his "Note of Interview with Herr Hitler, 29 January 1935," Lothian made no comment on Hitler's behavior or character. In this respect, the report was strikingly different from those of British diplomats who had met Hitler. Lothian clearly took Hitler at his word when he declared himself determined to avoid war.[175] For some five weeks after the interview, Lothian received a series of messages from Ribbentrop and Conwell-Evans that he passed on to the Foreign Office. Lothian now considered it his mission to act as intermediary between Germany and Great Britain for the purpose of promoting better relations between them. He took this role so seriously that he refused to sign any protest denouncing Nazi barbarities, although in private he had told Ribbentrop that the persecution of Christians, Jews, and liberal pacifists stood in the way of better relations between their two countries.[176]

When Germany remilitarized the Rhineland in 1936, without doubt the single most egregious violation to date of Germany's treaty obligations, Lothian expressed regret that Hitler had resorted to such illegal methods to attain his goals; but at the same time he contended that the "one-sided demilitarization" contradicted the "concession of equal rights to Germany." Therefore he opposed the imposition of any sanctions on Germany, a stance that amounted to allowing it to escape any punishment for violating international agreements.

A well-known appeaser by now, Lothian had no difficulty arranging a second meeting with the Führer early in May 1937. Lothian was again accompanied by Conwell-Evans, and this time Hitler invited Göring and Schacht, the minister of economics, to attend. The stated goal of the English visitors was to secure further information about the aims of the Nazi leaders. At the start, Hitler was "in a grave mood," but after an hour, by which time he had no doubt sensed that he faced a very sympathetic audience, the "atmosphere became considerably lighter, and there were smiles all around."

The chancellor made the same speech he delivered to all foreigners he sought to impress with his reasonableness: he assured his guests that he wanted to preserve peace, that Germany planned to annex only territories populated by Germans, and that his country aimed at nothing more than the revision of the unfair portions of the Treaty of Versailles and a reassertion of its "rightful position in the world." Eventually, this objective would mean the return of Germany's colonies, without which the country would not be capable of feeding its people. In resolving these issues, Hitler assured Lothian, "common sense would triumph, and . . . [t]he two peoples [German and English], racially akin with the finest qualities, would not commit suicide" by waging war against each other.

After returning to England, Lothian wrote a report in which he concluded that the international situation "was both more dangerous and more soluble than I thought." He was certain that Hitler's aims were entirely reasonable. The chancellor was not interested in "dominating other nations but only [in securing Germany's] own rights and her place in the world." Lothian was also convinced that National Socialism was a "fundamentally popular movement" and that "Hitler's power rests on popular support." This was demonstrated repeatedly by the plebiscites in which Nazi policies received overwhelming approbation by the German people. Lothian cited without any critical comment Hitler's claim that plebiscites should be considered "the form of democracy appropriate to Germany." In fact, Lothian asserted that if Hitler "disappeared, some of the extravagances like the persecution of the Jews and the propagation of paganism might disappear also, but as a military and air power Germany would remain as strong and resolute as ever." Lothian trusted that once Germany's legitimate grievances were satisfied with appropriate concessions, the country would return to the League of Nations and then even the controversy over armaments could be resolved. Lothian sent the account of his visit to Germany to Prime Minister Chamberlain and indicated that he would like to discuss it with him.[177]

For several years Lothian was a fervent appeaser, but he was not a rigid ideologue. He underwent a gradual but complete change of mind even before the outbreak of war on September 1, 1939. When Hitler marched into Austria in March 1938, Lothian became uneasy about Nazi behavior. Still, he refused to denounce the Nazis, claiming that the action was "inevitable and justified." Nevertheless, he now advocated "some kind of national service," without, however, abandoning his opposition to war, which, he contended, would "reduce the whole world to communism."[178] But during the turbulent events in 1938 he decided to read *Mein Kampf* and quickly concluded that he had misjudged Hitler, who, he now believed, must be resisted, by force if necessary. When Hitler ordered his troops into Prague in March 1939, Lothian totally reversed his former opinion about the German leader, whom he now called "a fanatical gangster who will stop at nothing to beat down all possibility of resistance anywhere to his will."[179] In April 1939, he publicly announced his change of mind in the House of Lords.

Shortly after the war broke out, Lothian was sent to Washington as ambassador with the specific mission of securing American support for Britain's struggle against Germany. By all accounts, he acquitted himself very well, but his efforts were short-lived since he died in 1940 at the age of fifty-eight.

THE FAILURE OF APPEASEMENT

The chief architect of appeasement, Prime Minister Chamberlain, clung tenaciously to his benign views of Hitler, not because he admired Nazism or subscribed to the doctrines of pacifism. He was not indifferent to Britain's security, and in April 1938, several months before his major effort at appeasing Hitler was launched, the government adopted a program to enlarge the Royal Air Force; within two years it was to have at its disposal twelve thousand airplanes, and if war erupted, Britain would have the capacity to produce twenty-one hundred planes a month. In short, Chamberlain did not rule out the possibility of military conflict, but he was determined to do all in his power to avoid the horrors of World War I; he had no doubt about his ability to handle the dictator. Throughout the 1930s, Chamberlain never spoke of Hitler as an unstable person whose policies were unfathomable. He had persuaded himself that he understood the man and could reach agreements with him that would be reasonable and acceptable to most Europeans. During the second half of September 1938, Chamberlain traveled to Germany three times in desperate attempts to ward off war, and after the prime minister yielded to Hitler's demands regarding the annexation of the Sudetenland, then part of Czechoslovakia, he told his sister that the leader of Germany "was a man who could be relied upon when he had given his word." Even after he led Britain into war on September 1, 1939, Chamberlain continued to believe that full-scale hostilities could be avoided.[180]

Germany's rapid and ruthless subjugation of Poland did not lessen his optimism. On October 8, 1939, he insisted that the Nazis were insufficiently confident in their military prowess to engage in total war unless "they are forced into it," and he had no intention of provoking them. "My policy," he wrote to his sister, "continues to be the same. Hold on tight. Keep up the economic pressure, push on with munitions production and military preparation with the utmost energy, take no offensive action unless Hitler begins it. I reckon that if we are allowed to carry on this policy we shall have won the war by spring [of 1940]."[181] By late November 1939, Chamberlain was convinced that Hitler's failure to take the offensive "can only be explained . . . by the state of 'abject depression' in which I believe he has been plunged owing to his inability to find any opportunity of doing anything." He ridiculed the idea of a German invasion of Britain, calling it "fantastic." The war, he assured his sister, was going badly for the Führer. He also had a "hunch" that a "great many Germans" were already admitting to themselves that their country could not win, and that by the spring this attitude would be so widespread that the war would be over. Once that happened, Hitler and his entourage must be deposed and Hitler himself "must either die or go to St. Helena or become a real public works architect, preferably in a 'home.'" Still clinging to the widely held view that Göring was a moderate, Chamberlain was willing to let him "have some ornamental position in a transitional government."[182]

In fairness, it should be noted that by this time Chamberlain acknowledged that he was not suited to be a "War Minister." He could not bear to cope with news of losses incurred by the British military, and when he learned, on October 15, 1939, that 833 British sailors had died on a battle-ship sunk by a German U-boat he was tempted "to hand over responsibility to someone else." Now he referred to Hitler as an "accursed madman" who was responsible for the carnage. "I wish he could burn in Hell for as many years as he is costing lives."[183] It had taken Chamberlain six and a half years to reach an understanding of Hitler similar to that of Rumbold and Phipps. Chamberlain's faith in the essential rationality of all human beings, his abhorrence of war, and his supreme confidence in his own judgment had prevented him from realizing sooner that the riddle of Hitler had in fact been solved three months after the Nazis assumed power.

Had the leading officials in Britain (including Chamberlain) heeded the advice of their ambassadors in Berlin in the first years of Hitler's rule, they would have reined in the Führer while Germany was still militarily weak. More specifically, they would have stopped him from marching into the Rhineland in March 1936, an aggressive move that historians consider to have been a turning point in the "whole international situation." The German action was a flagrant violation of the Treaty of Versailles, and the success of Hitler in defying the West without firing a shot emboldened him to undertake further aggressive measures without fear that the European powers would stop him.[184] If British statesmen in the years from 1933 to 1935 had acknowledged the validity of the conclusions about the German leader reached by their ambassadors in Berlin, namely, that Hitler was not a riddle at all, the history of the twentieth century might well have been different and that century would not now be known as one of the bloodiest ever.

Of course, Britain could not have been expected to take decisive action alone against Germany. It would have needed the support of other democratic countries, and especially of the other two most powerful democracies, France and the United States. Their stance also depended on how the political class assessed Hitler and Nazism. That, in turn, depended to some degree on how the French and American diplomats in Germany understood the new order in Germany, the subject of the next two chapters of this book.

CHAPTER TWO

The French Diplomats

In mid-December 1933, nearly eleven months after Hitler's advent to power, Maurice-Joseph-Lucien Saugon, the French consul-general in Hamburg, received a long letter on the tense relations between Germany and France from an "old German diplomat" who was deeply disturbed by political trends in his own country. The "old German diplomat"—let us call him X—deliberately ended his missive with an illegible signature, but Saugon recognized that the author was a thoughtful and well-educated man who wrote a "very pure" German. X asked the consul-general to forward his letter to higher authorities in Paris, who, he hoped, would find his views helpful in formulating policies toward Germany. As protocol required, Saugon also sent the letter to the French embassy in Berlin, so one can assume that it crossed the desk of André François-Poncet, widely regarded as the most prominent and most influential of all the emissaries who served in Nazi Germany.

X's letter was long, insightful, prophetic, and very courageous. Had it been intercepted by the police and traced to its author, X would surely have been incarcerated in a concentration camp, if not shot immediately. But X took those risks because he believed that it was his duty to warn the leaders of France of impending dangers so that they would not be taken by surprise by Germany's diplomatic moves. In X's view, the tense relations between Germany and France constituted the principal source of conflict in Europe, but until the rise to power of National Socialism it seemed possible that the two countries would resolve their differences by negotiation. "This prospect no longer exists," he wrote.

X placed the blame for the new state of affairs squarely on the Nazi leadership. He pointed out that until 1933, Germany had been ruled by a government and parliament that at least to some extent represented the will of the people, and foreign statesmen could be confident that agreements signed by the chosen leaders in Berlin would be honored. If a German statesman refused to uphold a treaty, he would be challenged in the Reichstag, and if he persisted, the question would be put to the people in new elections. But conditions had changed fundamentally, and there was no longer any "guarantee" that treaties concluded by Germany would be honored. The Reichstag now consisted of "compliant puppets of Mr. Hitler who must vote yes or no according to instructions. The will of the people is not represented at all in any organ of the government." One man ruled the country with the help of a political party, which, in turn, imposed its will on the nation with the liberal use of the bayonets of the Reichswehr and Hitler's "brown army" (the SA).

Stark and irreconcilable differences over key political issues now divided France and Germany, according to X. The primary goal of the National Socialists was to rearm Germany, whereas France yearned for "security against an enemy who in the course of 100 years has devastated the land three times." X warned that France should not expect friendly relations with Germany, which was governed by a "clique" that for fourteen years had been wedded to only one goal, revenge for the defeat in 1918. To achieve that nationalist goal, the clique relied on a popular speaker who had fashioned an ideology that was nothing but a "monstrous [set of ideas] plagiarized from Fascism and Bolshevism."

In X's view, no intelligent, enlightened, and thoughtful person who had read Hitler's *Mein Kampf* could put any stock in the author's declarations in favor of international peace, and he warned that the Führer and his supporters were only angling for time to position themselves to achieve three goals: control of the government "in order to enjoy the fruits of power"; completion of the military training of German youth; and, finally, the acquisition of sufficient quantities of military hardware, "which is now being produced secretly in Italy." X was certain that for the Nazis the agitation against the Treaty of Versailles was simply a pretext to arouse nationalist sentiment among the people. Neither Hitler nor his followers had ever tried to secure changes in that treaty; their only interest was to undo the outcome of World War I. As a result, the "militaristic spirit" in Germany was now ten times as powerful as it had been under Kaiser William II early in the twentieth century. Moreover, in "the country of racism no one thinks of upholding agreements with foreign countries."

André François-Poncet, French ambassador to Berlin from 1930 to 1938, conferring
with Hitler at a social event. Courtesy AKG London.

X did not advocate a preventive war against Germany, but he did urge France and other powers to exercise "the utmost energy, [and] firmness" in dealing with Hitler and to reject any kind of compromise or agreement based "on empty promises." France should maintain strong ties with friendly powers in the League of Nations and under no circumstances engage in negotiations with Nazi Germany, which in effect he dubbed a rogue state. Agreements with Hitler would be nothing but "scraps of paper."

On December 19, 1933, one day after he had mailed this letter, X sent another one that expressed even more alarm over the international attitude toward Nazi Germany. He had just learned from French newspapers that three prominent Frenchmen (Édouard Daladier, Bertrand de Jouvenel, and Foreign Minister Joseph Paul-Boncour) had spoken out in favor of negotiations with Germany to reach a general agreement on outstanding issues, an approach with which François-Poncet agreed.[1] X was appalled: "Such a proposal contains such a danger for France that one must ask one-self whether these gentlemen on the Pariserplatz [location of the French embassy in Berlin] have become prisoners of the Reichskanzlei [office of the German chancellor]. In France, we Germans have been accused of hav-ing forgotten everything and of not having learned anything. That is in part psychologically true of our people, but why do the responsible French statesmen and diplomats commit the same mistake?" X repeated his previ-ous warning: dealing with Nazis will produce only disappointments. The only correct policy for France was "unyielding firmness." X predicted that once "Hitler holds on to the little finger of Mr. Paul-Boncour, then he (see *Mein Kampf*) will want the whole arm. Hitler's Germany knows no bounds and has no inclination to adapt to a peaceful Europe. France has the right and duty to act in its own interest, the interest of Europe and in the interest of humanity to make it absolutely clear to this Germany, which represents only a minority . . . [that] despite the pretense of an election on 12 Novem-ber [1933], its policy should be: THIS FAR AND NO FURTHER!"[2]

X gave this advice to French statesmen when the Nazis had been in power less than a year, but ample evidence already supported his judgments about the new regime. With amazing speed, the Nazis had transformed Germany from a democracy to a ruthless dictatorship. In foreign affairs, Hitler's gov-ernment had demonstrated that it would pursue a radically new path by withdrawing from the League of Nations and embarking on a program of rapid rearmament. The French government could have spared itself much pain and suffering had it followed X's advice.

The government's reaction to X's letter is not known, but the authori-

ties in Paris were clearly not swayed by the arguments, if for no other reason than that the national mood was not conducive to an assertive foreign
policy. Large sectors of the public cringed at the very thought of any action
that might lead to military confrontations such as they had endured during World War I, when 1.3 million Frenchmen lost their lives and many
others were crippled for life.[3] Moreover, very few among the political class
paid much attention to Hitler's stated goal of ending France's position as a
major power, a message he had delivered unmistakably in *Mein Kampf*. As
the French were "the inexorable mortal enemy of the German people," he
declared, there would have to be a "final active reckoning with France. . . .
Germany actually regards the destruction of France as only a means which
will afterward enable her to finally give our people the expansion made
possible elsewhere."[4] It is doubtful that many French people had ever read
these words because publication of a French translation of *Mein Kampf*
completed in 1934 was legally enjoined in response to the petition of Eher
Verlag, the publishing house of the Nazi Party. The French political class
was not disturbed by the popular ignorance of Nazi intentions. In fact,
when Franklin Bouillon, a deputy in the French parliament, quoted Hitler's
words about relations between Germany and France in the Chamber of
Deputies, he was met with a round of sharp criticism. It was not considered
wise to alarm the people.[5]

In any case, the French political class did not take Hitler seriously; they
regarded him as "something of a half-crazy stooge" who would not remain
in office very long.[6] This attitude was not restricted to educated citizens in
France. Many well-informed Germans, who had seen the Führer, had lis-
tened to his provocative speeches, and had witnessed the violence committed by his followers, could not believe that a man as extreme and irrational
as Hitler could hold on to power for more than a short period in a country as culturally advanced as Germany, a country known for decades as a
Rechtsstaat (state based on law). It was simply beyond the capacity of many
people to grasp the ideological fervor of Hitler and the growing number
of his followers, their determination to implement the new program, and
their ruthlessness.

Even well-educated Jews in Germany, who had special reason to be
alarmed, thought of Hitler as a passing phenomenon. Hitler's accession
to power, they believed, was only one more in the long procession of gov-
ernmental changes that had taken place in the previous two years. Ernst
Marcus, a successful lawyer in Breslau, summed up the views of sophisticated Jews in 1933 as follows: "Let . . . [the Nazis] into the government

for six months [and] they themselves will run away from it." Six years later, after Marcus had left Germany, he acknowledged that he had misjudged the significance of Hitler's rise to power. On January 30, 1933, "the world had changed with one blow," but few realized it at the time.[7]

Moreover, during the years from 1933 to 1939 the people of France faced a myriad of domestic crises so severe that many citizens were disinclined to pay much attention to developments in a neighboring country, even one as threatening as Germany. The Great Depression of the late 1920s, which reached France in 1931–32, caused a substantial increase in unemployment, and as a consequence many Frenchmen focused on eking out a living. Then in 1934 a major scandal erupted over the illegal trading of stocks by Serge Stavisky, which led to street riots in Paris. The political system was too fragile to cope with so many upheavals. In just seven years no fewer than fourteen different governments held the reins of power, a state of affairs not conducive to the adoption of bold policies and programs. The political instability of France will be discussed in more detail later in this chapter, after a consideration of how French diplomats in Germany kept Paris abreast of developments in Nazi Germany and of the dangers the new regime posed for France. That, too, is a complicated story because French emissaries never provided their government with as penetrating and clear-cut an assessment of Nazi leaders as Rumbold sent to London.

THE POLITICS OF FRANÇOIS-PONCET

In addition to the embassy in Berlin, France maintained consulates in six other German cities, and officials in all of them produced some interesting and informative dispatches on developments in Germany. But by far the most influential and most comprehensive ones were written by the ambassador himself, and when the government in Paris debated policy on Germany, it focused on the information he had submitted. François-Poncet was a powerful personality and his knowledge of German and German affairs was extensive, as were his contacts with influential people in Berlin. He was also a man of enormous energy, personal charm, and ambition. During his seven years as ambassador to Germany (from September 1931 until October 1938), he sent reports to Paris that covered a vast array of subjects: political, social, and economic developments in Germany; his meetings with government leaders, including numerous ones with Hitler; relations between Italy and Germany; diplomatic negotiations between

Germany and Poland; Russian policies in Ukraine; the conflicts between the Nazis and the Evangelical Church; and the persecution of the Jews, to mention only the most important ones. Often his dispatches ran to seven printed pages, and in one day during the Czech crisis of September 1938 he produced six long reports. He was an acute observer of events, he read the German press omnivorously, and he knew how to turn an interesting phrase. Supremely confident in his own judgments, he was not shy about expressing his opinions or giving advice to his superiors in Paris.

François-Poncet first took interest in German affairs as a young man. Born in 1887 in Paris into an educated middle-class family—his father held the position of counselor of the Court of Appeals—he attended the highly regarded Lycée Henri IV and upon graduation in 1906 began to study Germanistics at the École supérieure, also a prestigious institution. In 1907 he continued his studies at the Universities of Berlin and Munich, from which he graduated in 1909 after having written a thesis on Goethe's *Wahlverwandschaften* (Elective Affinities). For two years, he occupied various academic positions and in 1911 received a fellowship that enabled him to resume his literary and historical research in Paris. He published several articles on German cultural themes and in 1911 a short book in support of the French government's proposal to extend the period of military service. He argued that such an extension was necessary to reinforce the "esprit public" of young Frenchmen as well as to strengthen France against Germany, which, he believed, had embarked on a program to establish "German hegemony in Europe," an endeavor widely supported by the people. François-Poncet admired Germany's cultural achievements, but he was troubled by the enthusiasm of the German nation for the creation of a "militaristic state." During World War I, François-Poncet served as a lieutenant in the French army; in view of his expertise in German affairs he was assigned in 1916 to the Ministry of Foreign Affairs, which sent him to Switzerland, where he was engaged in secret work consisting mainly of following internal developments in Germany and sending reports on his findings to Paris.[8]

When the war ended, Robert Pinot, the influential general secretary of the Comité des Forges (Committee of Heavy Industry), took an interest in François-Poncet's career and appointed him to an important position; he was to study developments in industry, technology, and the economy in general, both within France and in foreign countries, and produce daily reports to be published in the *Bulletin quotidien*, a journal widely read by businessmen in Paris. A moderate republican during his years as a student, François-Poncet now became a confirmed conservative, although he was sufficiently flexible to work with centrists and moderate leftists. He was strongly committed to the free market and to the sanctity of private property, opposed government intervention in the economy, and warned businessmen against making far-reaching concessions to labor unions. He favored a republican form of government, but his support for democracy and universal suffrage was less than enthusiastic. He thought that "responsible elites" should be the guiding force in running France. By the mid-1920s, François-Poncet had himself become a man of means, having married the daughter of a wealthy steel magnate.[9]

His growing number of contacts within the affluent and influential community of Parisian businessmen helped him launch a political career in 1924. In the elections that year he won a seat in the Chamber of Deputies, where he quickly rose in the esteem of his colleagues. Seven years later, he was appointed ambassador to Germany, a prestigious post because of the ongoing negotiations over various aspects of the peace treaties imposed on that nation after World War I. And within two years, in 1933, the ambassadorship to Berlin became the most important diplomatic post in the world. For a man as ambitious, imaginative, and cunning as François-Poncet, the assignment seemed ideal.

But it was also an assignment rife with pitfalls, and contemporaries as well as historians raised many questions about François-Poncet's effectiveness in Berlin. In the book he published after World War II, *The Fateful Years*, he tried to burnish his reputation. Without entirely ignoring some of his favorable impressions of Hitler, the Frenchman emphasized his distaste for the dictator's policies and his antipathy toward the German leader. He contended that Hitler had made no secret in 1933 of his intention to "proceed to eliminate the Jews altogether" and to "reintegrate the foreign policy of the German Reich." In the book, François-Poncet also referred to the Führer as a man who was little more than "a polemicist, an agitator in public meetings, an ungenerous fanatic." When Hitler marched into Czechoslovakia early in 1939, he revealed his true nature, according to François-Poncet: "All Hitler's personality and the personality of every German is here reflected. He was a *Nimmersatt* (glutton), a man never sated; he lacked all sense of proportion; he set a value only upon what he did not yet possess; he was urged to extremes by a demon."[10] The book does not include any reference to François-Poncet's flirtation with Fascism or to his favorable views of Mussolini. Nor does it fully describe his complicated relations with Hitler and his inconsistent appraisals of National Socialism.

This is not to say that all the criticisms of François-Poncet's reporting from Berlin are warranted. For example, the claims made in 1942 by the American scholar Elizabeth R. Cameron that the ambassador unequivocally favored Nazism are far-fetched. Cameron wrote that it was "known" that François-Poncet harbored "enthusiasm . . . for the National Socialist System" and that he was suspected of having advanced diplomatic proposals "behind closed doors."[11] On the other hand, François-Poncet's reputation in diplomatic circles as "the Führer's favorite ambassador" seems justified.[12] He conducted interviews with Hitler or spoke to him at meetings more frequently than any other foreign emissary—at least eighteen times during slightly more than six and a half years. Hitler himself is known to have had a special liking for the Frenchman; in the book *Hitlers Tischgespräche im Führerhauptquartier 1941–1942* (Hitler's Tabletalk in the Führer's Headquarters), published in 1951, Hitler is quoted as praising the ambassador for his "worldwide vision" and for being well versed in European culture and blessed with a conciliatory nature. Hitler also appreciated his "great generosity with pralines." Finally, François-Poncet was a fighter on the international scene with wide-ranging influence. "The extent of his contacts," Hitler pointed out, "is demonstrated by the fact that he once ordered a whole carriage full of pralines from France" to be distributed to his acquaintances.[13] Not even Sir Nevile Henderson, the most notable appeaser among diplomats in Berlin, tried so hard to curry favor with Hitler.

But Hitler also noted, correctly, that François-Poncet had committed a major blunder in assessing the inner workings of the Nazi Party, a blunder that proved to be helpful in persuading the Western powers not to rearm. The ambassador's frequent claim to have seen conclusive signs that Hitler's movement was riven by factional conflict between the SA and the Reichswehr persuaded many in the West that Germans would once again fight each other, as they had during the Middle Ages. This "prattle" by the ambassador, Hitler believed, had lulled the West into pursuing a policy of disarmament for several years, and by the time leaders in France and England realized their mistake, Germany had enhanced its military power to such an extent that nothing could be done by foreign countries to reverse the tide or to persuade the Nazi leadership to abandon its expansionist foreign policy.[14]

Nevertheless, it is inaccurate to label François-Poncet an outright admirer of Nazism or even a committed appeaser. His position on the Third Reich was not that firm; he often changed his mind on major issues, and in his dispatches he tended to focus on specific events rather than on the ideology of National Socialism. Moreover, he was a fervent patriot, and when he feared that Germany's policies would harm his country he sent warnings to his superiors in Paris. He rejected Nazi doctrines of racism, and although he did not write with the same passion or frequency as the American diplomats about the Nazis' persecution of Jews, he did make clear his distaste for Hitler's anti-Semitism. Quite often, his dispatches revealed the dark side of the New Order in all its horrors even if he did not always advocate strong measures by the Western powers to curb Hitler. In short, one cannot put a label on his political views or his recommendations on how to deal with a remilitarized Germany, which makes his diplomatic career both enigmatic and interesting. But it also throws doubt on the quality of his work as an ambassador in Germany at so critical a time in the twentieth century, when firmness and steadfastness as well as perspicuity were needed.

François-Poncet arrived in Berlin in September 1931 full of hope that relations between France and Germany could be put on a sound and friendly basis, not only because he admired German culture but also because he favored stronger industrial ties between the two countries, which, he believed, would bring economic benefits to both. He was aware, of course, of the economic and political crisis in Germany, but for about a year he paid relatively little attention to domestic politics and even less to the Nazis, whose strength was growing. On July 28, 1932, he reported to Paris that in the upcoming elections the Nazis might win between 200 and 245 seats in the Reichstag, giving them the largest representation there, and that this, in turn, would lead them to demand a share of political power in Prussia and in the republic as a whole. François-Poncet was close, ideologically and personally, to the German Nationalists, the staunchly conservative party, and he had persuaded himself that they would not allow the Nazis to take over the government. He was also confident that the Nazis would not succeed in taking power by force. He noted that late in 1932, when a Reichstag deputy asked General Kurt von Schleicher, the minister of defense, whether the Reichswehr would oppose such an attempt by the Nazis, the answer was unequivocal: "Cela va de soi!" (That goes without saying!)[15]

But a month later, François-Poncet worried about the possibility that the new Reichstag, which had been elected on July 30 and in which the Nazis held 230 of the 608 seats, would be not only anti-republican but also hostile to capitalism. He calculated that the socialist parties of various ideological shadings (Social Democrats, Communists, and Nazis) would control 452 votes, more than the two-thirds needed to change the Constitution. But his anxiety lessened when he realized that the Nazis' commitment to socialism was far from clear-cut. Hitler, he noted, had received large sums of money from Fritz Thyssen and other leading industrialists, and he would therefore be unlikely to turn against them. The ambassador suspected that Hitler might be playing a "double game"; he spoke favorably about socialism during the campaign merely to attract the support of the masses, but there was reason to doubt whether he intended to destroy the existing economic order. On the other hand, François-Poncet was not convinced that Hitler would prevail on this issue if the Nazis took over the government. He thought that the Nazi movement was seriously split on the most appropriate economic system for Germany. Senior party members such as Gregor Strasser and Count Ernst zu Reventlow were genuinely committed to socialism. In view of the "contradictory tendencies" within the party, François-Poncet found it "impossible to discern which one will prevail."[16] In saying this, François-Poncet revealed a serious misunderstanding of National Socialism: he was not yet aware of the enormous and even mystical power that Hitler wielded within the movement. True, differences on issues surfaced within the party, but in the end it was up to Hitler and to him alone to decide on the party's stand on key questions. Dissenters could not challenge his authority successfully.

In the Reichstag elections of November 6, held because no party had been able to form a majority government, the Nazi vote declined from 37.2 percent of the popular vote to 33.1 percent, and the party's parliamentary representation slipped from 230 to 196. Four days later, François-Poncet concluded that Hitler would never gain a majority in the legislature and that his chances of appointment as head of government were therefore "remote," although Nazism would henceforth be very likely to play a major role in German politics. The "National Socialist ideology has penetrated the entire public life of the country," and the 196 "racist" deputies would certainly be an important force that no government could ignore. The crucial question was how the loss of votes would affect Hitler: would he become wise or, on the contrary, would it make him more revolutionary? The ambassador was not sure.[17]

It is a sign of the political turbulence and uncertainty in Germany in late 1932 that within five weeks François-Poncet again changed his mind. On December 15, 1932, he wrote to Édouard Herriot, the foreign minister, that three paths to power were now possible for Hitler. He could stage a coup d'état, he might win a majority in the Reichstag in the next election, or he might collaborate with other parties to form a government. Hitler had tried force in 1923 and had failed, and his chances of gaining a majority in the Reichstag seemed highly unlikely, leaving open the one option that he actually adopted.[18] Over the next few weeks, the intrigues in the circle around President Hindenburg and among party leaders mounted at a dizzying pace, and so did rumors about the next moves of various parties. The Nazis were believed to be losing support and were finding it hard to raise money, deterring them from contemplating another electoral campaign. The financial crisis—the Nazis were said to have accumulated a debt of fifteen million marks, an enormous sum at the time—also made it hard for them to decide on a firm political strategy. According to press accounts, Hitler sought a rapprochement with the former chancellor, Papen, so that he could obtain "new credits" from industrialists. In return, Hitler was apparently willing to give "certain political assurances." On January 25, 1933, François-Poncet wrote that the internal situation in Germany was so tense and confused that it increasingly "assumes the character of a battle between two forms of dictatorship, the dictatorship of a party or of the military" (meaning General von Schleicher).[19] Three days later, he wondered whether the country might be on the verge of discarding the Constitution altogether.[20]

That possibility loomed even larger on January 30, when the official announcement that Hitler had been offered the chancellorship contained no word on the conditions, if any, that the new leader had been obliged to accept. The only reassuring news for the ambassador was that the rightwing Nationalists had agreed to serve in the new government. As soon as he heard that Hitler had become chancellor, François-Poncet contacted several rightists to find out more about the dramatic political change. All of them sought to put his mind at rest by telling him that "Hitler had become reasonable" and that he would be eager to reach an understanding with France. François-Poncet was not convinced. Even if Hitler himself wanted good relations with France, no one could be sure that his "troops, exalted by his assumption of power, will permit him to do as he wishes." The ambassador also feared that the Fascists in Italy, Hungary, and Austria would now feel emboldened to pursue aggressive policies.[21]

THE AMBASSADOR'S VACILLATIONS ON HITLER

Nine days later, François-Poncet sent a biographical sketch of Hitler to the Foreign Office, in which he elucidated the history and ideology of Nazism. It is comparable to Rumbold's famous analysis of Nazism sent to London on April 26, 1933, even if not as incisive and sweeping and not as brilliantly written. But it was perceptive in pointing out the foibles of

Hitler, his ability through his powerful oratory to move masses of people to follow him blindly, his deep hatred of the West and especially of France, and his ruthlessness. The dispatch certainly should have alerted his superiors in Paris that they—and France—now faced a formidable adversary. Because it is so forcefully written, the document makes possible comparisons between François-Poncet's views in 1933 and those he held in the following six years, and thus facilitates an evaluation of the argument of his critics who considered him inconsistent and misguided, and therefore ineffective as an analyst of Nazi Germany.

To understand Hitler, François-Poncet contended, one had to keep in mind that he was an autodidact; he had not progressed beyond secondary school (*Realschule*),* and although he read a lot as an adult, he limited himself to those authors whose ideas he found congenial: Arthur D. Gobineau, Houston Stuart Chamberlain, Paul de Lagarde (the first two advocates of racial doctrines and the third a fervent anti-Semite), and to a lesser extent Nietzsche. Once he had adopted their ideas, he held on to them with "unshakable fervor" and showed no interest in thinkers who held views different from his. "If intelligence consists essentially of a critical spirit," François-Poncet wrote, "then Hitler is not intelligent." On the other hand, as a demagogue Hitler was intelligent in the way he presented his ideas to rouse public support. He never hesitated to repeat his views; nor did he ever consider alternative positions as plausible. In addition, he possessed certain "feminine characteristics" such as tendencies to be sentimental and to suffer "a sudden nervous collapse." Whenever he lapsed into one of these states during a speech, he appeared to succumb to "hysteria," during which he tended to advert to various major events in his life, most notably his attempted coup d'état in Munich in 1923.

Hitler was also a man of uncommon determination and stubbornness. After his party declined by two million votes in the elections of November 6, 1932, he appeared to be "finished as a political leader." The Nazi Party was out of money, support for the movement had declined, and Hitler himself was being challenged for the movement's leadership by Strasser. Many of his followers were discouraged, but he refused to give up. He took all the necessary measures to silence the opposition within his party, and he exuded an air of confidence. Most important, he never lost faith in his ability to persuade the masses to follow him, and within weeks he succeeded in reaching the heights of power, in good measure because the political class

---

*He left school at the age of sixteen without taking the examinations necessary for a degree.

proved to be unable to take the necessary measures to prevent his appointment as chancellor. Leaders of other parties had underestimated Hitler, a "hypnotist [who] mesmerized the crowds [at meetings]"; he never doubted that he was leading a crusade and that he could persuade the masses that in following him they were engaged in advancing not simply a political program but a sacred cause.

To the entranced masses it was irrelevant that Hitler's doctrines were full of contradictions or simply false: "the masses who have suffered from war, inflation, and who today are going through a[n economic] crisis are hungry for programs [that promise action] rather than indictments [of those responsible for the state of affairs]." Hitler seemed to offer such a program, which helped him achieve electoral successes, but François-Poncet predicted that as head of the government he would be judged by his actions, not his agitation and promises. Uppermost in the ambassador's mind was the foreign policy Hitler would pursue. Here, too, the doctrines and pronouncements of the Führer were not sufficiently reliable as guides to his future actions. Yet on several issues he had maintained a consistent stance for several years, and on these his rhetoric should be taken seriously; from 1927 to 1931, his "propaganda was founded above all on hatred for France, on the elimination of reparations, [and] on [the necessity of] revising the [Versailles] treaties." In addition, Hitler espoused as a major foreign policy goal the annihilation of Communism, which he saw as a fatal threat to Germany and to Europe. He also had not wavered on one domestic matter, his determination to "purify" the country's administration, denoting the Nazis' intention to dismiss Jews and political opponents from the civil service.

The picture that François-Poncet drew of Hitler and his movement was essentially accurate and also frightening, which made the conclusion to his lengthy dispatch perplexing: it seemed to dilute his negative depiction of the new government. The Nazi Party, he declared, faced "numerous and complex problems"; hence, it was impossible to predict how the political situation in Germany would evolve over the "next few months." Some knowledgeable people in Berlin had told the ambassador that Hitler had entered into a "secret agreement"—with whom it was not clear—to restore the monarchy, although perhaps not in the near future. François-Poncet did not rule out this possibility, for it was hard to rule out anything when it came to a man "so nervous, [and] also subject to depressions and even to crises of hysteria."[22] Despite this divergent conclusion, François-Poncet's description of Hitler and Nazism included many warning signs that should have alarmed its readers in Paris.

For several weeks after Hitler's appointment as chancellor, François-Poncet alternated between exposing the anti-democratic measures of the new government and declarations of uncertainty about its future course. He was forceful in denouncing the elections of March 5, 1933, which yielded a decisive victory for the Nazis and therefore strengthened the Führer's hand. He pointed out that by no stretch of the imagination could the voting be said to have been free, despite all the promises Hitler had made to Hindenburg that he would not tamper with democratic processes. The ambassador cited several government measures that violated Hitler's commitments: the newspapers of the Social Democrats and Communists had been shut down and the two left-wing parties prohibited from organizing meetings; only parties friendly to the Nazis were permitted access to the radio; and citizens were subjected to various forms of intimidation and intense pressure to vote for the Nazis.

Many Germans, in François-Poncet's view, approved of these measures because the Reichstag fire of February 27, which had been set by a Dutch Communist, Marinus van der Lubbe, had persuaded the "simple-minded and naïve masses" that the security of the country and public order were endangered and that a Bolshevik attempt to seize power was imminent. The ambassador also invoked German history to explain the success of the Nazis in winning the support of the masses. Germany was a country in which the traditions of individualism and free speech were "infinitely less well developed than the spirit of gregariousness, admiration of force, the fear of coups, and [the tradition] of docility with regard to authority."[23] A month later, on April 5, the ambassador informed Paul-Boncour about additional violations of the rule of law: the government had sponsored a boycott of Jewish businesses on April 1 and had ordered the arbitrary arrests of Jews. These measures were further indications of Hitler's penchant for repressive measures against German citizens, in this case those he considered racially inferior.[24]

His first meeting with Hitler, on April 8, gave François-Poncet an opportunity to test his perceptions of the Führer's personality and, more important, to probe his intentions toward France. General von Blomberg, the minister of defense, was present, and it was therefore appropriate for the ambassador to initiate the discussion by reminding his host of a recent declaration he had made to the Reichstag that he had "peaceful intentions" toward other countries, and especially France. François-Poncet pointed out that in view of the new regime's "propaganda" on matters of foreign policy he feared that the future looked bleak. How could Hitler reconcile his recent public stance in favor of peace with his previous pronouncements? More specifically, the ambassador asked the chancellor how he conceived of relations between Germany and France.

Without hesitation, Hitler declared, "my government is sincerely and profoundly pacifist. We are convinced that a war, even a victorious one, would be costly in sacrifices for the entire [human] species, more costly than could be justified." In any case, he said, the main tasks of the government were to solve the problem of unemployment, to provide food for the hungry, and to overcome the economic crisis in general. "The solution to such problem[s] cannot be found in war!" Then Hitler turned the tables on François-Poncet and asked him why his government refused to allow Germany to bolster its military defenses since France was doing exactly that. He found it odd that France had "a sort of phobia against Germany"; it seemed to him far-fetched to believe that a country of sixty-nine million people that had just been vanquished militarily and had been thoroughly ruined could become a major power in the foreseeable future. The Nazi propaganda to which François-Poncet had referred did not mean, Hitler insisted, "that we are belligerent." The ambassador shot back that the Poles feared that their borders were not secure and that a rearmed Germany posed a threat to them. He also reassured Hitler that France was firmly committed to peace.

The ambassador and the Führer did not iron out their differences, yet François-Poncet ended his report to Paris on a positive note. Unlike his British colleagues Rumbold and Phipps, he found nothing strange in Hitler's behavior. On the contrary, he thought that "during the entire conversation the chancellor was courteous and amiable, not at all upset, and definitely more open than certain of his predecessors; [he was] always very prudent and careful not to touch on subjects with which he was not familiar." François-Poncet ended his dispatch with a call for cordial relations between Germany and France.[25]

The simultaneous singling out of the dangerous aspects of Nazism and favorable aspects of Hitler's character—as if the two were separate—came to characterize François-Poncet's dispatches. Thus, on April 19, 1933, he informed Paul-Boncour that Germany had been hypnotized and was in a state of intoxication; the people were filled with a "collective arrogance." At the same time he noted that all that passion lacked a solid underpinning. The economy had not improved, the financial system had not been stabilized, and the reforms of political institutions and the administration had achieved little more than to transfer power to reliable Nazis. But François-Poncet was troubled, as he indicated a few weeks later in a dispatch of August 31, by the extraordinary emphasis the Nazi leaders placed on military training of young people, who formed a large cadre of reserves. "Germany has now become a vast camp of military instruction." Officers of the Reichswehr were deeply involved in the program, and the ambassador predicted that the country would soon have a trained force of one million men, far more than the one hundred thousand permitted by the Treaty of Versailles.[26]

Nevertheless, François-Poncet could not resist pointing out that Hitler's attractive personal traits appealed to many well-meaning Germans. He had met various prominent people who had told him that even though they did not support Nazism they had found Hitler to be a man of charm, quite different from the person depicted by many of his political opponents. This theme was advanced with special force by Kurt Schmitt, who was appointed minister of economics after Alfred Hugenberg's departure from that office in the summer of 1933. The Frenchman met Schmitt at about this time and was impressed by the new minister, who claimed to have been won over by Hitler after recently meeting him. Only then did Schmitt realize how impressive Hitler was as a leader, he said. In this regard, Schmitt was not truthful. Although he had not been a member of the Nazi Party, as early as mid-1931 he had contributed two and a half million marks to Hitler's movement, which François-Poncet may not have known. He simply knew that Schmitt was a loyal member of Hitler's cabinet, and his personal contacts with him had persuaded the ambassador that the minister was a "man of good will. His honesty is evident, his patriotism is sincere and merits sympathy." Schmitt also struck the ambassador as a man of candor and integrity who worked with Hitler's subordinates without realizing that they were duplicitous.[27]

François-Poncet made his most favorable and, one might add, most dubious, comment about Hitler on May 9, 1933. After recounting Hitler's numerous attempts to overcome the mistrust of foreign statesmen and his frequent affirmations of peaceful intentions, the ambassador wrote the following: "When Hitler swears that he wants nothing as much as peace and denies that he harbors any bellicose intentions, one can grant that he does not lie." Germany, according to François-Poncet, was in no condition to wage war, and consequently the Führer adopted a nonbelligerent foreign policy. Hitler's primary goal was to secure for Germany "the means to speak, in Europe and in the entire world, the language of a great power." He also wanted to bring about changes in the postwar treaties, in particular with regard to the Polish Corridor, a region that had been severed from Germany. These goals, the ambassador suggested, went far in explaining Hitler's domestic program: Germany, the Führer believed, could restore its "liberty and honor" only by destroying Marxism and democracy and unifying the "Reich under the symbol of the swastika."[28]

François-Poncet believed that, given Germany's weakness, the best policy for France and its allies was to seek an agreement with Hitler on rearmament. The agreement should be structured in such a way as to enable Western countries "to control, to watch, to constrain, for as long as possible, the [country's] rearmament." The ambassador conceded that the approach he proposed might be criticized as simply gaining time for the West to consider other options. But this breathing space would be significant, since what Germany would be like in one year, let alone five years, remained unpredictable. In other words, François-Poncet still considered it likely, or at least possible, that the country might turn away from Nazism.[29] As he had suggested in a dispatch two weeks earlier, on April 27, 1933, "nothing . . . permits us to affirm that [Hitler] retains control over men and over events."[30] The ambassador was never again this explicit in depicting Hitler's control over Germany as so shaky, but for the next few years this view tended to be an undercurrent of his thinking and his recommendations to his superiors in Paris on how to deal with the new authorities in Berlin.

In fact, as early as mid-November 1933, François-Poncet's thinking had shifted and he now contended that the new regime enjoyed wide support. In the plebiscite of November 12, the Nazis scored an impressive victory, and although the ambassador knew that it was a charade in which 96.3 percent of eligible voters had participated, he feared that the Nazis would seize upon the victory as constituting a mandate to pursue their program without restraint. Eight months earlier, in the elections of March 5, Hitler's party had received seventeen million votes; now that figure had jumped to over forty million. True, government officials had shepherded people to the polls who were retarded, sick, or very old and many others who simply did not wish to vote, but the outcome of the vote nevertheless demonstrated to the world that the National Socialists were efficient in "persuading" the populace to do their bidding. It also demonstrated that the opponents to the New Order were politically impotent. Nazism had evidently not exhausted itself. On the contrary, Hitler could claim that the people supported him and that they were grateful to him for having restored the honor and grandeur of the German nation.

François-Poncet hoped that Hitler would now assume the mantle of statesmanship, that he would resist becoming intoxicated by his victory, and that he would avoid extremist goals. Although the ambassador thought that Hitler might adopt such a position, he was not sure that the Führer's supporters would follow him on the path of moderation. After noting the danger of an "inflamed Hitlerism" that would cast aside restraint, press for revision of the Treaty of Versailles, and step up rearmament, François-Poncet returned to his previous disdain for Nazism: "The Hitler movement, installed in the heart of Europe, constitutes an immense peril. It rests on an ideology inflated with fanaticism and violence. In what direction will its dynamism finally move? What prize will it pounce on? There is no infallible means of measuring the sincerity of Hitler; but there are a thousand reasons to attribute to him and his regime hidden and alarming motives." Or, as he put it nine days later, the Nazi leaders were "above all, mystics of a political doctrine. They are inspired by the ideas of race, authority, and morality." François-Poncet found some solace in the fact that the Nazis still lacked a practical program, especially in the critical field of the national economy. As if to reassure Paris that he had not lost his way, the ambassador told Paul-Boncour that he was not under any illusion about Hitler's aims, and he advised the foreign minister that to frustrate the Führer's aggressive moves France would have to be "firm, flexible as well as smart."[31]

On November 24 and December 11, François-Poncet again met Hitler. And once again the ambassador noted that Hitler was "amiable and cordial" during most of the first meeting, although he began the conversation with a vehement protest against the charge in the French journal *Petit parisien* that he and all his supporters were "impostors." Judging from the ambassador's initial account, it was a strong but short protest. Five days later, however, François-Poncet elaborated on Hitler's outburst, calling it "a veritable explosion" of "venom" and "indignation." The ambassador tried to reassure Hitler that the editors of the French journal were serious people and that they must have seen some documents on the Nazi leaders that they believed to be authentic. Unwilling to tolerate any criticism, the Führer made it clear that he was not mollified.

Eventually, François-Poncet steered the conversation to a more serious subject, German plans to rearm. He referred to recent statements by leading Nazis that focused on "honor" and "equality of rights," which suggested that they were committed to increasing expenditures on the military. Hitler tried to deflect the charge by emphasizing his "horror of war" and by suggesting that all the great powers immediately launch a program of substantial disarmament. If they agreed, Germany would not demand permission to expand its military machine any further. But he did not believe that other powers—he mentioned France, Poland, and Russia—would accept his "sensible" proposal, and he therefore would demand that Germany be permitted to increase the size of its army to three hundred thousand men, two hundred thousand more than permitted by the Treaty of Versailles. He would be prepared, he said, to sign a convention outlawing chemical and bacteriological warfare as well as the bombardment of civilian areas in the event of war. Finally, Hitler promised that he would reenter a reorganized League of Nations, one that resolved international conflicts rather than exacerbated them.

Two weeks later, at the second meeting with Hitler that fall, François-Poncet announced that France had "reservations" about the Führer's proposal for disarmament. The French cabinet had concluded that in view of the many statements by Hitler on the subject and his decisions since coming to power, that was no longer an option. The major sticking points were his insistence that Germany be permitted to maintain the SA and to enlarge the army to three hundred thousand men. The Nazis claimed, as they had in conversations with British envoys, that the SA was a purely political organization, which was patently not the case. And after 1933, the SA increasingly took on the character of a full-scale military force: it was divided into sections, companies, battalions, and regiments, and it also commanded its own motorized units. All the members received extensive military training. As already noted, by the end of 1933 the SA had grown into a formidable force. Understandably, the French and British governments insisted that the SA, which the German authorities on December 1 declared to be an "official" institution, constituted a significant reserve that could quickly be mobilized. Hitler also let it be known that he would not disband the SS. The two Western governments regarded these two military organizations as a critical bone of contention that stymied every attempt to reach an agreement with Germany during the first years of Nazi rule.*

In a second dispatch on the interview of December 9, François-Poncet provided interesting additional information: he now reported that the Führer had behaved differently from the way he had conducted himself at his previous meetings; this time he was "surly" and "disagreeable" and appeared to be generally "displeased and anxious." He claimed to be "astonished" that France would not give up its views on disarmament. He insisted that only if the major powers changed their position would Germany modify its stance, and he reiterated that he did not intend to dissolve the

---

*On the British view of the SA and SS, see pp. 32, 42, 60–61 above.

Brownshirts.[32] Hitler and François-Poncet continued to discuss the issue of the two paramilitary organizations at several meetings early in 1934, but the Führer would not budge. In a conversation with Foreign Minister Neurath, the French ambassador pointed out that the amplification of these two paramilitary organizations equipped Germany with the largest military establishment in the world. He tried to prod Neurath into voicing his own opinion by stating that he could not possibly expect France to "give its blessing to such a system." But neither the foreign minister nor any other Nazi leader would retreat from the claim that the SS and SA were purely political bodies. This conceit had become a part of Nazi orthodoxy.[33]

Nevertheless, François-Poncet clung to the position that some agreement might yet be possible because Germany was too weak to sustain an aggressive foreign policy. But he now watered down the expectations. Early in 1934 he proposed that the goal of total disarmament be abandoned in favor of "limited and controlled rearmament." "Any agreement," he argued, "even a mediocre one . . . [would be] better than none." He ruled out the imposition of sanctions because neither Great Britain nor Italy would agree to them; even France would probably demur. Years later, François-Poncet claimed that he never expected Hitler to "scrupulously observe limitations and rulings imposed by an international convention: I knew he was a cheat." But he thought that an agreement on partial disarmament would "embarrass him and slow him down; that the institution of a board of surveillance, to which complaints might certainly be addressed, would hamper the freedom of his movements; and that abuses cited by this board would place him in a poor position both before nations too readily inclined to trust him and before his own people. I also believed that publicity given to his acts of fraud, constituting a warning and an alarm more arresting than ambassadorial reports, would incite our government and the whole country to devote all their energies, all their labor, and all their ardor to increasing the strength of our military apparatus."[34]

On May 30, 1934, François-Poncet framed yet another argument designed to buttress his position on the limitation of rearmament. He did so in response to a question he had posed to himself: will the Nazis be guided by party doctrines in formulating future policies? His answer, radically different from some of his own earlier views and certainly from those of Rumbold or the American diplomats in Germany, was that, "In reality, the politics practiced by the leaders of the Third Reich is a politics of 'circumstances,' whose characteristic feature is its opportunism." In short, in formulating state policies, Hitler and his subordinates reacted to specific problems and were not putting into effect preconceived notions about how German society ought to be organized or about the relations between Germany and other countries. François-Poncet did grant that an overarching goal of the Nazis was to achieve autarky (*autarcie*), but even this pursuit was not a matter of "dogma" for them.[35]

Senior officials in the French government were not persuaded by the ambassador's rearmament proposal, and their reasoning was even more dubious than François-Poncet's. André Tardieu, the former prime minister and now minister of state, thought that an agreement with Hitler on disarmament was unnecessary because he "won't last much longer, his fate is sealed!" Moreover, he contended that any treaty with Hitler would only "consolidate his power," and if he went to war, "not a month would elapse before he would be deposed and replaced by the Crown Prince." The flippant comments by Tardieu on Nazi durability displayed the widespread lack of understanding of conditions in Germany among the French political class. *Le Temps*, one of the most important newspapers, had all along dismissed the Führer as a "demagogue" and "house painter," whose tenure in office was bound to be short. The prime minister, Gaston Doumergue, also found the ambassador's proposal unrealistic. Only the foreign minister, Louis Barthou, thought it had merit.[36] It is now clear that the French government was right not to support the ambassador, but not for the reasons it gave. An agreement for partial disarmament would not have deterred Hitler from pursuing his goal of reestablishing Germany as a major military power.

THE NIGHT OF THE LONG KNIVES

Not long after François-Poncet made his assessment of Nazism as an opportunistic movement, he sent the Foreign Office his sharpest, and most incisive, condemnation—on moral and ideological grounds—of Hitler and his party. The ambassador's latest change of mind was a reaction to what was until that date the single most brutal action by the Nazi leadership. For some time in 1934, Hitler and his closest collaborators had come to doubt the political reliability of Ernst Röhm, the head of the SA. An ambitious adventurer, Röhm was a close friend of Hitler in the 1920s and had participated in the failed putsch of 1923, for which he was sentenced to prison for three and a half years. In the early 1930s, he played a significant role in building the SA into a potent force, and after the Nazis' ascent to power he was determined to transform the SA, under his leadership, into a people's militia that would spearhead a second revolution—a "German revolution"—although he never spelled out the social program he favored for the radical reordering of the country's institutions. He also wanted the paramilitary organization to be merged with the Reichswehr, a move that was correctly considered a threat to the traditional military leadership. But Hitler preferred not to antagonize the generals, whose participation was essential to Germany's rearmament and any campaign of conquest the Nazis might wish to initiate. At the same time, the Führer was reluctant to move against Röhm, a long-standing friend and supporter. True, Röhm was known to have voiced criticisms of the Nazi government, but he always professed his loyalty to the party and to Hitler.

Eventually, however, the Führer, egged on by several senior Nazis as well as the leaders of the Reichswehr, grew to suspect that Röhm, who enjoyed great popularity within the party, was hatching a plot against him.*He was also troubled by Röhm's unconcealed homosexuality. He therefore gave the order to assassinate Röhm and his alleged accomplices on June 30, soon to be known as the "Night of the Long Knives." Within a matter of hours, at least seventy-seven people—and according to reliable sources, many more—were shot to death in cold blood in various locations in Germany. Among them were the former prime minister, General Schleicher, and his wife, and several Nazi Party leaders now condemned as rivals by Göring and Himmler. Numerous other prominent political figures thought not to be sympathetic to the New Order were also executed.[37]

The elimination of Röhm both strengthened the Reichswehr politically and boosted the loyalty of the military to the New Order. General von Blomberg, the minister of defense, drew closer to the Nazi leaders and accepted more and more of their ideas, including the "Aryan paragraph" promulgated by the Nazis on April 7, 1933; it had ordered the dismissal from the civil service of Jews and opponents of the regime. Blomberg now referred to the army "as the sword of the German people who are united under National Socialism."[38]

François-Poncet was shocked by the massacre, and he was further shocked and offended by charges carried in the German press that France and he himself had been involved in the plot concocted by Röhm and had actually given him weapons for his militia, to be used in the event of a government attack. The charge was based on the following flimsy evidence: (1) François-Poncet was known to have good relations with General Schleicher, one of

---

* On this event, see also above, pp. 35–36.

the men accused of participating in the conspiracy; (2) at a reception given by Count von Bassewitz, the chief of protocol, the French ambassador was seen talking at length with Röhm; and (3) numerous German emissaries had recently visited France to "test the waters," and Schleicher himself had been in France "on a mysterious voyage."[39] To the ambassador's astonishment, the German press swallowed the charges and publicized them widely. François-Poncet complained to Neurath and warned that the "newspaper campaign," stoked by Goebbels, could lead to a serious deterioration in relations between France and Germany. Neurath "formally denied" that there was any basis to the charges against France and assured the ambassador that he had urged the newspapers to desist from implicating France in the Röhm affair, but despite his best efforts the rumors continued to be widely disseminated.[40]

François-Poncet also expressed surprise that the German government had not published any documents to prove the existence of a plot to overthrow Hitler. Neurath responded that such a step was "not opportune" because it would stir up "too much emotion" in the country. But the foreign minister understood that a "primitive plan" had been scheduled for August or September. Röhm, however, had learned that the police were close on his heels and therefore moved up the date of the putsch to June 30, when Hitler and his ministers were to be arrested by followers of Röhm. The Führer decided that he had no time to lose and ordered his subordinates to unleash the massacre before the other side could strike. François-Poncet urged Neurath to make these facts available at least to the diplomatic corps in Berlin because, as he put it, "the events of 30 June were not such as to evoke sympathy abroad for the Third Reich." Neurath simply repeated that he had ordered the press not to cast suspicion on foreign powers. For the rest, he predicted that the excitement would soon abate. But François-Poncet observed that "he did not have the demeanor of someone who was very sure of this."[41]

In diplomatic circles, few accepted the government's claim that Röhm had plotted to remove Hitler from power, and certainly no one believed that foreign powers were involved. To be sure, there had been bad blood between several leading figures in the Nazi Party (Göring, Himmler, and Reinhard Heydrich) and Röhm, it was no secret that Röhm favored an agenda different from Hitler's, and—most troubling to the Nazi leadership—Röhm had not discouraged the emergence of a personality cult of his own within the SA.[42] Still, most foreign diplomats thought it highly unlikely that he would have staged a coup. But they all agreed that as a result of the bloodbath the influence of the Reichswehr had increased immeasurably.

François-Poncet drew one other conclusion from the bloody events, one that he had occasionally voiced earlier: Nazism was a deplorable and dangerous political movement. The massacre, he thought, indicated the strength of "radical and almost Bolshevik" tendencies within Nazism.[43] Thirteen days after making these comments, the ambassador contended that the Führer fully supported these tendencies: "there is no doubt that Hitler himself ordered the massacre." The bloody event had brought to light "the psychology or rather the pathology" of Nazism. Hitler had revealed himself to be "veritably a deranged [man] affected by two madnesses: the madness of greatness and the mania for persecution. This vegetarian, this ascetic about whom it is said that he suffers from the weakness of not being able to separate himself from his old comrades and who finds no joy in music,* has assumed a sinister bearing as a demagogue. [In front of an audience] his hoarse voice has an unbelievable pitch of ferocity; he acts like a man possessed [*possédé*] by rage. . . . When such a man is the leader of 60 million people and controls all the levers of power, he constitutes a peril to Europe that no one should conceal from himself. I have already indicated it, and I insist on it: *one must fear the day that Hitler has a decidedly favorable opportunity* [to make his moves on the international scene]."[44]

Equally troubling to François-Poncet was the definition of treason in the two-hour speech that Hitler delivered to the Reichstag on July 13 about the events of June 30. "In matters of treason," he exclaimed, "it is not the act that is important [but rather] the state of mind!" That is, for Hitler, mere opposition to him was tantamount to treason. "This was the reasoning applied at the time of the [French] Terror; it is applied by the Bolshevik regime," the ambassador noted; and now Hitler, who considered himself the "supreme judge," applied it with unspeakable "inhumanity" and "cynicism." This approach to the law conformed with Göring's declaration to a gathering of procurators: "The will of the Führer, that is the law." François-Poncet could not understand why the world did not "tremble at assertions so monstrous that they subvert the fundamental notions on which civilization rests and to which [we are] accustomed."[45]

The death of President Hindenburg on August 2, 1934, intensified François-Poncet's apprehensions about Europe's future. Although the president had been old and feeble and too much under the sway of a circle of ambitious and reckless sycophants, he still exercised great moral authority in the

---

*François-Poncet was wrong; Hitler did enjoy music.

country as well as in the army; and he was the only person who could have restrained Hitler. The Führer, the ambassador believed, had lived in fear that one day the president would abandon him, just as he had abandoned two previous chancellors, Brüning and Schleicher.

Hitler wasted no time in taking advantage of the new turn of events. As soon as news of Hindenburg's death reached him, he assumed the functions of chief of state, as the Constitution stipulated. But the question of whether an election would now be held for the highest post in the land, as the Constitution also stipulated, was simply ignored by the cabinet; the ministers raised no objection to Hitler's plan to act as both president and chancellor, making him the "master" of one of the great countries of Europe. The political elite and the public remained passive as these events unfolded. Seventeen days after Hindenburg's death, a plebiscite was held on Hitler's assumption of his new position; over 90 percent of the eligible voters went to the polls and of these, 89.9 percent supported the "constitutional" transfer to Hitler of "unlimited power as head of state, head of government, leader of the Nazi Party, and Supreme Commander of the armed forces."[46] The Nazi leaders were disappointed that the margin of victory was not larger. In François-Poncet's view, the elevation of Hitler to the position of "supreme magistrate of the Reich" was "[not] reassuring for the future of Germany, Europe, or for peace."[47]

The trust in Hitler's word that the ambassador had declared only a few months earlier had dissipated. On August 8, he told the French foreign minister that he did not believe that the Führer could have been honest in informing Ward Price, a reporter for the *Daily Mail*, that Germany accepted its present borders. Even Hindenburg, Brüning, or Stresemann, all much more moderate than the Führer, would not have made so conciliatory a declaration, which the German people would not support. Nor did François-Poncet credit Hitler's renunciation of all claims to the colonies that Germany had possessed before World War I. On the other hand, Hitler was truthful in not giving up on the demand for the incorporation (*Anschluss*) of Austria into a Greater Germany. On this issue, François-Poncet mocked Hitler—which he had rarely done in his previous dispatches—for mistakenly claiming that Germany and Austria had long been united in a "Germanic community" until Austria decided on a split. "Knowledge of history is not his forte."[48]

One senior member of the embassy, the chargé d'affaires, Pierre Arnal, offered a somewhat optimistic assessment of Germany's recent past. He believed that the bloody Night of the Long Knives had brought the era of revolution to a close. Now that Hitler had eliminated Röhm and could count on the support of the armed forces (Reichswehr), the chancellor fully sided with the "conservatives" in the Nazi Party. He understood that the terror that had swept over the country for the first fifteen days of July had taken a terrible toll, and therefore wanted to reestablish order and "bring about a [period of] calm that the country had never known since the accession [to power] of the [Nazi] regime." Having made this optimistic prediction, Arnal adopted the stance of his superior, the ambassador. He concluded by warning that Germany was so volatile and Hitler so impetuous that no one could speak with much confidence about the future course of events.[49]

GERMANY AS A MILITARY THREAT

In the midst of the growing signs of Nazi ruthlessness and brutality at home, the French military attaché, General Gaston Renondeau, a major source of French intelligence on Germany, found disturbing evidence that Hitler's government was making extensive preparations for a long military conflict. The general based his report to Paris on data collected by a British official considered thoroughly reliable. The data indicated that Germany had launched a major program to obtain large quantities of raw materials, most notably fuels. Several firms—among them I. G. Farben and the Braunkohle Zwangsgemeinschaft—had made arrangements to acquire industrial equipment by January 1937 that would make possible the production of two million tons of fuel. Other industrial firms were to produce three hundred thousand tons of synthetic fuels by hydrogenating carbon. In addition, the German authorities had set a high priority on discovering new processes for manufacturing synthetic rubber. General Renondeau concluded with a clear warning that "Germany has formally decided to replace all the raw materials that are not found on its soil and that are indispensable during war with synthetic products manufactured in its country. The projects, carefully examined, are now on the verge of being realized."[50]

A few days after François-Poncet had forwarded the general's report to Paris, he himself sent a dispatch on rearmament based on intelligence he had received from a person simply identified as a well-placed and reliable "informer," who had revealed that members of the SA and SS were receiving six and eight weeks of military instruction from lower-ranking officers of the regular army. In addition, many young men were sent to camps on the pretext that they would work on the land but instead spent most of their time on military training. And when they "worked," they participated in the "construction of underground shelters" clearly designed for military purposes. According to the informer, the military were currently paying special attention to the training of pilots. The ambassador learned the exact locations of "aeronautic centers" in fifteen regions of Germany. François-Poncet concluded that despite Hitler's many pronouncements in favor of peace, the "feverish" pace of rearmament proved that the chancellor was preparing for the "eventuality of war."[51] In light of these warnings about Germany's focus on rearmament, it must have been puzzling and frustrating for officials in Paris to read the ambassador's frequent confessions that he could not be sure about Hitler's intentions. Indeed, he ended this report, written on October 25, 1934, with a series of questions that betrayed his own confusion about the Führer's plans: "Is he thinking of provoking . . . war? . . . Is he afraid? It is difficult to pierce his true feelings from one day to the next."[52]

François-Poncet's vacillations continued throughout 1935, in many ways a pivotal year in the consolidation of Hitler's power. On January 13, a plebiscite on the future of the Saar held in accordance with the provisions of the Versailles Treaty greatly bolstered Hitler's prestige in Germany. Almost 91 percent of the residents voted in favor of reunification with Germany, a clear sign that most ethnic Germans were prepared to overlook Nazi extremism for the sake of nationalist goals. In the ambassador's view, the vote undermined the view of those who believed that the Nazi revolution would somehow collapse, that it was merely a passing phase, or a "nightmare" that would dissipate. "The plebiscite in the Saar region removes all doubt that this revolution has created a new and durable state of affairs; it proves the pointlessness of making a distinction between a Hitlerian Germany and an anti-Hitlerian Germany. There exists only one Germany and it is with this one [country] that the powers must come to terms."

In the same dispatch, François-Poncet noted that since the electoral victory the German press had been more moderate than in the past and that Hitler himself "speaks a language more conciliatory" than usual; these developments might lead some of his radical supporters to fear that he was abandoning his intransigence and that he might even be thinking of returning to the League of Nations. "For this very reason, we would be wrong to minimize their importance." The ambassador was further encouraged by an assurance he had received from the German Foreign Office that the government would not "remilitarize" the Saar and would not build a new airport there. But as was his wont, François-Poncet also warned that it might be too soon for France to be sure about Hitler's course in foreign affairs. He again advocated a "wait and see" approach by his government.[53]

It did not take long for Hitler to make a move that undermined the ambassador's advice. On March 16, François-Poncet received a call from the chancellor's office inviting him to a meeting with Hitler, who showed his guest the text of a new law establishing obligatory military service in Germany and increasing the size of the army to twelve corps and thirty-six divisions. Hitler asserted that Germany had the right to enlarge its army and again vowed not to attack any other country. He also repeated his disavowal of any thought of German hegemony in Europe. François-Poncet responded that as the representative of a country that had signed the Treaty of Versailles he felt obliged to register a protest against Germany's new law; and he made a point of stressing that over the preceding two years France had not increased the size of its military forces. Hitler's reply was brief and, at least on the surface, reasonable: he declared that he was always ready to debate this issue. As was true of his previous meetings with Hitler, François-Poncet did not detect any aberrant behavior on the chancellor's part.[54]

But when two senior British officials were reported to have made favorable comments about the Führer, François-Poncet, always suspicious of Britain's intentions in foreign affairs, exploded. The outburst had its origins in a visit that Sir John Simon, the foreign minister, and his subordinate Anthony Eden had paid to Germany, during which they met Hitler privately on March 24, 1935. The Führer's lieutenants quickly spread the word that the British guests had been impressed by their host as an "absolutely candid" leader who delivered his arguments forcefully and persuasively. And the two Britons had found Hitler to be altogether reasonable.* Sir John had never challenged him and left the meeting convinced that the chancellor was "an honorable and serious partner" in tackling international issues. In a private conversation, the British ambassador, Sir Eric Phipps, gave François-Poncet the impression that Hitler's subordinates were not "absolutely" wrong in making these claims. As related by François-Poncet, rather than being a dictator who ordered the decapitation of women and the shooting of his friends, Hitler had struck Simon as "well brought up and amiable[; he] spoke on all matters thoughtfully [and] was capable of arguing with shrewdness." Phipps also confirmed that Simon was so impressed by Hitler that in the future the foreign minister would not favor any new European international arrangements that were concluded without Germany's participation.[55]

---

*On the visit to Hitler by Simon and Eden, see also above, pp. 60–61.

François-Poncet was scathing in his reaction to Simon's assessment of Hitler. The ambassador conceded that Hitler could be gracious and could give the impression of being moved by honorable sentiments. But François-Poncet warned that Sir John had not taken the full measure of the man. Hitler was also a person of "brutal arrogance, [who was] violent, devoured by the madness of [his own] greatness, . . . obstinate, stubborn and mean to the point of madness." Simon had placed his trust in a "primitive brute."[56] François-Poncet seems to have forgotten that too often he himself had dwelled on the apparently attractive features of Hitler.

When François-Poncet returned to Berlin on June 23, 1935, after a one-month stay in Paris, he was amazed at the change in the political climate. When he left, the mood had been downcast, mainly because the League of Nations had condemned Germany for rearming in violation of the Treaty of Versailles. Moreover, it had seemed that several European powers—France, the Soviet Union, Czechoslovakia, and Romania—were planning to isolate and encircle Germany. But by the end of June, the atmosphere was entirely different. The British government, which sympathized with Germany's resentment of the punitive measures of the Treaty of Versailles, had signed a naval agreement with Hitler that allowed Germany to build a navy 35 percent as large as the Royal Navy. The British government looked upon the treaty as a way of limiting German rearmament, but the Germans were pleased to be permitted to exceed the limits set by the Treaty of Versailles, and they also saw the agreement as a first step toward creating an alliance with Great Britain against France and the Soviet Union. But the French and Italians were disturbed because they had been kept in the dark during the negotiations. "The naval accord of London," François-Poncet noted, "had banished the clouds [in Germany] and had brought back the sun." The Nazis considered the agreement a complete transformation of the international situation because Germany was now no longer isolated. It enhanced Hitler's prestige, and his followers were now confident that within a few years their country would reemerge as "the foremost military power in the world."[57] Writing after World War II, François-Poncet argued that all along British political leaders had underestimated the military threat posed by the Nazis and that they therefore bore much responsibility for the West's failure to stop the rearmament of Germany.[58]

Days after his return to Berlin, the ambassador received an unsettling report from General Renondeau on Germany's expansionist plans. The general had been sent a remarkably candid account of those plans by Major Friedrich-Carl Rabe von Pappenheim, a soldier who within another eight years rose to the rank of lieutenant-general and who at times also worked as a diplomat. Pappenheim was well-informed and appeared to be echoing the words of senior officials in the German government. "The proposition is simple," according to Pappenheim. "Germany is a country that suffocates under present conditions; endowed with a powerful dynamism in the midst of people for whose weakness it has contempt, it is not content with amputated territories that are broken into pieces." As a country of sixty-five million soon to grow to one hundred million, Germany must secure *Lebensraum*. Pappenheim assured his interlocutor that "Germany did not plan to expand in the west, but rather in the east, northeast, and the south." A primary goal was to reoccupy the Danzig Corridor, then under Polish rule; Poland was to be compensated in part with land severed from Lithuania and in part from the Ukraine. And if Czechoslovakia was dissolved, part of its territory would go to Poland, the rest to Germany. Pappenheim also indicated that Germany would soon have an army of four hundred thousand and that by 1936 it was expected to be even larger. He was sure that all these ambitions could be accomplished quite easily: neither France nor Great Britain would prevent them because they would be preoccupied with maintaining their empires. Germany, Pappenheim assured the French diplomat, had no intention of meddling in the colonial affairs of these two countries. It was an astonishingly frank description of Germany's plans that could leave the authorities in France with little doubt about the dangers that confronted Europe.[59]

After the annual meeting of the Nazi Party in Nuremberg on September 11–17, 1935, François-Poncet sent his first detailed account of the persecution of the Jews to Paris. In his view, it was at that meeting that Hitler, who for a long time had been silent on the internal divisions within National Socialism, made it clear that he sided with "the old guard, his first companions in the struggle for the realization of the revolutionary program." The party congress extolled the army and lauded the ideas of Streicher, Goebbels, Himmler, and Robert Ley, all of whom espoused a "new war against Jews, Catholics, [and Marxist] revolutionaries." Immediately after the congress adjourned, the government promulgated new laws that officially defined the Jews as a race and placed a series of new restrictions on them: "Aryan" women under the age of forty-five could no longer work for Jews as servants, and intermarriage, as well as any sexual relationship between Jews and Aryans, was prohibited. This prohibition was consistent with Streicher's contention that even one sexual encounter between a Jewish man and an Aryan woman would make it impossible for the woman ever to produce a "pure-blooded Aryan child."[60] In François-Poncet's view, the laws were further evidence that Hitler and the other leaders of the Nazi Party were bent on "exterminating the Jews of the Reich by means of a slow strangulation more terrible than the pogroms." Despite these ominous signs of Nazi brutality, François-Poncet saw a ray of light. Ever the optimist, he thought it was still "premature" to conclude that the "army has abandoned all thought of resistance and that it is resigned to complying with all the wishes of the [Nazi] Party." His evidence for this optimism was not very strong. All he could come up with was the reaction of the Reichswehr to a speech by Göring during the Nuremberg ceremonies on the "law of the flag": the officers were "stony faced," which he interpreted as a sign of apprehension.[61]

On November 21, 1935, François-Poncet had his last interview of the year with Hitler, and once again the ambassador's reports on the meeting are inconsistent, if not contradictory. In his first dispatch (a telegram), he noted that the Führer had responded "with much amiability and in a very cordial tone," even though he also delivered a long criticism of the recently concluded pact between France and the Soviet Union, which he insisted was directed against Germany. In a second telegram, François-Poncet indicated that the German newspapers had reported positively on their meeting, which gave the ambassador hope that Germany and France might be able to discuss critical issues in a calm atmosphere and that they might yet reach agreements acceptable to both.[62] But six days after the interview, the ambassador wrote a much longer dispatch in which Hitler's behavior was described as much more bombastic and aggressive. "On 21 November I had in front of me an elated and spirited man who embarked on a vehement tirade as though he were addressing a crowd of several thousand people, after which he seemed to be like a battery emptied of its electricity." Hitler had clearly reflected in advance on what he intended to say and made his points forcefully. He expressed strong disapproval of the Franco-Soviet pact, voiced concern over the friction between Italy and Abyssinia, and reiterated his wish for better relations between Germany and France. In the course of the interview, Hitler delivered "frequent and frenetic" attacks on the Jews and the USSR, but François-Poncet passed no judgment on Hitler's bizarre behavior.[63]

François-Poncet's repeated comments about Hitler's good behavior are puzzling because he knew that his British counterpart, Sir Eric Phipps, was sending assessments of the German leader that were quite different from his. The French ambassador met Phipps in mid-December, only days after his encounter with Hitler, and during the conversation Phipps noted that he was "struck" by the negative tenor of his own recent conversation with Hitler, during which the Führer was more acerbic than he had ever been with the French ambassador.[64] Phipps noted that Hitler was "puffed up" and not at all in a mood to agree to "reasonable" suggestions. The British ambassador was annoyed that the account in the press of his talk with Hitler, drafted under the direction of Neurath, falsely claimed that the discussion of a pact on air warfare (to avoid targeting civilians) and the limitation of rearmament had made progress. Why François-Poncet sent the Foreign Office this report on his meeting with Phipps as an addendum that he specifically marked "secret" is not clear.[65] Could it be that the ambassador did not want it to be generally known that in his presence Hitler tended to be more restrained than he was in meetings with the British ambassador?

THE MARCH INTO THE RHINELAND

On March 7, 1936, Hitler made his most daring and provocative move yet in international affairs by sending German troops into the Rhineland, an area fifty kilometers east of the Rhine that had been declared a demilitarized zone in 1919.* Germany's violation of the agreement regarding this area did not surprise François-Poncet. On March 6, he informed Paris that he had learned from a "generally well-informed" source that on March 2 the Führer had asked several senior Reichswehr officers how long it would take to occupy the demilitarized area and how much time they would need to organize adequate defenses against a French attack.[66] Hitler considered such a move very risky and ordered the army to be prepared to retreat in the event of strong resistance by the French military. For the allies, this was almost certainly the last time that they could have taken forceful action against Hitler without risking a major conflagration. Germany was still too weak to defeat the French, and a retreat by the Reichswehr would have been deeply embarrassing and a sharp political blow to the Führer.

For the French ambassador, the aggressive move by Germany once again raised questions that he had not been able to answer to his own satisfaction. Had the leaders of Germany lied all along when they declared that they would respect the treaty provisions concerning the Rhineland? Had Hitler once again adopted the views of the most radical and most violent Nazis? François-Poncet now believed that Hitler had always followed a single pat-

*For more details, see above, pp. 44–46.

tern in the conduct of his foreign policy. In leaving the League of Nations, in announcing the expansion of the army on March 16, 1935, and now in sending his troops into the Rhineland, Hitler was following a preconceived plan to expand German power. "[Hitler's] ambition is not limited to reestablishing Germany's sovereignty. The Third Reich has decided to go . . . further than William II." The Nazis' next move, the ambassador predicted, would be the annexation of Austria; Göring had bluntly stated that intention in various pronouncements. Hitler would then make Czechoslovakia his next victim, having ultimately set his eyes on the establishment of "German hegemony in central Europe. . . . If England gives way, if it surrenders, then Hitler will win. If it defends the principles of morality, then Hitler's cause will fail." The German people, the ambassador asserted, did not want to repeat the mistake of 1914, and if their country faced unyielding opposition, in the end they would turn away from provocative policies.[67]

François-Poncet believed that the French government was paralyzed, and he warned the leaders in Paris that they would regret their failure to respond to the "brutal action" of March 7 with an "act of the same character." Unable to secure British support for a strong stand against Germany, afraid that the citizens of France would reject a response to Germany that might lead to military conflict, and still befuddled about Hitler's ultimate goals, the government did not follow the ambassador's advice. There was no serious attempt to explain to the nation the likely consequences of advance into the Rhineland. After two or three days of uncertainty, the statesmen of the Western powers "recovered their serenity" and decided to ignore Hitler's move. The governments offered a variety of reasons for their inaction, and the result was predictable: the Führer could boast of another bloodless victory on the international scene.[68]

Hitler's self-confidence rose immeasurably. On March 18 he dissolved the Reichstag and called for elections to enable the people to express their views on the latest developments. The electoral campaign proceeded as had all the others under Nazi rule, except that the public was more cowed than ever before. The Nazis scored their greatest electoral victory yet: out of forty-five million ballots, 98.8 percent backed the march into the Rhineland.

François-Poncet fell into despair and once again raised doubts about Hitler's sincerity in avowing his peaceful intentions. The ambassador was distressed by France's military weakness, which prevented the country from standing up to the new Germany. He likened the relationship between the two nations to a sexual relationship in which "Germany assumes to itself the role of the [dominant] male." He ended the dispatch with a strong indictment of the Nazis that suggested his growing awareness of a link between their conduct of affairs within Germany and their conduct of foreign policy. "Isn't it too much to expect . . . us to believe," François-Poncet wrote, "in the sincerity of men who have burned their Reichstag, assassinated their own supporters when they have become a nuisance, and violated without shame . . . international agreements that their country had freely signed?"[69]

A month later, on April 21, François-Poncet once again debated with himself whether the Führer wanted peace or was preparing for war. He concluded that the dictator was not eager to engage in military conflict, especially since his moves had met with no resistance. He had achieved his goals without bloodshed; why not continue with his successful strategy? But then the ambassador raised a consideration to which he—unlike his British colleagues Rumbold and Phipps—had not always paid adequate attention: Hitler's character. He now referred to "his fits of brusque exaltation and fanaticism, his rashness as a gambler that excites the determination of his most reckless friends." The Führer was aware that his past successes had resulted from daring gambits on his part, and François-Poncet warned that the West must expect the Nazis, whose ideology was fundamentally bellicose, to behave as they invariably had since coming to power.[70]

Two weeks after he composed these thoughts, on May 6, the ambassador received news that confirmed his worst fears. Ignoring promises they had made only two months earlier, the Nazis had begun building fortifications in the Rhine region. The work was scheduled to be completed by wintertime, and then "Germany would be sufficiently prepared to wage war."[71] François-Poncet was now convinced that Germany's move into the Rhineland had undermined France's credibility, especially among central European nations, which France had promised to protect. He feared that several of them, most notably Austria and Czechoslovakia, would not be able to withstand Nazi encroachments.[72]

In the summer of 1936, Germany took another large step in enhancing its military. The government announced that the period of service for military recruits would be increased from one year to two. François-Poncet urged his government to pursue a two-pronged policy: rapid rearmament coupled with a proposal to Germany for the negotiation of an agreement to limit the arms race. If France and its allies did not rearm, the ambassador advised, then "in one or two years Hitler will go to war."[73]

Any lingering doubts that François-Poncet may have had about Hitler's grandiose designs on Europe should have been swept away during an extraordinary meeting they had on September 2, 1936, in Berchtesgaden, which began with a free-wheeling discussion of international affairs. The ambassador repeated his country's eagerness for amicable relations with Germany, urged Hitler not to intervene in the Spanish Civil War, and then voiced his concern about tensions in Europe. In his response, Hitler claimed that the situation was more critical than his guest realized and contended that Western statesmen failed to understand what was causing the tensions. "Europe," Hitler declared, "has been eaten away by Bolshevism. Distributing endless sums of money, the Soviets have so far undermined Poland, Czechoslovakia, Romania, [and] France." He warned that a terrible upheaval, organized by the Comintern (the Communist International), could break out at any moment. "Only two men were determined to defend civilization and the traditions of [the European] continent: he himself, Hitler, and with him Mussolini. They might perhaps perish [in the endeavor]. But history will honor their memory as the two courageous champions of a great humane cause." Hitler then boasted that he was a better European than was generally realized.

That did not end his comments on the current situation in Europe. He also launched into what François-Poncet called a "tirade" on Germany's economic needs. Both France and Britain could rely on colonies to supply them with needed goods. Those countries must understand that Germany, too, could not do without an adequate supply of raw materials. As the leader of that country, he had to make good on his promise to its sixty-seven million people that he would find work for them as well as an adequate supply of food. "Germany," he said, "demands" that other powers freely and in a friendly manner make it possible for it to acquire the necessary products. "Otherwise, it will procure them in other ways." But, as usual, Hitler added that he wished for nothing but peace.[74]

THE END OF FRANÇOIS-PONCET'S
TENURE IN BERLIN

The dispatches to Paris that François-Poncet composed during his last twenty-two months in Berlin, roughly from January 1937 until late October 1938, tended to be more consistently critical of Hitler and Nazism than those of previous years; yet they still held out hope that the West could somehow reach an agreement with Germany and that war could be avoided. On the one hand, on March 17, 1937, he told Yvon Delbos, the foreign minister, that there was no doubt that some among the leadership of the Third Reich were "sincere partisans of a Western entente," which they viewed as the "most solid foundation for peace." How much influence they would exercise would become clear only "over the coming weeks and months."[75]

On the other hand, about a month later, the ambassador gave a chilling account of the celebration of Hitler's birthday on April 20. Many citizens, in a state of rapture, marked the event by extolling the "resurrection" of the German army and the reoccupation of the Rhine territory. The celebrations took place "in an atmosphere of idolatry and cultism, evoking in certain aspects the cult that surrounded Roman emperors." The military marches harked back to the most elaborate such spectacles of Imperial Germany. Hitler's photograph was prominently displayed on virtually all streets to drive home the point that he had restored the country's power and prestige. According to François-Poncet, it seemed as though the Führer was portrayed as some sort of "Germanic deity" and that the cult surrounding him was designed to supplant Christianity. In the evening before these celebrations, Goebbels delivered a speech, widely reprinted in the press, that lauded Hitler as "one of the greatest figures in history, as a being of superhuman will, a person with a sharp intelligence [and] a phenomenal memory, capable of confounding any technician on questions in his specialty; a man of encyclopedic knowledge, [who] knows by heart the smallest details of Greek or Roman history as well as the tonnage of any German or foreign warship." The ambassador concluded his dispatch with a statement that could be taken as a warning to the French government: the grand display of April 20 amounted to further evidence of Hitler's megalomania and boded ill for European countries standing in his way.[76] It was certainly not the description of a leader who could be restrained by domestic pressures from pursuing his ambitions. It is therefore surprising that François-Poncet continued to believe that moderates in the Nazi Party might yet influence the Führer's policies.

Totally unexpected events early in 1938 further strengthened Hitler's grip on power. On January 12, General Werner von Blomberg, the minister of war and an ardent admirer of the Führer, married a young woman twenty years his junior in the presence of his five children, the bride's mother, and Hitler and Göring; the last two acted as witnesses. Blomberg's wife had died, and lacking friends he yearned for female companionship. But within days of the marriage, rumors circulated in Berlin that the general's new wife had been a lady of ill repute; even worse for devoted Nazis, she had been photographed in scanty attire by a Czech Jew who was her lover. According to the historian Ian Kershaw, unverified rumors circulated that Hitler was so upset by this news of racial defilement and by his having kissed the hand of the minister's new wife that he bathed himself seven times in one day to wash away the stain.[77]

A few days after this shock, on January 24, Hitler learned of another scandal, this one involving Colonel-General Werner Freiherr von Fritsch, commander in chief of the army, also an admirer and loyal follower of the Führer. Fritsch, it was charged, had been involved in 1936 in a homosexual relationship with a young man. The evidence was skimpy at best, but Hitler and his leading lieutenants were deadly afraid that as a result of the two scandals the government would become a laughingstock and lose popular support. On January 27, Hitler dismissed Blomberg and eight days later fired Fritsch.

In a dispatch of February 10, François-Poncet drew two conclusions from the dismissals: they proved that there were still deep ideological differences and conflicts between the conservatives in the military leadership and the extremists in the Nazi Party; and they represented a continuation of a trend initiated after the bloodbath of June 30, 1934, that is, the increase in Hitler's power over the military. The correctness of the second conclusion quickly became evident. Hitler assumed the title of "Supreme Commander of the Armed Forces" (*Oberster Befehlshaber der Wehrmacht*), which marked a major shift of power from the traditional army leadership to the National Socialist Party.[78]

François-Poncet's interpretation of the conflict between the army and the Nazi Party was rather complicated and not altogether convincing. He pointed out, correctly, that a fairly large number of the army's leaders, who were traditional conservatives, opposed Hitler's economic and social policies, as well as his campaign against the Jews and Christianity. But he went on to assert that this dichotomy proved that "behind the façade of totalitarian regimes . . . the same strife, the same political conflicts are waged as in other regimes," and thus one could not be certain of the outcome in Germany. The future, he insisted, was "problematic and covered with clouds."[79] François-Poncet seems to have forgotten his own descriptions of Hitler's unchallengeable hold on power and his ruthlessness in exercising it. Such charismatic and unprincipled leaders do not often rise to the top in all societies, especially not in democratic countries.

On February 16, six days after raising doubts about the dangerous consequences of Hitler's dominance over the army, the ambassador changed his mind: he now believed that one result of the dismissal of Blomberg and

Fritsch was that Germany might initiate a "more active phase" in foreign policy. It even seemed likely that the Reich was poised to launch "an adventure."[80]

A week later, on February 23, François-Poncet assessed Hitler's leadership in some ways more critically than ever before. In the report, he evaluated the Führer's three-hour address to the Reichstag of February 20 on the recent scandals. Never had Hitler expressed himself with more resentment and more threats; nor had he ever been as peremptory in his demands. He also harshly denounced the foreign press for its critical comments on German internal affairs. To defend his own conduct, he referred to crises in other countries, drawing attention in particular to the "orgies of the guillotine" at the time of the French Revolution. Then he unleashed a personal attack on Anthony Eden, the foreign minister of Britain. Hitler's delivery "betrayed the profound arrogance of a man who was more and more emotional and given to megalomania, and who, moreover, suffering from insomnia, increasingly had to resort to soporifics."[81]

Within weeks it became clear that Hitler was now bent on radical action on the international scene. On March 12, 1938, German troops marched into Austria, and despite the "brutality, suddenness, and scope" of the invasion, Hitler's bold decision to annex the German-speaking land evoked great admiration among the people, who at the same time felt relieved that the danger of a European war had been "deferred, if not eliminated."[82]

In mid-June the Nazis launched a new campaign against the Jews, another sign of a shift to extremism. The ambassador informed Paris of the stepped-up drive to expropriate Jewish property and the numerous indiscriminate arrests of Jews, many of whom were "trembling like hunted beasts and seeking ways of running away." François-Poncet viewed this new wave of persecution as a typical reaction of the Nazis to "difficulties that exasperate them." They were now holding the Jews responsible for the worldwide hostility toward them, especially in Anglo-Saxon countries. But the ambassador also noted that the Nazis were looking for pretexts to deprive the Jews of their assets.[83]

In the midst of these turbulent events, François-Poncet received an unusual request from Paris. The Foreign Office asked him to evaluate two articles in the distinguished British journal *The Economist*, which examined conditions in Germany and surprisingly concluded that the country was considerably weaker than Imperial Germany had been in 1914 and would therefore not risk a "general conflagration." The editors of *The Economist* were not sympathetic to Nazism; nor can they be classified as out-and-out appeasers. But they had persuaded themselves that Germany might well be restrained by the country's economic vulnerability, which the editors demonstrated with a careful analysis of the failure of the Nazis to achieve their economic goal of autarky. In any case, "the German people to-day have no more stomach for a great war against adversaries of their own caliber than the French or the English or the Americans. . . . The Germans do not want to fight, and Herr Hitler certainly knows it. We believe that the Führer has the will to peace."[84]

When his staff had completed its analysis of the articles, François-Poncet added his own views. He thought the editors had made a serious attempt to understand Nazi thinking and Nazi policies, but he rejected their conclusions as "a bit too optimistic." True, Germany still faced many economic difficulties, but he considered it a mistake to assume that the Nazi leaders acted like leaders in the West when it came to military matters. Hitler and his lieutenants had great faith in their huge army and air force, as well as in Germany's efficient industry, and they could count on a population imbued with National Socialist ideals and the traditions of obedience to orders from above. In any case—and this was a critical point for the ambassador—the Nazi leaders were not guided by reason but by "sentiment." Hitler followed his emotions and led a movement whose driving forces were excitement and exaltation. Finally, François-Poncet warned that Nazi leaders were often inclined to underestimate their adversaries, whom they tended to think of as "disunited, feeble, hesitant and cowardly."[85]

~

François-Poncet's last involvement in a major diplomatic negotiation in Germany took place in September 1938 during the crisis over Hitler's demand that Czechoslovakia surrender its control over the Sudetenland, a region with a German-speaking majority. The Czechs rejected the demand and were prepared to resist by force if Hitler ordered his troops to march into the disputed area, but British prime minister Chamberlain was determined to avoid war, even if it required far-reaching concessions. During the second half of September 1938, he traveled to Germany three times in desperate attempts to ward off a military conflict. François-Poncet closely followed the intense negotiations and perceptively commented on them. After Chamberlain's first visit, he noted that Hitler and his close collaborators had interpreted the prime minister's appearance in Germany as a sign of weakness by Britain. The event inflated all the Nazi leaders with a sense of triumph, pride, and self-confidence, coupled with contempt for their adversaries. At the same time, their "ambition and appetites" increased enormously. In their private conversations, the Nazi leaders went so far as to speak of Europe as if it were "their property."[86] François-Poncet granted that the Czechs had mistreated the Germans in their country, but he was also convinced that the Nazis were behind the unrest among the Sudeten Germans. Simply to give in to Hitler would be a mistake, but to oppose him would lead to war, for which France and Britain were unprepared. At a meeting with Hitler on September 28, the ambassador presented him with a memorandum that proposed the following solution to the crisis: Hitler would be permitted to occupy three parts of the Sudetenland on October 1, but an international commission would accompany the German army to indicate which areas were to be taken over. Other contested areas would be permitted to decide their future by plebiscite.

The ambassador warned Hitler that if the German army marched into Czechoslovakia without an agreement with Western powers, "you will be the aggressor . . . [and] you will provoke war which will become a general war" involving England, France, and Russia. Eventually, other countries such as the United States and some South American nations would join the conflict and "soon the entire world will be against you." Hitler remained calm throughout the one-hour meeting, even while criticizing the Czechs for persecuting his "compatriots" and expressing surprise that France and England opposed his occupation of the Sudeten territories. Other than that, Hitler refused to give the ambassador an immediate response on the proposed settlement.[87] But one day later, after Chamberlain had made another quickly arranged trip to Munich, a settlement was reached, and it contained many of the provisions in François-Poncet's proposal. It avoided war, but not for long.

On the whole, François-Poncet was pleased with the outcome of the deliberations in Munich, but he feared that Hitler's acquiescence would be short-lived. The Nazis' boasts about their victory and constant repetition that Germany was now a world power—a "nation of 80 million people [*sic*] who will not allow themselves to be intimidated by anyone"—made him uneasy. On October 4, he wrote to Georges Bonnet, the foreign minister, that Western democracies should learn some important lessons from the recent crisis. They should reaffirm their desire for peace but also eliminate the causes of internal weakness in their countries and concentrate on rearming as quickly as possible.[88]

These were not François-Poncet's only proposals to preserve peace. He now conceived of a new, and rather far-fetched, diplomatic maneuver. During the negotiation over the Sudetenland it had become known that Mussolini had sent messages to Hitler urging him to be conciliatory, and the Duce's intervention at one critical point had been effective. François Poncet concluded that if peace was to be preserved, if Hitler was to be prevented from provocative adventures, Mussolini would be the man to use his influence on the Führer. As the ambassador put it, Mussolini was the "key to the future," and the Frenchman was eager to encourage the Italian dictator in his supposed role as preserver of the peace.

For at least a year, François-Poncet had been convinced that Mussolini was not willing to play second fiddle to Hitler. In a dispatch of September 29, 1937, he gave free rein to his ruminations in discussing the outcome of a four-day meeting between the two dictators, even though neither government had issued any official announcement on the high-level talks. The diplomatic corps in Berlin, according to François-Poncet, agreed that Mussolini did not want to give "*carte blanche* to the Nazis." It was even possible that "he demanded a renunciation of all violence" by Hitler. François-Poncet concluded by acknowledging uncertainty about the dictators' intentions, but the thrust of his comments was that Mussolini could be relied upon to exert a moderating influence on the Führer.[89]

In the fall of 1938, François-Poncet asked the Foreign Office for a transfer to Rome and in early October he left Berlin. In Rome he quickly discovered that he had misjudged Mussolini. There was little hard evidence that the Italian dictator could exert the kind of wide-ranging influence over Hitler that François-Poncet had assumed. On the contrary, Hitler dominated the relationship between the two. Moreover, it was now clear that a lasting, peaceful relationship between France and Germany was an illusion. Nevertheless, it continued to be the ambassador's dream, despite his later claims that by 1938 he had abandoned it.[90]

Soon after Italy declared war on France on June 11, 1940, François-Poncet returned to his home country and lived in Grenoble, where he avoided any involvement in public affairs. In August 1943, the Germans imprisoned him, which made it easy for him to disavow his previous advocacy of good relations with the Nazi regime. After World War II, he once again was honored with senior positions in the government and was elected to the prestigious Académie française. Initially, he was an adviser to the French government on German affairs; from 1949 to 1952, he served as high commissioner in Germany; and from 1953 to 1955, he was the French ambassador in Bonn. For the next twelve years he held the post of president of the International Red Cross, and once again came under suspicion of having been sympathetic to Nazism: he was accused of having helped Klaus Barbie, a notoriously brutal Nazi official in France, escape to Bolivia.[91] The charge was never proven.

ROBERT COULONDRE TAKES OVER
AS AMBASSADOR

In late 1938, Robert Coulondre, who had ably served as ambassador to Moscow, replaced François-Poncet in Berlin. A civil servant with a long career in the Foreign Service, he has been praised as a "determined and clearheaded diplomat." In his memoirs, published in 1950, he claimed that in the 1930s he had clung tenaciously to a twofold strategy: Hitler must be reined in, and for this approach to succeed the West must join forces with the Soviet Union.[92] But the diplomatic documents published several decades after the memoirs tell a somewhat different story. Coulondre's perception of National Socialism was not strikingly different from that of his predecessor, François-Poncet. This is hardly surprising, since Foreign Minister Georges Bonnet was determined to avoid war and was therefore unlikely to pick a person for the most important diplomatic post in the world who held radically different views from his own.[93]

That Coulondre was generally following in François-Poncet's footsteps became clear in the two dispatches he sent to Paris on his first meeting with Hitler on November 22, 1938, only days after his arrival in Germany. Hitler, the ambassador reported, made a "good impression" on him. The chancellor spoke to him "with calm, with simplicity and with clarity; at no time did I have the feeling that he was hiding his thoughts." He did not become animated until the end of the discussion, when he declared that he knew the meaning of war and that "even a change in the frontier between the two countries [that is, Germany and France] is not worth the sacrifices that it would cause." He declared, as he had so often, that he wanted good relations between Germany and France. Coulondre responded in an equally friendly manner and stressed that the French government and people were eager for rapprochement with Germany.

Coulondre offered an interesting, though unconvincing, interpretation of Hitler's conception of international relations. The Führer's contention that military action was not warranted to secure a change of frontiers meant that he did not subscribe to the law of the jungle, which places no restrictions on human behavior. Instead, Hitler was a proponent of the "law of force," according to which frontiers between nations were binding, and they were binding not because they were established by treaties but because they reflected the military realities in the balance of power between adjacent countries. In view of this "Nazi doctrine," the ambassador counseled that although he favored collaboration between France and Germany for the preservation of peace in Europe, such cooperation could be fruitful only if France was strong. A weak France would not be able to make its voice heard in Europe and would not be able to protect itself and its empire against the "covetousness of the Germans."[94] Coulondre's theory might have been persuasive had the Nazis not demonstrated all too often that they were not squeamish about spilling blood.

Not long after the meeting with Hitler, Coulondre met Göring and Goebbels, both of whom were cordial and expressed the hope that relations with France would be amicable. Coulondre was reluctant to draw "premature conclusions," but he now believed that even the most "intransigent" Nazi leaders wanted Germany to be on good terms with France.[95]

The reporting on internal developments in Germany after François-Poncet's departure from Berlin was as comprehensive as it had been over the preceding five years, and in some respects more perceptive. For example, on November 15, 1938, Hugues Barthon de Montbas, the chargé d'affaires at the embassy, analyzed the events of Kristallnacht with a sure eye for the important details, terming that night "the ultimate offensive of National Socialism against the Jews." The German public, he pointed out, was "not deceived" by official statements that the action had been prompted by the assassination in Paris of the diplomat Rath by a German Jew. People knew that the government was using the incident as a pretext for a renewed campaign against Jews and the seizure of significant portions of their assets. And the government had stepped up measures to isolate them from the rest of the nation. Some people believed that the assassination had been engineered by Nazis, and many even believed that Goebbels, who had recently lost favor in Hitler's eyes because of a marital scandal, had planned the action to burnish his reputation among ardent Nazis.[96]

Montbas made the interesting point that, ever since the assassination of Rath, the Nazis had waged a new campaign against "international Jewry," which had tended to replace the long-standing campaign against "international Bolshevism." The Nazis justified the new emphasis by claiming that "the Jewish enemy" planned to undermine the worldwide influence of National Socialism. It was a battle cry, the Nazi leaders believed, that would arouse much sympathy among the German people.

Montbas also raised a series of intriguing questions about the larger significance of Kristallnacht: Were the Nazi leaders abandoning all pretense
of moderation, and were they prepared to strain relations with the United
States and Great Britain, where the anti-Jewish violence evoked extensive
criticism of the German government? Did the new anti-Jewish campaign
mean that the "spirit of accord" reached at Munich was no longer in effect? Was a "stable" relationship between the West and the Third Reich
impossible? Finally, did the attacks on Jews mean that Nazi Germany was
committed to violence as a principle and that Hitler would not hesitate to
subjugate any people he considered his country's adversary? The last question is especially noteworthy because it touches on a very difficult and important issue that is still debated by scholars and politicians: Is there a direct
link between a government's domestic and foreign policies? Or, to relate
this discussion directly to our topic, did the Nazis' unhesitating resort to
violence against the Jewish population at home mean that Germany would
act just as ruthlessly toward foreign countries? In his last sentence Montbas observed that several diplomats from smaller countries believed that
"if there were no changes in the domestic conditions of the Third Reich, a
European conflict could well be inevitable."[97]

To add to the diplomat's anxiety, an analysis completed by the Berlin
embassy on December 14, 1938, depicted in unprecedented detail the scope
of Germany's expansionist goals. On the basis of a careful reading of many
journals and newspapers, the staff reached conclusions that must have jolt-
ed officials in Paris. German ambitions in central Europe were well known,
but this report pointed out that Hitler had much more in mind. The Nazi
leadership aspired to expand into the Near East and the Gulf of Persia,
so that the Reich would be able to exploit the economies of Turkey and
Iran. The pre–World War I dream of a railroad from Berlin to Baghdad was
to be realized, placing Germany in a powerful position to dominate the
economies of a vast region.[98] The authors of the report were convinced that
Hitler's grip on political power was now so overwhelming that he could
lead the country into adventures that even some Nazi officials who still
retained a sense of proportion might consider unrealistic. In addition, early
in 1939, one of Ambassador Coulondre's "collaborators" had talked to a
senior German official whose work put him in frequent contact with the
Führer, and he had indicated that since the settlement of the conflict over
the Sudeten region "all the leaders of the Reich are convinced that the Führer is infallible." The senior official also said that although Hitler genuinely
wanted peace, Germany was bolstering its military forces so rapidly "that

in four or five years no power in the world will be capable of defeating" the country.[99]

In the meantime, the Nazis imposed a new list of restrictions, most of them purely spiteful, on the Jews. On December 15, 1938, Coulondre sent the foreign minister a description of the measures that, in the ambassador's view, were to prepare the ground for the creation of a ghetto that would consign the Jews to the "margin of society." Economically as well as socially, the Jews were to be isolated. Jews were no longer permitted to appear on certain streets and in certain public places; on Saturday, December 3, the day of "national solidarity," Jews were not to leave their homes between 12:00 noon and 8:00 p.m.; Jews could no longer attend the theater, concerts, museums, or sports events; as of December 31, Jews would not be allowed to own cars, and those not clearly identifiable as Jews would have to adopt the name "Israel" or "Sarah"; and Jews could no longer attend universities or technical schools. Toward the end of the long dispatch, Coulondre speculated whether these restrictions would be followed by "other, more radical measures." In the very last sentence he predicted that if one of the persecuted, in an attempt to seek revenge for the suffering of his people, succeeded in assassinating a Nazi, the SA or the SS "would not hesitate in bringing about the disappearance in blood of those they call the descendants of Judas."[100] Coulondre showed real insight into Nazism even though he was too cautious in his prediction; the bloodshed occurred even without the provocation he mentioned.

Despite the mounting barbarism of the Nazi regime and the growing international tensions, in early 1939 Coulondre believed that the public mood in Germany, which was hostile to war, together with the severe shortages of goods, might lead Hitler to curb his aggressive designs. People resented the "orgy of grandiose construction" of buildings for senior officials at a time when ordinary people could not buy essential foods. The police had discovered the following graffiti on the wall of the new Reich Chancellery in Berlin and on walls and sidewalks in several sections of the city: "*Kein Kaffee, keine Butter, kein Ei, Aber eine neue Reichskanzlei*" (No coffee, no butter, no eggs, but a new Reich Chancellery). Among workers discontent was especially intense, and Coulondre was certain that the public mood was quite different from that of 1914, when many people enthusiastically supported the country's war effort. Ever the optimist, Coulondre thought that the widespread disquiet could influence Nazi leaders into being more cautious in pursuing their expansionist goals.[101]

The ambassador reached this conclusion three weeks after learning some astonishing details about a meeting the Führer had held on January 26 with thirty leading officers of the army, navy, and air force. The German press had reported on the meeting in general terms, but a "well-informed source" provided the French embassy with unsettling details. Hitler delivered a brief speech in which he insisted on "blind obedience to his orders." He let it be known that he did not want any officer to say to him, "I cannot accept responsibility for this or that operation." The Führer reminded the assembled group that in September 1938, General Ludwig Beck had made such a comment to him, and by October he was no longer in service. "I alone," Hitler told the officers, "bear the responsibility [for Germany's policies and actions]. Whoever is not pleased with that can leave." Hitler thereupon walked from one officer to another and waited for each one to take an oath of obedience to him. He then clasped the hand of the officer in his two hands. In this vein, a senior German officer told the French military attaché in Berlin that henceforth opposition to Hitler's plans by senior officers could not be expected. In fact, the Führer became so confident of Germany's unity and strength that he now embraced Ribbentrop's position that Western powers would readily accede to Germany's territorial demands.[102]

The approach of Coulondre to diplomacy during his service in Berlin can be characterized as embracing a sound comprehension of the issues tempered by excessive caution. This approach was especially pronounced on March 13, 1939, in his reaction to Germany's forcible annexation of Bohemia and Moravia, the two regions of Czechoslovakia that had retained their independence after the Munich agreement. Coulondre was shocked by the Nazi aggression, but when the British ambassador Nevile Henderson, himself a committed appeaser, proposed that Britain and France register a protest—a very mild one—by recalling their emissaries from Berlin, the Frenchman demurred. "I told . . . [Henderson] that it was up to our government to decide on it, but that I personally do not favor it." Coulondre offered several reasons for his position: a break with Germany would not induce Hitler to change his policy; once relations with Germany had been severed, it would be very difficult to restore them; Italy would be the only country to benefit from such a break because it would be the only state with influence on Hitler that retained a diplomatic delegation in Berlin; finally, and most important, the withdrawal of French and British diplomats would run the risk of strengthening the hand of Nazi extremists who argued for "immediate war." Coulondre believed that Hitler and a majority of the Nazi Party did not want to go to war just then, and that both

France and Britain needed more time to rearm before entering into military conflict.[103] The ambassador did not reckon on the likelihood that failure to make a telling response to Hitler's aggression would encourage the Führer to conclude that the West would never respond forcefully to his violations of international law.

WHY PARIS IGNORED ITS DIPLOMATS

It is difficult to evaluate the reporting of French diplomats in Germany during the Nazi era, especially that of François-Poncet, by far the dominant figure among his country's emissaries in Berlin. His long service in the German capital, his knowledge of German history and politics, and his frequent meetings with Hitler gave him the reputation of a particularly acute analyst of German affairs. Always well informed on current events, he was not shy about airing his opinions; often his judgments were trenchant, but too often he seemed to forget what he had said previously. His inconsistencies can be bewildering. He frequently described Hitler as unprincipled and brutal, yet he also contended on one occasion that if the Führer claimed to be a man of peace, he should be given the benefit of the doubt and be believed. For much of his tenure in Berlin, the ambassador advocated negotiations with the regime to achieve an agreement on slowing the process of rearmament, which Germany had initiated soon after the Nazis came to power. He clung to this position despite the Führer's numerous violations of international agreements. Coulondre, the successor to François-Poncet, did not deviate in any fundamental way from his views.

François-Poncet's recommendations on policy disregarded the sage advice of the "old German diplomat," or X, who had warned French officials in late 1933 not to negotiate with the Nazi regime because it represented a radically new political movement that was determined to implement its program of territorial expansion and racism at all costs. Nevertheless, it would be a mistake to suggest that the two French ambassadors considered Hitler a "riddle" in the sense that Sir Maurice Hankey, quoted in the Introduction, believed he might be after having attained power: a "new Hitler" who wished to "extricate himself, like many an earlier tyrant, from the commitment of his irresponsible days." The French diplomats in Germany did not see Hitler in that light. Although many of their recommendations were naïve and their prognostications of Hitler's course of action inconsistent, they did not think that he would change his colors completely. They repeatedly produced assessments of Nazism that revealed a sound understanding of Hitler and of his most prominent subordinates. Beginning as early as February 8, 1933, and ending shortly before his departure from Berlin late in 1938, François-Poncet alone sent no fewer than ten dispatches to the Foreign Office that contained detailed and insightful accounts of Hitler's extremism and psychological fragility. And the military experts attached to the French embassy in Berlin sent additional reports to Paris that verified Western suspicions of Germany's extensive preparations for war.

Conceivably, François-Poncet would have been more effective in persuading his superiors in Paris to take a firm stand against Hitler's aggressiveness had he been consistent in his evaluations of the Nazis, and certainly historians would now treat him with more respect. On the other hand, if French statesmen had read his dispatches with care, they would have been aware of the dangers that lurked in Berlin. The French diplomats in Germany differed with X not so much on the character of Nazism as on the best way to deal with its aggressiveness. The differences with X concerned strategy and tactics, and in politics a sound grasp of the ideology and moral principles of an adversary does not count for much if it is not accompanied by wise strategy and tactics.

François-Poncet's and Coulondre's frequent inconsistency on policy matters, despite their generally correct assessments of Hitler's character and the radicalism of Nazism, was no doubt deeply ingrained in their character. But it was also a trait that fit well with the reluctance of their superiors in Paris to act decisively in foreign affairs. The country's political instability, a long-standing feature of modern French history, was not congenial to strong, decisive leadership. In the years from 1933 to 1940, fourteen governments ran national affairs, and during that period the Foreign Office underwent eight changes in leadership. As the historian Jean-Baptiste Duroselle has pointed out, the rapid turnover in top personnel did not encourage diligence on the part of political leaders, although some of them were clearly able and conscientious. Even the most imaginative and dedicated foreign ministers remained in office too short a time to develop and implement long-range policies or some sort of "master plan." To make matters worse, several ministers were "amazingly irresponsible." For example, Joseph Paul-Boncour, who held the post of foreign minister during the critical period from mid-December 1932 until late January 1934, failed to read the dispatches from French ambassadors in their entirety; he asked his subordinates to summarize them in no more than three lines.

After an interlude of nine days following Paul-Boncour's departure from the post, Louis Barthou took charge as foreign minister. Barthou was a creative and diligent official who perceived Germany as the "enemy" and sought to form new alliances for France and to invigorate existing ones, only to be rebuffed by Britain, which opposed the isolation of Germany. In any case, his tenure in office was cut short after only eight months when he was assassinated together with King Alexander of Yugoslavia, who was visiting France. The next foreign minister, Pierre Laval (from mid-October 1934 until late January 1936), claimed to be following Barthou's policy, but he was devious and his unpredictable behavior did much to confuse the public about the threat emanating from Germany. Moreover, he did not take his work seriously, evidenced most dramatically by his failure to prepare himself for meetings with major foreign leaders, among them Mussolini. During the requisite planning sessions, Foreign Office officials spent much of their time telling anecdotes and jokes. Such irresponsible behavior was not rare.[104]

The mood of the French people was also not conducive to the pursuit of a robust foreign policy. The average person was most concerned with the impact on France of the world depression, which did not hit the country until 1931, but when it did, it proved in some respects to be more damaging than in other industrial countries. It lingered for an exceptionally long time; France was the only major industrial power that did not regain its 1929 level of production until after World War II. The economic situation was so dire that between 1931–32 and 1935, just when Hitler was intensifying Germany's rearmament program, France reduced its military budget by 32 percent. The historian Julian Jackson has argued convincingly that France's failure to resist Germany's march into the Rhineland should be attributed in large measure to the country's economic decline.[105] Not until 1935 did France increase its spending on the military, but even then outlays were "faltering" and insufficient to alarm the Nazis.

There were other reasons for the widespread pessimism and political lethargy in France. Proportionately, the country had suffered more casualties during World War I—some 1.3 million deaths—than any other nation, and after the conflict ended, the birthrate declined sharply. Despite the recovery of Alsace-Lorraine in 1918, the country's population between 1911 and 1920 fell by two million.[106] To many people, the thought of another military conflict was anathema. Not surprisingly, this heightened atmosphere of anxiety and helplessness was fertile ground for the emergence of numerous groups advocating one form or another of pacifism. To be sure, the pacifist movement was not as large and well organized in France as in

Britain, but it was large enough and sufficiently vocal to draw the attention of political leaders. By 1936, more than two hundred pacifist organizations had been formed, and quite a few of them could count on the support of well-known intellectuals and members of the political elite.[107]

Early in 1934, the tensions within French society exploded into a riot in the center of Paris by thousands of people protesting against the illegal financial schemes of Serge Stavisky, which had caused turbulence in the stock market. Minor riots had taken place during the evening hours for some weeks, but the demonstration on February 6 was massive and much more violent than in any previous incident. By midnight, the Place de la Concorde, where fifteen people lost their lives and some fifteen hundred were injured in numerous skirmishes, looked like a battlefield. Historians still differ over whether the bloody events can be considered a genuine insurrection carefully designed to overthrow the government. The opposition seems likely to have had a less ambitious plan; it wanted the Radical government to be replaced by a more conservative one.[108] That happened, but it did not bring about political stability: over the next two and a half years, five different people served as prime minister.

In June 1936, French politics underwent a transformative change with the establishment of a socialist government. A major reason for the change was that the riots had shocked many people into believing that the unrest was directed at undermining the democratic order. To prevent such a political upheaval, the left-wing parties—the Socialists, Radicals, and Communists—joined forces to form the Popular Front, which won a majority of 306 out of 608 seats in the Chamber of Deputies in the elections of May 1936. Léon Blum, the head of the government, which did not include any Communists, was an intelligent, well-informed, and cautious man who succeeded in introducing many progressive changes in economic and social policies. Under his direction, the Chamber passed legislation that legalized strikes, mandated twelve days of annual leave for workers, and limited the work week to forty hours, to mention only the most notable measures. In foreign affairs, however, Blum did not fare well. Because the Radicals opposed support for the democratic forces in the Spanish Civil War, Blum adopted a policy of nonintervention, which irritated many of his supporters on the left.

But on the more urgent question of how to respond to Nazi Germany's increasingly aggressive moves, Blum's judgment was simplistic and unsound. A visionary who has been described as a "pacifist, antimilitarist intellectual," he believed that the answer to international strife, no matter how intense, was disarmament, unilateral if necessary. Blum deplored Nazism, and he indicated that if Hitler attacked France he would favor resistance. But his greatest concern was that a strong response by France to German nationalism would reinvigorate French militarism and a "general war atmosphere," as well as reactionary sentiment. He had argued in 1934 and 1935 that if France embarked on disarmament, the "world conscience" and "universal reprobation" would "force Hitler to comply." He also believed that negotiations with Hitler and Mussolini could be productive, an opinion he had voiced in December 1934 and repeated on several occasions: "When the question of peace with Germany and Italy is involved, we are ready to shake all hands, even hands stained with blood." As prime minister, he told the Senate that he believed Hitler when he proclaimed his commitment to world peace. Blum justified his faith in the Führer by stating: "We do not intend to doubt the word of a former soldier who for four years knew the misery of the trenches."[109] Thus, when Hitler sent his troops into the Rhineland on March 7, 1936, Blum and his party had been able to come up with no better advice for the government than to act "with calm and sang-froid." Still, by the time he became prime minister three months later, the threat to France had grown so intense that he had no choice but to initiate a program of stepped-up rearmament.[110] In much of Europe, this move did little to raise the stature of France, now widely regarded as having lost its standing as a major power.

One unforeseen consequence of the advent to power of the Popular Front was the growth of ultra-right-wing movements in France that hated the Left more than they feared Fascism or Nazism. During the first three years of Nazi rule in Germany, a series of leagues sympathetic to the extreme Right had emerged in France, but only in 1936 did they become large enough to pose a threat to the Republic. The two most successful ones, which were solidly reactionary if not fully Fascist—the Croix de feu led by Colonel François de la Rocque and Action française led by Charles Maurras—enlisted an estimated several hundred thousand supporters. Their goal was a political system based on "order, stability, authority and a return to the old elites."[111] The outright Fascists aimed for more radical change: their slogans were "Better Hitler than Stalin" and "Better Hitler than Blum."[112]

It was a general, Maurice Gamelin, a strong supporter of the Republic, who clearly understood the impact of social and political unrest—especially in the first half of 1936—on France's conduct of foreign policy. "It made many of us lose sight of the dangers of Hitlerism and fascism at our doorstep because behind the 'Popular Front' one saw the specter of Bolshevism.

Therein lies the origin of the slogans that disfigured the soul of the nation: 'Better Hitler than Stalin' and 'Why die for Danzig?'" Similarly, Paul Reynaud, a political leader of the Alliance démocratique, a center-right party, bemoaned the fact that many French citizens subscribed to what he called "conditional patriotism," which meant that they would fight for their country only if the government was not in the hands of leftists.[113]

In this climate of political and social turbulence and declining patriotism, only a statesman of extraordinary wisdom and uncommon courage could have steered France into a path of resistance to Nazi Germany. But men with such sterling qualities are rarely to be found in politics, in France or anywhere else. When the Popular Front was forced to leave office after a brief, second tenure in April 1938, Blum was replaced by Édouard Daladier, whose understanding of foreign affairs outstripped by far his resolve to stand up to a dictator as tenacious and ruthless as Hitler. Daladier knew that the Führer could not be trusted to keep his word and was certain that within a few months of securing the agreement of the Western powers in 1938 to his seizure of large parts of Czechoslovakia, he would make new demands for territorial expansion. But the French prime minister yielded to the wishes of Chamberlain when it became evident that he could not persuade the British leader to change course. Daladier confessed to his colleagues, "I am not proud [of capitulating],"[114] but he remained in office until 1940, by which time Nazi Germany was on the verge of delivering its final blow to France.

It was a tragic ending to the Third Republic, all the more so because it could have been prevented. French statesmen had received ample information on the nature of Nazism from their senior diplomat in Germany and from a former German diplomat as early as 1933, but institutional instability, abhorrence of armed conflict, and weak political leadership doomed any possibility of successful resistance to Nazism.

CHAPTER THREE

The American Diplomats

American diplomats serving in Nazi Germany faced an especially challenging assignment. Their task was to report on domestic developments in a country of little concern to most people in the United States who, ever since the end of the world war in 1918, had embraced the doctrine of isolationism. Deeply rooted in American history, the doctrine specified that the United States should avoid all entanglements, political or economic, in the affairs of other nations, because in the past they had only led to the expenditure of blood and treasure by the American people without significant benefit to the United States.

The ramifications of this widely held attitude toward the rest of the world, and particularly to the Old World, were numerous and far-reaching. The Senate refused to approve the entry of the United States into the League of Nations, and various steps were taken to keep contacts with foreign countries at a minimum. Most notably, Congress imposed high tariffs on foreign goods and placed sharp limits on immigration. Even after Hitler's assumption of power and the growing danger of military conflict on the European continent, the isolationists argued that the squabbles three thousand miles from the American continent had no bearing on the vital interests of the United States. On June 20, 1938, these sentiments were cogently formulated in a letter to Sumner Welles, the under secretary of state, by Hugh R. Wilson, who a few months earlier had been appointed ambassador to Germany: "Twenty years ago we tried to save the world and now look at it. If we tried to save the world again, it would be just as bad at the end of the conflict. The older I grow the deeper is my conviction that we have nothing to gain by entering a European conflict, and indeed everything to lose."[1]

Yet the American embassy in Berlin as well as the eleven consulates in other German cities showed keen interest in the political, economic, and social developments in Germany, and produced many impressive reports. This interest is all the more surprising because two of the three ambassadors during the Nazi era were not professional diplomats and knew little about the political and economic situation in Germany, and not much more about the tense relations between several European countries. Both had been successful in their fields, one of them first in the law, then in business, and, finally, for five years as a senator from Kentucky; and the other as a professor of American history. Although they mastered at least the rudiments of diplomacy, they did not acquire an acute understanding of Hitler and his movement, which they held in contempt. The third ambassador to Berlin assumed office early in 1938 and occupied the post for only ten months. His strong support of appeasement handicapped him as an analyst of the crisis in international relations simmering in Europe, but even he sent reports to the State Department that accurately described the domestic turmoil in Germany and the brutality of Nazism.

All three ambassadors were fortunate that the professional staff in the embassy and consulates in Germany were, with few exceptions, remarkably accomplished. Most knew German and had a good grounding in history and political science, which enabled them to make astute analyses of the New Order being created by Hitler. Two of the sharpest critics of Hitler's regime, Raymond Herman Geist and George Messersmith, were of German descent, which probably helps explain both their passionate commitment to their work and their sensitivity to the gruesome behavior of the Nazis.

Geist was so appalled by Nazi anti-Semitism that he did his best in various ways to facilitate the granting of American visas to German Jews, and, according to Richard Breitman and Alan M. Kraut, the diplomat "could perform wonders" to get Jews released from the clutches of the Gestapo. "On occasion, Geist himself went into the [concentration] camps to get the people out."[2]

The American diplomats began to pay serious attention to the National Socialist movement in 1930, and even at that early date they warned that the emergence of Hitler's party might be an ominous development. Over the next nine years, the Americans occasionally stumbled and came up with interpretations that were off the mark, but on the whole their reports, which concentrated on concrete policies and events rather than on ideology, were comprehensive and incisive. Gerhard L. Weinberg, a leading specialist on Hitler's foreign policy, correctly suggests that the "American government was perhaps better informed than any other" on conditions in Germany.[3] To most American diplomats who observed events firsthand, neither Hitler nor Nazism was a riddle, and they provided Washington with ample information for the crafting of sound policies regarding the New Order.

Despite his lack of credentials as a diplomat, Frederic Sackett, the U.S. ambassador in Berlin from February 1930 until shortly after Hitler's rise to power, was not ill-cast in his new role. He was intelligent, diligent, and insightful and quickly acquired sufficient information about German and European politics to handle the new assignment; it did not take him long to sense that Germany was in the throes of a great upheaval. By the end of the year, he concluded that the Nazi leader was a rabble-rouser totally unfit to govern. Early in December 1930, Sackett reported having hoped that by this time the "wave of recklessness and disgust" that had prevailed at the time of the Reichstag election in mid-September would have subsided. But to his chagrin, a series of local elections on November 16 and 30 "revealed a distinctly disturbing tendency." Despite Chancellor Heinrich Brüning's best efforts to stem the political tide moving in Hitler's direction, "Hitler's lieutenants, who are constantly gaining greater experience in demagogism, have been able to exploit local causes of unrest and discontent." As a consequence, the Nazis had made substantial gains in the elections in Bremen and elsewhere, which demonstrated that Hitlerism "is still in full flow."[4] Sackett decided that he could be most helpful to the moderate forces in the country by working closely with Chancellor Brüning to shore up the Weimar Republic. In Washington, Secretary of State Henry Stimson was also "troubled" by developments in Germany, especially by the widespread disorder, but he was less pessimistic. In a memorandum he wrote a few days before receiving Sackett's report, he indicated that he was not yet willing to write off Germany. After all, in the United States there were also Communists "and violent elements which were as bad as those in any other country," but that did not mean that they represented a dominant force in society. Stimson thought that the same could be true of Germany.[5]

For a variety of reasons, American ambassadors had considerably less contact with Hitler and other senior Nazi officials than their British or French colleagues, and that might explain why they tended not to dwell on the personal attributes or ideology of the Führer, both of which, we now know, bore significantly on his conduct of affairs. George A. Gordon, the senior political analyst in Berlin during the early 1930s and on occasion the chargé d'affaires, was a stickler for protocol and insisted that no one on the embassy staff was to meet with opponents of the government, then led by Chancellor Brüning.[6] Gordon was a well-educated career officer with years of experience, and his word carried considerable weight in the Foreign Service and at the embassy. Sackett, however, was his own man, and when Gordon temporarily left town in December 1931, the ambassador disregarded the injunction and decided to meet Hitler. Not much is known about that meeting except that it reinforced the ambassador's unflattering view of Hitler as a "fanatical crusader." Sackett found Hitler's personality generally unappealing, and he became more convinced than ever that "he is not the type from which statesmen evolve." Hitler talked "vigorously," but "he never looked me in the eye." Sackett concluded that if Hitler came to power, his government would surely fail.[7]

Even after the Nazis took over the government, American diplomats continued to maintain their distance from Hitler and his coterie. They distrusted and disliked him intensely. Gordon, who made no effort to keep his feelings to himself, was soon declared persona non grata at the Foreign Office, which limited his opportunities to obtain information on the private views of his counterparts in the German government. During his four and a half years in Berlin, Ambassador Dodd also avoided personal contact with the Führer and met him privately only three times. None of these encounters was quite as revealing as those between Hitler and the British and French diplomats.

For their reports, American diplomats in Berlin relied primarily on information in German newspapers, discussions with businessmen and a few Weimar politicians, and extensive accounts of local developments written by American consuls in different parts of the country. If the American assessments of the political and social scene were intellectually less sparkling than those of their British colleagues, they were nevertheless extremely valuable because they often contained details not widely available at the time, as well as insights into the workings of the Nazi regime. Appalled by the Nazis' disregard for democratic principles and their frequent resort to violence, the American diplomats did not hesitate to depict the new regime in all its depravity.

Gordon set the tone for the political reporting at the American embassy. He wrote a compelling analysis of National Socialism as early as September 15, 1930, immediately after the Reichstag election in which the Nazis emerged as a party to be reckoned with. To the surprise of many observers, the Nazis won 6.4 million votes out of a total of 35 million, and 107 out of 575 seats in the legislature. This marked a stunning jump of 5.6 million votes and 95 seats in two years.* It was a sign, Gordon asserted, of the "disgust and recklessness" pervasive in German society. People were now prepared to give their support to a "party whose leaders and promises are irrespon sible." Two days later, Gordon wrote to his superiors in Washington that he had examined the party's program and its campaign materials, and despite his best efforts, he could not find "any constructive element" in them: "when seeking to win votes from the Communists the National Socialist orators declared that as their social theories were similar, they appealed to them to vote for a Communist form of government directed by Germans rather than the same thing under the guidance of Moscow; when invading Nationalist territory, the party spokesman emphasized their adherence to the principle of private ownership of property." A recurring theme of the Nazi campaign was that all "the country's evils flowed from Semitism, international banks, the Young Plan,† the Treaty of Versailles and all other international treaties with any provisions which might be considered objectionable from a chauvinistic point of view." Gordon was convinced that Hitler intended to establish "a reactionary dictatorship with, however, not even a suggestion as to the alternative measures contemplated for remedying the conditions complained of."

Elaborating on these statements, Gordon attributed the large vote for the Nazis to two factors: the "reckless frame of mind" of many Germans and the ignorance of the younger generation of the "horrors and hardships of war"; their only concern was the huge debt that had resulted from the war and that threatened to burden them for the rest of their lives. Still, Gordon did not think that the situation was hopeless; the republic, as he put it, had been dealt a "body-blow," but not necessarily a "knock-out blow." He argued—and most historians would now agree with him—that if "all sincere supporters of the Republic" joined forces, if "strong leaders with a strong program could be evolved from the present welter," many "reckless" supporters of the Nazi Party would return to the traditional parties, and the Weimar Republic could still be saved. But he warned that if they failed "to sink their personal and doctrinal differences, then indeed a serious situation will present itself."[8] Gordon returned to this theme a week later, when he observed to the secretary of state that the most disturbing fact about the current political situation was that the "parliamentary parties lying between

*For more details on the election, see above, pp. 17–18.

†The Young Plan, adopted in 1930, reduced the annual reparation payments that Germany would be required to hand over to the Allies for the cost of World War I. But the cost was still substantial and the payments would have to be made for fifty-nine years.

the extremists to Right and Left have not yet learned their lessons: they still do not realize that they should unite on the most fundamental issue, the maintenance of a republican and parliamentary form of government." Instead of collaborating, they continued in their old ways, endlessly "jock-eying, bickering and bargaining." Gordon singled out the distinctly right-of-center People's Party for special rebuke because it refused to compromise with the "socialist doctrines" of the democratic Left.[9]

The Nazi leaders knew that the diplomats at the American embassy harbored serious misgivings about their movement, and they had persuaded themselves that this was merely the result of misunderstandings. One day after the September election, a party official called the embassy to request a meeting at which a Nazi spokesman would explain the National Socialist program and seek to clear up all misconceptions. Gordon could hardly refuse, although he insisted on an "informal" gathering. On September 16, Arno Schickedanz, the Berlin representative of the *Völkischer Beobachter*, the leading Nazi newspaper, appeared at the embassy eager to set the record straight. Schickedanz seemed to be an ideal spokesman for National Socialism. As a participant in Hitler's failed putsch of 1923, he belonged to the prestigious circle known as the "Old Fighters" (*Alte Kämpfer*), and he was close to Alfred Rosenberg, a member of the party since the early 1920s who was regarded as one of its "arch-ideologues," the "philosopher" of the Nazi movement.[10]

Schickedanz wasted little time before proceeding to the heart of his mission, to correct the erroneous impressions in the West about Hitler's movement. Schickedanz stressed that Hitler's primary goal was to end the economic depression in Germany, which had desolated the country. In his view, the causes of Germany's plight could be traced directly to the burdens imposed by the Treaty of Versailles and the insistence by the West that Germany alone had caused the outbreak of war in 1914. His party, Schickedanz reiterated time and again, merely wished to secure fundamental changes in the treaty and the abrogation of all financial obligations placed on Germany. But he declared unequivocally that his party did not intend to achieve its goals by force or, as he put it, by resort to "violent and illegal measures." Fear of military aggression by Germany was "absurd" given the restrictions on rearmament imposed under the treaty. Schickedanz also rejected the charge that Germany permitted the existence of various "semi-military organizations, such as the Stahlhelm* and others" (the latter clearly a reference to the Nazi SA and SS). "Concluding his remarks in this field he said

*Association of War Veterans.

it was unthinkable that Germany could attempt to cope with the combined armed forces of France, Poland and Czechoslovakia, and that at any rate, as far as his party was concerned, it entirely realized the complete impossibility at the present time of attaining its objects by force."[11]

Of course, the key words in this statement were "at the present time," and this nuance was not lost on Gordon. Nevertheless, the American diplomat was impressed by Schickedanz's demeanor: he did not give the impression of being a "hot-headed 'wild man' as the Nazis are often depicted in the local press." He was quite young, about thirty-five, well mannered, and although clearly a true believer, he "expressed himself throughout in moderate and restrained terms." Schickedanz, Gordon acknowledged, made as strong a case as he could for his party, "but it obviously cannot stand up under the slightest analysis." He never explained how the party planned to achieve its goals, and Gordon concluded that "on his own showing, its policy is one of sheer opportunism." The plain purpose of the interview, as Gordon saw it, was to impress upon the world that the Nazis did not intend to take power "by violent and illegal measures."[12] The chargé d'affaires was not won over, as his later dispatches would demonstrate.

About a year after this meeting, the embassy was asked to respond to a memorandum on the political situation in Germany prepared by officials at the State Department, who had based their analysis primarily on newspaper reports. Interestingly, at this time the analysts in Washington were considerably more pessimistic than their colleagues in Berlin. "Hitler's position," the memorandum contended, "both on the basis of votes cast and psychologically, is unquestionably obtaining increased strength and there is a general expectation that his group will attain power soon, either as a part of the present Government or in charge of the Government." The memorandum also suggested that both in its economic program and in its stress on nationalistic slogans, Nazism resembled Mussolini's Fascism.[13]

The embassy quickly responded with its own analysis, which depicted a much less dire situation in Germany. The diplomats in Berlin acknowledged that the Nazis had greatly increased their electoral support in September 1930, but they insisted that the assumption that Hitler's party would continue to grow "in geometric progression" was "undoubtedly erroneous." The party might secure the support of 35 percent of the electorate, but it would not come any closer than that to 50 percent and therefore would not be able to form a government by itself, although it might form one by establishing a coalition with the Catholic parties (the Center Party and the Bavarian Catholic Party). The embassy also rejected the notion that Na-

tional Socialism could be likened to Italian Fascism. Although both emphasized chauvinism, Fascism was based on "the idea of a cooperative state,"
whereas Hitlerism harked back to the "old Hohenzollern and Prussian idea
of strong centralization, imperialism and expansion." Moreover, anti-Semitism, a major feature of the Nazi program, was absent from Fascism.[14]

Throughout much of 1932, the reports by American diplomats reflected
the confusing state of affairs in Germany. Chancellor Brüning could not
count on adequate support in the Reichstag to cope with the growing economic crisis, and he could not calm the political waters; and by the spring,
President Hindenburg had lost confidence in him and requested his resignation, which was submitted on May 29. Two governments, virtual dictatorships, governed successively for the next seven months, but they, too,
turned out to be ineffective. During this period of intense political strife
and uncertainty, American diplomats sent divergent, even contradictory,
messages to Washington. On February 2, 1932, John Wiley, the counselor of
the embassy, reported that he had held discussions—in apparent violation
of Gordon's strictures—with Goebbels, Göring, and Hanfstaengl,* three
close adherents of Hitler, and had concluded that although the "present
course of events in Germany is somewhat disquieting," the outlook might
not be as bleak as many feared. He was certain that the Nazis "have become
more and more moderate." Wiley noted that he had been assured that "the
Nazi idea is not to harm a hair of any Jewish head, but to treat them as foreigners; to tax them, but not to subject them to military service; to deport
eastward as many Polish and Russian Jews as possible." Wiley was especially
impressed by Goebbels, whom he found to be "more intelligent than any
other Nazi I have ever met. He obviously has first-rate ability and much
personal magnetism." Goebbels had admitted to sharp differences within
the Nazi Party, but he seemed not to be troubled by them because "the final
decision . . . always rested with Hitler," whose judgment could be relied
upon to be sound.

Wiley also found Goebbels reassuring on Germany's foreign policy.
Goebbels had indicated that, once in power, the National Socialists would

*Ernst (Putzi) Hanfstaengl was an early supporter of Hitler, having been entranced by
him in 1922, when he heard him speak in Bavaria. In the early 1930s, he was one of Hitler's
closest associates. The Führer enjoyed his piano playing and his jovial personality. Hanfstaengl
came to be known as the court jester, but in 1937 he fell out of favor because of conflicts with
Goebbels, and, fearing he would be punished, escaped to Britain. In 1942, he moved to the
United States, where he had studied as an undergraduate (at Harvard). He worked on a project, funded by the U.S. government, entitled "Analysis of the Personality of Adolf Hitler." He
provided valuable information on Hitler's private life.

do their utmost to make Germany *bündnisfähig* (qualified to enter into alliances). Wiley added that he had been reliably informed that the "Nazis are doing their best to flirt with the French." They had let the French know that they were prepared "to reach an agreement with France in respect of both reparations and armaments." In the last substantive paragraph of his report, Wiley reversed course and cautioned that the outlook might not be as bright as his meetings with the three Nazi leaders had suggested. "The constant playing . . . [on] the political passions of the people [by the Nazis]," he cautioned, "is certainly not wholesome. The German mind, as the war demonstrated, is particularly susceptible to nationalist appeal."[15]

Several consular officials in different parts of Germany thought that the political crisis would be resolved by "a return of the [Hohenzollern] monarchy within the next year."[16] To add to the confusion, the German ambassador to Washington, Friedrich von Prittwitz und Gaffen, assured W. R. Castle, the under secretary of state, that the present government "would be likely to remain in power for a long time." He based his prediction on the assumption that Hitler was not "at all anxious to take over all the authority." Even if his party made "large gains in the next election," he might well attempt to form a government with the Nationalists, but the German ambassador never made clear why this would be Hitler's preference.[17] Ambassador Sackett made much the same argument in a dispatch of June 4, 1932, that he composed after a long conversation with Bernhard Wilhelm von Bülow, the state secretary in the Foreign Ministry, who contended that Hitler did not want a purely Nazi government because he "recognized that in his party there is no proper Cabinet material available."[18] The truth is that at this time no one could read the mind of Hitler on questions of short-range tactics; a wily politician, he knew how to conceal his intentions.

Shortly after the Reichstag election of July 31, 1932, from which the Nazis emerged as the largest party with 37.2 percent of the vote and 230 seats in the Reichstag, the reports from Berlin became more pessimistic, or perhaps one should say more realistic. On August 15, 1932, Sackett told the secretary of state that "Germany has for a long time past been in a situation which could well be termed a state of latent civil war."[19] A week later, Sackett informed Washington that ever since the election the Nazis had "perpetrated acts of atrocious violence at various places throughout the Reich from East Prussia to Bavaria." A total of nineteen instances of terrorism "resulting in deaths and serious damage to property" had been reported by the police. The worst violence took place in Königsberg, where Nazis, disappointed by their failure to win a local election for the Reichstag seat, "stoned shop-windows, burned gasoline stations after ringing false alarms to divert the fire brigades from these fires, attempted to destroy democratic or socialist newspaper offices by fire and sought out prominent members of the Socialist and Communist parties who were murdered or assaulted in their dwellings, some whilst they were in bed." In various parts of the country, Jews were also attacked. Several policemen and civil servants in Prussia were dismissed "simply because they were objectionable to the Nazis." The methods were everywhere similar, which suggested that they had been centrally and carefully planned. On various occasions, the government threatened to put an end to the lawlessness, but it rarely followed through with decisive measures.[20]

The State Department appreciated the detailed account of the grim situation in Germany, but it wanted analysis in addition to facts. More specifically, Castle, then acting secretary of state, asked Berlin on August 15, 1932, for a broad assessment of the political situation and for informed estimates of likely future developments. Sackett, no doubt chastened by the implied criticism, responded immediately that he had changed his mind about Hitler's intentions. "The keynote of the political situation," he wrote, "would seem to be Hitler's dogged intentions to rule alone. . . . Hitler, one of the biggest show-men since P. T. Barnum, and his silver-tongued lieutenant, Goebbels, are past adepts at twisting events to suit their fancies and purposes, and indefatigable spell-binders." Ever cautious, the ambassador spelled out four possible outcomes of the political struggles: Hitler might come to power as head of a coalition supported by the Catholic Center Party; the present government under Papen might be granted a "breathing spell"; the Nazis, having declined in popularity because of the widespread violence, would split between Hitler's loyal supporters and the radicals who favored a "more militant aggressive line"; or, finally, the Reichstag might be dissolved. Sackett thought that the most likely scenario was the fourth, which would be followed by new elections, but he conceded that all the alternatives he had listed were based on "conjecture."[21]

Within a few months, on January 30, 1933, Sackett's first scenario proved to be more or less on target, though not quite in the way he had foreseen. After intense intrigues at the highest level of politics and especially in the circle of advisers in President Hindenburg's office, Hitler came to power as the chancellor of a coalition that included only three Nazis (Hitler, Göring, and Wilhelm Frick) and nine conservatives, and it was widely assumed that under the circumstances Nazi influence on policy would not be decisive; nor were the three Nazis expected to remain in office very long. As became evident very quickly, this change in government marked a critical turning point in German, European, and world history. But at the time, most journalists writing on international affairs paid little attention to the political changes in Berlin: they showed far more interest in Franklin D. Roosevelt's impending assumption of office as president of the United States and in the upcoming World Economic Conference in London.[22]

Alfred W. Klieforth, the chargé d'affaires in Berlin in early 1933, was troubled by the change of government, but his reports suggested uncertainty about its significance. On January 31, he wrote, "[t]he new Government has thus far made no enunciation of policy. The reactionary and monarchist influence which predominates in the new Cabinet, however, indicates clearly what course it may be expected to pursue." Yet at about the same time he noted with a sense of relief that at a dinner party Dr. Schacht had quoted President Hindenburg to the effect that he had "obtained assurances from Hitler that he will observe the Constitution." To add to the confusion, in Washington the German ambassador, himself a staunch supporter of the Weimar Republic, assured Castle that the new government would not in any way change Germany's foreign policy.[23] Within a matter of weeks, the political class in Germany and the American diplomats were stunned by the speed with which Hitler and his supporters seized control of the levers of power and fundamentally changed the country's domestic and foreign policies. It may have been the fastest revolution ever.

On February 13, only fourteen days after Hitler became chancellor, Sackett informed Washington that although the cabinet members differed over social, economic, and financial policies, "the principal cohesive force is a fanatic chauvinism coupled with a common hatred of democratic government and the parliamentary system." To root out the republic, the Nazis placed their own people in key administrative positions. "The work of purging the administrative departments of democratic and republican influence set in with an avidity and swiftness unprecedented in German political life." The Reichswehr is "practically the only arm of the executive branch of the Government which they [the Nazis] do not control," and they were eagerly eyeing that branch. Three days later, Sackett wrote that practically all police commissioners throughout Prussia "had been replaced with reactionaries the Nazis could trust" and that Göring planned to use the Nazi Brownshirts (SA) as an "auxiliary police." Moreover, the government had taken steps to muzzle the opposition press, and by the end of February approximately 150 newspapers, most of them controlled by Social Democrats or Communists, had been shut down. The violence against members of the opposition parties had been so extensive and brutal that many citizens doubted whether the upcoming election for the Reichstag on March 5 could be "a free expression of the will of the people."[24] Sackett immediately realized that a new order—to use the Nazi terminology—was being imposed on Germany.

Leon Dominian, the U.S. consul general in Stuttgart, an especially astute observer, vividly described the nazification of rural areas. By mid-February 1933, a "band of National Socialists" had moved from village to village, terrorizing anyone suspected of not being sympathetic to the Nazi cause, and that automatically included Jews. The Nazis openly carried weapons, and groups of four or five of them could be seen almost daily and especially on weekends, frightening ordinary citizens with their "arrogant and swaggering attitude." They saw to it that local police chiefs were replaced with Nazi sympathizers. Dominian did not think that the Nazis would win the election on March 5, but that would not matter because they would most likely retain power by force.[25]

Dominian also described how the Nazis' "militaristic policy" had been translated into repressive measures. Early in 1933, they summarily dissolved the local branch of the "International Women's Organization for Peace and Liberty," only one of several societies in Stuttgart devoted to "cordiality between Germans and other nationalities" to be disbanded. Rotary Clubs were also on the Nazi list of proscribed associations. It had become risky for citizens even to utter the words "liberalism" and "democracy," because they aroused expressions of "positive hatred" by local Nazis. Dominian concluded that the country had reverted to the "political philosophy which guided its leaders since 1871 up to 1918." The new rulers of Germany "represent the cynical militarism of their predecessors of pre-Weimar days."[26]

The election on March 5 gave Hitler a clear majority in the Reichstag and hence the mandate he had sought to continue in office.* There could be no doubt, as Sackett put it, that "Hitler has won an unprecedented triumph. Democracy in Germany has received a blow from which it may never recover. . . . The much heralded Third Reich has become a reality. What form this Third Reich will finally take is not yet clear in these critical days of political confusion and uncertainty."[27] In a series of dispatches Sackett then described the measures taken by the Nazis to solidify their power: the continuous purging from public office of members of the opposition, the arbitrary arrest of citizens suspected of favoring democratic or left-wing parties, the closing of some Jewish shops, the continuing suppression of newspapers, the release from prison of five men in Beuthen who had been sentenced to

*For more details on the election, see above, pp. 106, 109.

death for brutally murdering an alleged Communist, and, finally, the establishment of concentration camps.[28] These accounts gave a vivid picture of Nazi conduct, but it was a subordinate, the chargé d'affaires Gordon, who comprehensively analyzed the aims of the National Socialists and their policies for achieving them. He based his conclusions on a close reading of Nazi literature; frequent conversations with political leaders, among them the former chancellor Brüning; and at least one conversation with Hitler.

NAZISM AS TOTALITARIAN

In his quest for an all-embracing explanation of Nazism, Gordon used a term for the New Order that anticipated one that was widely adopted by political scientists and historians after World War II, specifically after the publication in 1951 of Hannah Arendt's *The Origins of Totalitarianism*. On June 24, he wrote to the acting secretary of state that the Nazis, more than any previous political party, at least in the West, were guided by the principle of "totality," which meant that Germany was to be turned into an "exclusive one party state" in which all political and social organizations must be subordinated to the Führer. The Reichstag had been fully emasculated with the expulsion of the Social Democrats and Communists; these measures reduced the chamber to 446 deputies, leaving the 288 Nazis in a commanding position. They were only ten votes short of the two-thirds majority needed to change the Constitution. And they would surely find these ten among the Nationalists. This is exactly what happened on March 23 when they adopted the Enabling Act, which in effect granted Hitler dictatorial power.[29] It seemed likely that the Reichstag would not meet at all for the next four years.[30] Gordon predicted that "a new revolutionary wave" would soon sweep the country to further implement the principle of "totality." Other diplomats in Berlin, including the new American ambassador (Dodd) and Gordon's colleague, the consul Geist, soon began to use the more modern term. Geist, for example, wrote on December 19 that the Nazis had brought labor under their control with the creation of the German Labor Front (Deutsche Arbeitsfront), and thus had moved a step closer to the "realization of the totalitarian idea."[31]

Gordon's theory of totality was convincing, and the more he examined Hitler's regime, the more evidence he found to buttress his argument. As he put it, within one "crowded joyous week" in April 1933 the Nazis had made clear their intention not only to rule dictatorially but also to dominate all social and cultural institutions regardless of their political leanings. The Nazis outlawed the Nationalist combat units, various youth organizations, the Bavarian People's Party, the Christian trade unions, and the Social Democratic Party. At the same time, the government proceeded to nazify the institutions of learning, a process carefully described by Gordon. Teachers considered politically unreliable and all Jewish teachers were summarily dismissed, the curricula were changed, and students who had "fought for the national uprising" were given special privileges such as reduced fees and scholarships.[32]

According to Gordon, "the lengths to which this pace of achievement may lead are not pleasant to behold," and further measures by the Nazis to extend their control over public and private institutions could be expected. In fact, within short order the Stahlhelm, Bund der Frontsoldaten, a right-wing association of war veterans, was incorporated into the Nazi Party. The press owned by Hugenberg, a leading Nationalist who was a member of Hitler's cabinet, remained silent about these repressive measures, a dramatic indication of the extent to which Hitler had succeeded within four months in imposing his will on the country.[33] By the end of June, all potential sources of resistance except the Reichswehr and the police had been "either absorbed by the Nazis or largely, if not totally, crushed." The only institution that had offered serious resistance to the Nazis' implementation of the principle of "totality" was the Evangelical Church, which exerted considerable moral influence over its large following.[34] By early July, the Catholic Center Party, also regarded as an institution with moral authority, was dissolved. Even the Nazi leadership was surprised at the ease with which this party had been "annihilated." In a speech to an SA rally in Dortmund, Hitler himself said that it was inconceivable that only five months after the Nazi takeover of the government the Center Party "would haul down its flag."[35] To Gordon, it was now clear, "[t]he Nazi principle of 'totality' has become a fact; Hitler's triumph over the political parties is complete." Six months earlier such a development had been "hardly conceivable."[36]

ROOSEVELT'S AMBASSADOR, WILLIAM E. DODD

In mid-July 1933, William E. Dodd, Sackett's replacement, arrived in Berlin to begin a four-and-a-half-year tenure as ambassador that turned out to be controversial and at times embarrassing.* Dodd was not a profes-

*For a fascinating account of the experiences of Dodd and his family in Germany, see the recently published book by Eric Larson, *In the Garden of Beasts: Love, Terror, and an American Family in Hitler's Berlin*. Although Larson devotes many pages to the adventures and affairs

sional diplomat, but he had some impressive qualifications for service in Germany. For three years (1897–1900), he had studied at the University of Leipzig, where he wrote his doctoral dissertation on Thomas Jefferson. He had mastered German and had even published a book in German. After returning to America, he concentrated on the history of the American South and produced several well-regarded works in that field, as well as a study of Woodrow Wilson. In 1908 he began to teach at the University of Chicago, where he acquired a national reputation in his field. During his stay in Leipzig he had read widely on the history of Germany up to the twentieth century, but once he returned to the United States he did not keep up with contemporary German politics. He was a man of strong views, and he tended to cling to them dogmatically, a trait that at times prevented him from understanding political positions different from his own.

A passionate democrat—as well as Democrat—Dodd arrived in Germany with deep misgivings about Nazism, even though, like Rumbold, he harbored mild anti-Semitic prejudices. Yet in his early days in Berlin he was confident that he would be able to persuade Nazi leaders to moderate their policies, and for several months he remained convinced that Hitler himself was a moderate who could be prevailed upon to abandon the reckless course favored by the radicals in his party. During his meeting with the Führer in October 1933, the ambassador was taken in by Hitler's rhetoric in favor of world peace and wrote to the State Department that the "total effect of the interviews was far more favorable from the point of view of the maintenance of world peace than I had expected."[37] But, also like Rumbold, he was soon appalled by the Nazi persecution of the Jews, and his reports from Berlin often exposed the brutality of Hitler's anti-Semitism. He came to believe that the Nazi campaign against the Jews must be seen as symptomatic of the Nazi creed and was therefore a key to grasping the essential nature of Hitlerism. Over the next few years, this theme became central to many of the dispatches by his staff.

At first glance, it seems surprising that despite his somewhat benign view of Hitler, Ambassador Dodd, shortly after his arrival in Berlin, sent a series of detailed and candid dispatches to Washington describing the repressive nature of the Nazi regime.[38] But when it came to civil rights, Dodd could not hold his tongue. In one of his earliest messages, he reported that there

---

of Dodd's daughter, he also gives a vivid description of conditions in Germany's capital—especially in the political sphere—during the first four years of Nazi rule. Readers interested in pursuing the subject of Americans in Nazi Germany further might turn to Andrew Nagorski, *Hitlerland: American Eyewitnesses to the Nazi Rise to Power*, which appeared in early 2012. By that time, I had completed my study.

were about one hundred thousand political prisoners in Germany, many more than the official figure of eighteen thousand. He also pointed out that many Nazis incarcerated for serious crimes—often murder—were being pardoned, and after their release the criminals were "given a rousing ovation by the Nazis in their home town." Dodd spared no details in recounting the barbaric treatment by the Nazis of suspected opponents. He related the story of "Frau Luedemann, the wife of a former Oberpräsident in Silesia," who was imprisoned in the same camp as her husband because she had made "untrue assertions about conditions in the concentration camp." He told of the arrest and imprisonment without trial of family members of the former president of the Weimar Republic, Friedrich Ebert, for no reason other than that they were related to a Social Democrat. Dodd also noted that there were daily announcements of political prisoners having been shot while trying to escape. The brutality and sadism of the Nazis was thus well known in Washington as early as the summer of 1933.[39]

In mid-August, while Dodd was pondering these unappealing features of the New Order, he (and the chiefs of mission from other countries) received an unexpected and unwelcome invitation to attend ceremonies to be held in Nuremberg on September 2 and 3 at the time of the Nazi Party caucus. These party meetings or rallies were major public events attended by hundreds of thousands of Nazis and Nazi sympathizers to celebrate the achievements of the National Socialist movement. Hitler often made major policy announcements at these gatherings. The invitation to Dodd indicated that the German government would make all the travel arrangements, provide accommodations for chiefs of mission, and treat the foreign diplomats as "personal guests" of the Führer. The invitation caused "much perturbation" among all the ambassadors, with the exception of those who represented Fascist states, such as Italy and Hungary.[40]

Dodd immediately asked the State Department for "full instructions" on how to respond to this "entirely unprecedented" invitation, which he and several other ambassadors considered "provocative." He indicated that he would like to decline to attend if he could find a gracious way of doing so. He also let Washington know that if he and the British refused to attend the event in Nuremberg, "it would strengthen the hand of the liberal and peace forces in Germany." William Phillips, the acting secretary of state, adopted a cautious position: he did not think that the United States should take the lead in this matter because the British and French had much more at stake. But in the end the acting secretary left it up to Dodd to decide how to respond, not a very helpful or courageous stand. However, Phillips assured

Dodd, "we are of course prepared to support you in any decision you may make." By this time Dodd had concluded that acceptance of the invitation would be a "vicious precedent" that the Nazis could "exploit intensively." It would constitute an endorsement of the "present regime" and would thus weaken the domestic opposition to Nazism. The British ambassador initially favored acceptance of the invitation, but changed his mind and sent the Nazi authorities a note informing them that "urgent family reasons" prevented his attendance. The French and Spanish officials also found some excuse to skip the Nuremberg events, and Dodd followed his original instincts; he turned down the invitation on the ground, as he put it in his note to the Nazi organizers, "that I could not absent myself from Berlin long enough to have the pleasure of accepting." It was a minor rebuke and a minor setback for the Nazis.[41]

Dodd's revulsion at domestic developments in Germany was not simply a reflection of his democratic and liberal outlook. He also came to understand, as early as 1933, that there was a close connection between Hitler's foreign and domestic policies, and that the former would soon pose a danger to international peace. Dodd developed this theme in a series of dispatches in November 1933 in which he discussed at some length the referendum the government had prepared on the following question: "Do you, German man, and you, German woman, approve the policy of your Government and are you ready to recognize it as the expression of your own view and your own will and solemnly pledge yourself to it?" Citizens were to vote in circles marked "yes" and "no." The main purpose of this referendum, as Dodd noted, was to secure public approval for Germany's withdrawal from the League of Nations and from the Disarmament Conference in Geneva, two steps that created a measure of anxiety among the people fearful of another war. The Nazi authorities staged a massive campaign that included widespread intimidation of citizens to secure overwhelming approval of the question. Only a "hopeless minority" would have the courage to vote no. In fact, the Nazis succeeded in mobilizing support for their policies, perhaps far beyond their expectations: 96.3 percent of the voters cast their ballots in the affirmative, and in the election for the Reichstag that took place at the same time, 95.2 percent voted for the Nazi ticket. The Nazis had left nothing to chance. Even inmates at concentration camps supported the government: at Dachau, 2,231 prisoners voted in the affirmative; only 9 submitted invalid ballots, and only 3 voted no. At another camp, in Frankfurt, 67 out of 99 political prisoners allowed to vote gave their approval to Hitler's program.

Although it was obvious that the election had been rigged and that many

Germans had been cowed into supporting the authorities, Dodd concluded that the outcome nevertheless showed that very many Germans revered Hitler and that the overwhelming vote of confidence he had received meant that "he is now the undisputed ruler of Germany." Dodd was convinced that many people supported the Nazis largely because they approved of their foreign policy. Hitler and his subordinates certainly interpreted the electoral victory as approval for their audacious moves on the international scene. The Nazis were confident that they would succeed in pursuing their bold policies because, in their view, "the men who hold the reins in other countries are of an inferior caliber, and, if faced with a momentous decision, are certain to make concessions to Germany rather than take the risk of involving their countries in another war. It is the same line of reasoning with which the Nazis operated against the Weimar regime in Germany, and their phenomenal success in the field of domestic politics only tends to enhance the inherent danger of such logic." Dodd predicted that if the Nazis succeeded in their foreign policy moves, they would be able to divert attention from domestic problems and would then remain in power for a long time.[42]

NAZISM AND THE CHRISTIAN CHURCHES

In implementing the principle of "totality," the Nazis placed high priority on the integration into the New Order of the two principal Christian denominations, the Protestant (or Evangelical) and the Catholic. The diplomats in all three democracies paid close attention to this development, but the reports of American officials in Germany were the most systematic. Hence the treatment of the ongoing conflict between the Nazis and Christianity is included in this section, but the reader should keep in mind that the governments of the major democracies were kept abreast of it.

On April 21, 1933, Chargé d'Affaires Gordon sent a dispatch to Washington on the initiatives that the government had already taken to weaken the Christian churches, and thus again drew attention to the radical and in many respects bizarre aims of Hitler that amounted to a sweeping repudiation of cardinal tenets of Western civilization. For the next four years, American diplomats in Germany sent a stream of reports to Washington on the evolving conflict, and in view of the Nazi government's efforts to keep the details of the campaign against Christianity from the public, it seems that at least during the early stages of the rift, senior officials in the State Department were better informed on this subject than the German people.

According to Gordon, the Nazis aimed at nothing less than the creation of a "thoroughly 'Germanized Christianity.'" The new religion was designed to transform the Evangelical Church, whose membership made up about two-thirds of the nation's population, into a religion that would be "based on the 'trinity of the divine creation of state, nation and race' and would be imbued with a 'heroic godlessness.'" The "New Christians," soon to be known as "German Christians," were expected to disavow the Old Testament and replace it with the "old sagas and legends immortalized in the Wagnerian operas." Special attention was to be paid to the re-education of young Germans. The German Christians "apparently have in mind organizations of the evangelical German youth which would in effect be ecclesiastical storm detachments with a militaristic spirit, from which members for the regular storm detachments could later be recruited. In order to expedite matters, the Nazis are urging the appointment of state commissioners with the task of reorganizing the church." Throughout 1933, the New Christians became ever more determined to meld Nazism with Christianity. For example, when repairs on a church in Mainbernheim in Bavaria were completed in August, the workers placed a large swastika on the church tower. The point was to unite the Nazi symbol with the Cross of Christ.[43]

Another major concern of the German Christians was to rid religion in Germany of any ties to Judaism; they claimed that Jesus was not a Jew and that Christianity emerged not from Judaism but from a struggle against Judaism. Accordingly, they insisted on strict enforcement of the "principle of racial purity," or the so-called Aryan paragraph. Every official of the church not only had to be loyal to the Nazi Party but also had to prove that he was a pure Aryan. No one married to a non-Aryan, as defined in the Aryan paragraph, would be allowed to join the church. Ambassador Dodd observed that as late as September 1933 the newspapers in Germany had remained silent on these measures to give the impression that they had been implemented with very little controversy or opposition.[44]

In November 1933, Dodd added the following examples of how Nazi dogma was being infused into the Evangelical Church: "The Bishop of Brunswick is reported to have blessed the dead for their entry into Valhalla. Bishop [Joachim] Hossenfelder spoke of Horst Wessel's Storm Detachment in Heaven."* At a convention of German Christians in Saalfeld, Church-

---

*Horst Wessel (1907–1930) was a Nazi activist who joined the SA and was murdered under circumstances that are still unclear. The Nazis claimed that Wessel was killed by a Communist, making him a national hero. His stature as a martyr was enhanced because he had written the words for the song "Die Fahne Hoch," the anthem of the Nazi Party.

warden Julius Leutheusser declared, "[w]e have but one task; and that is, to become Germans—not Christians." The same church dignitary referred to Hitler as the "'Saviour' of all Germans." In a speech in June 1934, Göring insisted that the education of the country's youth must be controlled by the state alone. "If the Church says she comes first and then the people, I say that God did not create German Catholics or Protestants, but He gave them His soul in a German body with German blood." Nevertheless, Göring categorically denied that the Nazi authorities were hostile to religion or that they wished to prevent people from practicing their faith.[45]

The transformation of the nation's largest religious institution did not proceed without a considerable amount of friction. Hitler favored the changes, but he understood the sensitivity of the issue, and therefore publicly stated that he recognized the independence of the Evangelical Church and even granted that the program of the German Christians violated that principle. But in actuality he strongly supported outspoken Nazis in the church. For example, he frequently conferred with his friend Ludwig Müller, a clergyman who was a candidate for the leadership of the Evangelical Church. The Führer directed that Müller be granted free access to the government-controlled radio, and the authorities in Prussia withheld funds from churches that rejected the new trends.

Many pastors considered Müller unfit for the position because he lacked administrative experience and, more important, because he held views far out of the mainstream. It was widely assumed that he had become a viable candidate only because he had fawned over Hitler. On one occasion, he had predicted that history would honor the chancellor "for winning respect for the conception of blood purity." Müller had also announced that although he was prepared to baptize a Jew he would not allow the convert to serve as a pastor. If a baptized Jew set his heart on the profession of pastor, he should work as a missionary among the Jews.[46] It was primarily because of the government's support that Müller was elected Reich bishop (*Reichsbischof*) or head of the Evangelical Church on September 27, 1933.[47]

The formal installation of Müller a year later as the Reich bishop and primate of the Evangelical Church at the Protestant Cathedral in Berlin turned out to be a glaring demonstration of how influential the Nazis had become in the religious life of Germany. Several senior government officials attended the proceedings, as did many SS and SA men in their uniforms. They frequently gave the Nazi salute within the church. The service was broadcast by loudspeakers, but only a "moderate sized crowd" could be seen outside the cathedral.[48]

Within the Evangelical Church, strong resistance to the government's religious policies surfaced immediately after they were announced in 1933. About three thousand Protestant ministers voiced their opposition to the reform policies in general, but they were especially troubled by the government's insistence on enforcing the Aryan paragraph. One of the more outspoken opponents of the Nazi program was a young clergyman, Martin Niemöller, an interesting and unusually courageous person who rapidly rose to national and international prominence. But Ambassador Dodd was quick to point out—in December 1933—that the opposition to the German Christians was not necessarily directed against Nazism per se. Quite a few pastors who joined the opposition, initially including Niemöller, were in fact sympathetic to many of Hitler's aims. They were passionately patriotic, and Niemöller was always proud of his service as an officer on a U-boat during World War I. When war broke out in 1939, he was in a concentration camp, and yet he offered to return to duty on a U-boat, only to be turned down by Hitler. Niemöller and his colleagues objected to the new tendencies in the Evangelical Church primarily on doctrinal grounds; that is, they believed that sacred Christian doctrines were being wrongfully discarded. Indeed, Dodd claimed that "a victory by the moderate elements in the Church over the radicals is not likely to have any perceptibly adverse effects on the Hitler regime."[49]

Hitler pursued a more moderate policy with regard to the Catholic Church, which served the spiritual needs of about one-third of the population, and the result may have been to his advantage. Prior to 1933, the Roman Catholic Church had opposed Nazism more vigorously than the Protestant Evangelical Church, but after 1933 the situation changed and became more complicated. On the whole, German Catholics offered less resistance as well as less support to Nazism than the Protestants, who contained within their midst both ardent supporters and uncompromising opponents. Hitler conciliated the Catholics by signing a concordat with the Vatican on June 30, 1933, that voided all the dissolutions of Catholic organizations that had taken place during the first months of his rule; the concordat also committed the government to repealing "all [other] compulsory measures against priests and other leaders" of the Catholic Church that had been enacted. In return, the church agreed to remain aloof from politics. Hitler was now confident that he would be able to count on "citizens of the Roman Catholic faith" to support the National Socialist state.[50] He was not wrong, although some leaders of German Catholicism never became reconciled to Nazi Germany's religious policies.

Be that as it may, during the four years that Dodd served as ambassador in Germany he and his staff in the capital as well as in other cities focused on the struggles between the Nazis and the recalcitrant Evangelical ministers. Their reports could have left no one in doubt that the conflict was intense; in early 1934, about fifteen hundred clergymen "openly disavowed" Müller's authority by using their pulpits on Sundays to read protests against the administration's attempts to politicize the church. The Evangelical bishops of Bavaria and Württemberg went so far as to announce that they would not enforce Müller's order to pastors to desist from "public discussions" of church policies. The bishop of Württemberg also advised his parishioners that if they were forced by officials to choose between "an Evangelical or an Aryan faith. . . . 'Only a firm loyalty to the heritage received from our fathers can bring welfare and blessing to the National Socialist movement.'" The bishop sought to emphasize that although he did not harbor antinationalist feelings, he would ultimately be guided "purely" by ecclesiastical considerations. Such arguments did not sit well with the Nazis.[51] Nor did they take kindly to Karl Barth, a prominent professor of theology at Bonn University, when he added the following words to his oath of unlimited allegiance to Hitler: "in so far as I can conscientiously do so as an Evangelical Christian."[52] Barth was immediately removed from his post. Ambassador Dodd also learned that in various parts of the country Protestant pastors had been arrested for trivial infractions of government regulations. In one case, a priest was "taken into custody for having placed a small swastika flag over the entrance of his church on the anniversary of the Nazi revolution instead of hoisting a large one on the steeple." And Reich Bishop Müller suspended several pastors because they had used their pulpits to express opposition to his policies. In the winter of 1934, the bishop forced Niemöller to take a leave of absence, which apparently meant that he had been deprived of his parish. In some localities, the Nazis physically attacked clergymen who refused to hew to their line. "Windows have been broken in the houses of a number of ministers . . . only several days ago," Dodd reported on January 31, 1934; "the pastor of the prominent Wilhelm Gedächtnis Kirche was assaulted in his home by a group of rowdies."[53]

Nevertheless, the confessional pastors, as the opponents to Bishop Müller and the Nazi reforms came to be known, publicly continued voicing their rejection of the changes in doctrine and ritual, and they paid a heavy penalty for their courageous stand. In mid-March 1935, the American embassy learned "on what is believed to be good authority" that in Prussia alone five hundred pastors had been taken into custody or put under house arrest for several days because they planned to read a manifesto stating their religious convictions in their churches. Niemöller, now the leader of the opposition, was sent to prison even though he had made no effort to read the manifesto. In fact, he had gone into hiding but was apprehended by the secret police. To tighten its control over the confessional churches, the government in the spring of 1935 issued a decree prohibiting all teachers at seminaries from participating in the unfolding controversies over doctrine and appointments.[54]

When all these repressive measures failed to silence the confessionals or the Catholic critics of the New Order—the latter were especially distraught over the Nazi program of sterilizing mentally disabled people, a practice introduced in July 1933—the government decided to step up the campaign against the clerical opposition. On July 18, 1935, Göring issued an edict calling on local officials and the state secret police to "proceed with greatest energy against clerical adversaries of the Nazi regime." At the same time, Hitler appointed Hanns Kerrl as minister of church affairs. It was an appointment that brought a chill to everyone with reservations about the regime's policies. Kerrl was known to be close to Reich Bishop Müller and, in addition, had a reputation for resorting to violence in his dealings with political opponents. As president of the Prussian Diet, "he was wont to quell opposition by heaving ink pots and other light missiles" at those who disagreed with him, and many confessionals expected him to use similar methods against them even though there was speculation that he would first concentrate on disciplining Catholic Church activists.[55]

Kerrl took his time in imposing his will on the religious opposition, but within a few months he had made substantial headway in weakening it. He was no doubt encouraged by a speech Hitler delivered on August 11, 1935, in Rosenheim. J. C. White, counselor of embassy, cleverly noted in a dispatch he wrote "For the Ambassador [Dodd]" that the Führer, who had generally stayed in the background during the controversies with the religious opposition, now provided his supporters with a powerful argument in favor of silencing those who resisted his will. In a carefully crafted speech, he claimed that as the leader of Germany he was doing the Lord's work. "We have never feared a battle in the past, nor do we today. If . . . [our opponents] want a battle they can have it. We will throw them down so hard that for the next 15 years they will have no desire to continue the fight. . . . I may say to those who think they have a monopoly on Heaven's blessings that 15 years ago I had nothing but my faith and my will. Today the movement is Germany—today this movement has conquered the German nation and shaped the Reich. Would that have been possible without the blessing of the Almighty? . . . What we are, we have become not against the will of Providence, but by its will. . . . We will continue to have the blessing of Providence." White ended his dispatch with a warning that with "this unblushing claim that divine providence is on his side," Hitler had indicated that there "will be little quarter and no surrender" in the struggle with his Protestant and Catholic opponents.[56]

In September 1935, the Nazi authorities gave Kerrl "virtually dictatorial powers over Protestant church matters," and he used them with great skill. He combined harsh treatment of the dissidents—arresting some of the more recalcitrant activists—with a few conciliatory gestures, and by November 27, according to Dodd, both the Protestant and the Catholic Churches "were in a state of unrelieved confusion."[57] Some moderate confessional Protestants and some Catholic dissidents were now inclined to enter into agreements with Müller and his Nazi superiors. Several leaders of both churches, however, appeared ready to continue the fight because, as Dodd put it, "they are apparently now convinced of the anti-Christian character of Nazi-ism."[58]

By late 1936, the reporting by American diplomats on the religious conflicts tapered off. The volumes of documents published by the United States Department of State for the years 1937 and 1938 contain no dispatches entitled "Relations of the Nazi Regime with the Evangelical and Roman Catholic Churches." But this does not mean that Nazi pressure on the churches had ended. In 1937 the government dissolved various Catholic organizations throughout the country and in 1938 it concentrated on outlawing Catholic youth organizations.[59] Even without touching on the religious conflicts during 1937 and 1938, the numerous reports on the first four years of Nazi rule indicate that the diplomats passed on a wealth of information on the values and principles of government that animated the leaders of Nazism.* The Nazi views on Christianity were as primitive, distorted, and dismissive of Western traditions as their views on international relations, race, and the treatment of political opponents.

---

*A "nucleus of the Nazi hierarchy" continued to persecute the churches on a reduced scale even after the outbreak of hostilities in 1939, despite Hitler's call for a truce to promote unity for the sake of the war effort. See Conway, *Nazi Persecution of the Churches*, pp. 232–53.

William E. Dodd, American ambassador to Berlin from 1933 to 1937. Courtesy National Archive, College Park, Md.

George S. Messersmith, consul at the American embassy in Berlin from 1930 to 1934, then minister to Austria, and from 1937 until 1939 under secretary of state. Within the American diplomatic corps, Messersmith was the most prolific and outspoken critic of National Socialism. Courtesy National Archive, College Park, Md.

NAZI ANTI-SEMITISM

In many respects, then, by mid-1933 American diplomats in Germany and senior officials in the State Department were well informed about the ideology of National Socialism and the ruthless methods the party used to retain power and implement its policies. But initially the diplomats did not seem to understand the centrality of anti-Semitism to the thinking of the Nazi leaders, and they certainly did not suspect that Hitler was determined to drive the Jews out of Germany, much less exterminate them in all of Europe. This blind spot cannot be attributed to sympathy for anti-Semitism; although some of the American diplomats stationed in Germany during the 1930s were not enamored of Jews, they, as well as most State Department officials in Washington, were nevertheless appalled by Nazi policies toward them. In fact, as early as March 11, 1933, Ambassador Sackett informed Foreign Minister Neurath that the widespread attacks on Jews would "have a disastrous effect in America and in molding world public opinion." And Sackett was pleased that the British embassy had made a similar declaration to the German foreign minister. But, surprisingly, Sackett was easily mollified by Neurath, who assured him that there would be no "pogroms" against "foreigners," which was actually a reference to the isolated attacks on American Jews in Germany, and did not necessarily mean that there would be no attacks on German Jews. In addition, Sackett did not question the information he had received that Hitler himself had ordered his followers to cease molesting foreigners. Sackett thought that since German citizens were highly disciplined, Hitler's order would "bring about a cessation of the anti-Jewish demonstrations."[60] How he reached this conclusion is a mystery.

In any case, for a short period in early 1933 that was a widely held view by American diplomats in Berlin. They believed that Hitler represented "the moderate section of the party" and that he had succeeded in squelching the "violent radical wing" led by Göring and Goebbels.[61] As we now know, Hitler had not ordered his followers to desist from attacking Jews and, indeed, as a fervent anti-Semite, he was unlikely to have done so.[62] It did not take long for diplomats who had welcomed the decline in street attacks to realize that they had been mistaken, and they now stressed that the anti-Semitic campaign had taken a new and ominous turn by pointing to the dismissals of Jews from government positions, schools and universities, the practice of the law, and many other professions. The aim was clearly to oust Jews from all spheres of German culture as well as from the economy.[63] This campaign, as a dispatch noted on April 10, 1933, had been given new stimulus by a speech Hitler had recently delivered to representatives of Nazi medical associations; he vowed to purge "the German people, and especially the intellectual circles, of Jewish influence, declaring that the greatest achievements in the intellectual life had never been attained by members of a foreign race, but only by those who embodied Aryan and pure German intellectual energy. To permit an unduly large proportion of Jews in the professions could be interpreted as an admission of their intellectual superiority, which, he declared, must be resolutely rejected."[64]

Within the staff of the American embassy, Consul Messersmith became the most prolific and certainly the most influential exponent of the evils of Nazi anti-Semitism and of Nazism in general. Historians have often praised him for his "substantive" warnings about Nazism, and Nazi leaders were furious at him for that reason. Putzi Hanfstaengl, a favorite of Hitler and his court jester, was so angry at Messersmith that he spread the canard that he was a Jew.[65] But even Messersmith initially misunderstood Hitler's racism.

Messersmith was an interesting man whose rise to prominence in the diplomatic corps followed an unusual path. He was born in 1883 to a family whose ancestors had moved from Germany to Pennsylvania in the 1700s. Although he never completed his studies at college, he became a successful teacher with a strong commitment to reform along "progressive lines," and while still in his twenties he published a book on civics. His vigorous campaign for reform made him many enemies, and in 1913 he decided on a new career. He took the examination for the Foreign Service, which he passed, but officials considered him unsuited for a career as a diplomat because he lacked private means. He therefore joined the Consular Service, which handled the promotion of American commercial interests, the issuance of passports, and the verification of individuals claiming to be U.S. citizens. After a series of postings to consulates in Curaçao, the Netherlands, and Antwerp, he was assigned to Berlin in 1930. By now he was a respected official who had demonstrated strong sympathy for the disadvantaged, a trait especially noticeable in his work in Germany.[66]

As a person of considerable ambition, Messersmith resented not being allowed to write political reports, and during the hundred days between Sackett's departure from Berlin and Dodd's arrival, he simply ignored the restrictions and wrote a series of dispatches on conditions in Germany. Gordon, the chargé d'affaires during those days, did not appreciate his colleague's violation of the State Department's rules, and from that time there was bad blood between them.[67]

Eventually, Messersmith may have regretted his audacity because his first attempts at political analysis were shallow and inconsistent. In one dispatch, written on March 21, 1933, he reported on all the measures taken by the new government against the Jews and called them "disturbing."[68] Four days later, he quoted a particularly gruesome and prescient prediction of the Munich police president, SS Führer Himmler, later the architect of the genocide of the Jews, regarding a Jew's alleged attempt to assassinate Hitler: "I have the conviction that with the first shot, it will come in Germany to the greatest mass murders and pogroms that have ever yet been experienced in the history of the world, and no state and no police can stop it."[69] Yet at this time Messersmith sent other dispatches in which he claimed to have reliable evidence that the government was backing away from its anti-Jewish policies. He had heard from prominent Americans that Nazi leaders "are greatly concerned over the Jewish question." They now believed that they had made a serious mistake on the issue and were looking for ways to "modify" their "attitude toward the Jews." They were "searching for a solution which will enable them to keep . . . face both at home and abroad." Messersmith had also talked to several Nazi leaders who had convinced him that the prominent Americans were right. He cited the following evidence in support of his assessment: "the great conductor Klemperer has been practically persuaded to return to Germany and to undertake his former activities." Other "outstanding Jews," Messersmith contended, would soon follow Klemperer's example.[70] Messersmith allowed himself to be taken in; neither Klemperer nor other prominent Jews returned to Nazi Germany.

On March 25, two days after he wrote these words, Messersmith claimed to be certain that Hitler did not approve of the anti-Jewish measures. He informed the secretary of state that the Führer was believed "to be very moderate" on this issue. The real villain of the piece was Göring; the third person in the leading trio of the party, Goebbels, was widely believed to be wavering between the other two. Prominent Germans had told Messersmith that Hitler could soon be expected to issue a statement outlining the abandonment of "extreme measures" and promising a more moderate course on the Jewish question.[71]

Messersmith's relatively benign assessment of the future course of Nazi anti-Semitism lasted for about six months. By the summer of 1933 he realized that Hitler did not intend to let up on the anti-Semitic campaign, and by the end of the year the consul referred to the Nazis as "clinical psychopaths" who could be restrained only by force.[72] On November 1, 1933, he acknowledged that he had been mistaken in believing that the worst persecution of Jews had ended. "The attitude of the Government and of the [Nazi] party," he wrote to the secretary of state, "is still to eliminate them from active and gainful participation in any phase of German life." Having abandoned his view of Hitler as a moderate, Messersmith now referred to the Führer "as a man governed by his passions rather than by reason." Moreover, he conceded that Hitler was "the real head of the anti-Jewish movement," and that he was incapable of understanding that foreign unfavorable opinion of him was to a large extent a reaction to the maltreatment of a helpless minority. On these issues, as we now know, Messersmith was right, but it is questionable whether he fully understood the cause of the Nazis' hatred of Jews. He thought that the "deepest fundamental reason for the action against the Jews in Germany is not so much racial as one of competition." Historians have recently demonstrated that the seizure of Jewish property was an important motive behind the attacks on them, but it is not true that racism was a secondary factor. The two cannot be easily separated. But Messersmith was right in his conclusion—he referred to it as his "personal opinion"—that "no moderation in the Jewish policy" will be effected "until there is some radical change in the Government which will enable it to turn about-face on this question."[73]

This change of heart did not prevent him from making a dubious prediction about the Third Reich; he was convinced that the German economy was so brittle that the entire political order created by Hitler was bound to collapse, and he urged Washington to apply economic pressure on Germany—by reducing their bilateral trade—to speed up the process of disintegration.[74]

In May 1934, Messersmith was transferred to Vienna, where he assumed the post of minister to Austria, a move accompanied by a promotion from the consular to the diplomatic service. He continued to believe that Nazism was destined soon to collapse, perhaps within two months, but a visit to Berlin in March 1935 disabused him of his optimism. In conversations with long-standing friends he learned that the Nazis were stronger than ever. He very much regretted the failure of European democracies to take steps to weaken Hitler, although he strongly opposed any American undertaking along these lines. The United States should limit itself to rendering moral support to the democracies that pursued a policy of collective security. Even though by now he frequently deplored the treatment of the Jews, he adamantly opposed their large-scale immigration into the United States on the ground that the newcomers would compete with natives for work.[75] At bottom, this position was not far removed from that of the isolationists.

Not until October 1937 did Messersmith fully abandon his view on the imminent collapse of Nazism. In a memorandum for his superiors in the State Department, he now advocated a firm stand by the United States against Germany, which, he had come to believe, was bent on crippling Great Britain and then attacking the United States. Messersmith had become convinced that ultimately the differences between the "haves" (the democracies) and the "have nots" (Germany, Italy, and Japan) were not over economic issues; their differences stemmed from "a basic clash of ideologies." The three aggressive countries subscribed to the "doctrine of force and of might and to an entirely different international morality" from that which prevailed in France and Britain. Messersmith warned that if the Western democracies failed to defend their interests by "all peaceful methods at their command," they would inevitably have to resort to force. He recognized that their citizens abhorred war, but he warned that this sentiment paralyzed the governments from taking appropriate action to defend their values and interests. The leaders of the "Fascist states," aware of the popularity of pacifist doctrines in the West, had no compunction about pursuing aggressive policies. In Messersmith's mind, his argument was irrefutable: "It is not that proof is lacking but that truth is being ignored."

The memorandum impressed Hull and he immediately showed it to President Roosevelt, who found it so persuasive that he came out strongly against a proposal of Under Secretary of State Sumner Welles, an ardent advocate of appeasement, to convoke a world conference to foster understanding among world powers. Welles thought that Germany and Italy would surely attend and that both countries would be willing to enter into an agreement, although they would insist on concessions that he considered reasonable, such as access to raw materials.[76]

Within the State Department, the subject of Nazi persecution of the Jews became a matter of "deep concern" as early as mid-March 1933. Secretary Hull was apprehensive about reports, confirmed by leaders of major Jewish organizations, of an upcoming mass meeting of protest scheduled to be held in New York City on March 27. Hull did not wish to sanction anti-Semitism, but the information he had received from the American embassy had not convinced him that the situation in Germany was so grave as to warrant mass protests or official protests by the U.S. government. He asked Ambassador Sackett to provide him "with an exact picture of what is taking place. Please therefore telegraph us the facts as you see them, after consulting the principal Consulates, by telephone if necessary, with a view to ascertaining the situation throughout different parts of the country."[77]

A day after sending this telegram and before he had received any reply from Berlin, Hull held a press conference at which he distributed a reassuring statement by Göring that the German ambassador to the United States had passed on to the State Department. Göring promised to maintain "law and order under all circumstances" and pointed out that he had dismissed fifteen SA men because they had acted "on their own authority." Finally, Göring declared, "if one considers that during the last weeks a revolution was witnessed one will have to admit that it passed with very little bloodshed." Hull ended the press conference with an announcement that no official protest against the treatment of the Jews would be considered until the State Department received a reliable account of conditions in Germany.[78]

Hull was cautious and preferred not to ruffle feathers; he therefore made every effort to avoid criticizing the new regime in Germany. He hoped that the Nazis would soon stop the attacks on Jews and that he would then not be obliged to break his silence. He complained that he was "under heavy pressure" to take some action, and he feared that the "monster mass meeting" to be held on March 27 in New York, and other rallies in Chicago, Boston, Philadelphia, Baltimore, Cleveland, and seventy additional locations, would place him in an untenable situation. He was convinced that "outside intervention has rarely produced the results desired and has frequently aggravated the situation." To defend his policy of nonintervention, he tended to refer to the "alleged mistreatment of Jewish nationals," and he would clutch at any sign, however dubious and misleading, that suggested that Hitler was committed to restoring law and order.

But pressure on Hull and President Roosevelt to condemn the Nazis did not let up, throwing doubt on the claim by some historians that American Jews and American organizations in general were far too silent on Hitler's anti-Semitism.[79] Within weeks of Hitler's ascent to power, Stephen S. Wise, a prominent Reform rabbi and the leader of the World Jewish Congress, did his utmost to alert Americans to the bestiality and dangers of Nazism. He visited Secretary Hull to plead for a statement of condemnation of German persecution of the Jews, and he called for an economic boycott of Germany. He warned that the Nazis were not attacking only German Jews but world Jewry.[80]

Rabbi Wise was not the only person in the United States to call for the strong denunciation of the Nazi persecution of the Jews. The archives of the State Department contain hundreds of messages, pleas, and petitions from all parts of the country urging the government to issue formal and strong protests against Germany's mistreatment of Jews. In addition, many appeals were sent to senators and congressmen, who often called on the government to take action.

It would be tedious to summarize all of these appeals, but reference to a few of them will indicate that many Americans understood the seriousness of the anti-Semitic campaign by the Nazis. On March 23, 1933, only weeks after Hitler came to power, the Louis Marshall Club of the Young Men's Hebrew Association of Mount Vernon, New York, wrote to Hull to express its horror at the "conditions of barbarism" in Germany and to press for diplomatic protests against the persecution of the Jews. "With bowed heads and prayers upon our lips, we urge you to stop this 'madman' before he becomes a Frankenstein to the world." The letter continued with a warning that the "lesson of history is that the black brigade of anti-Semitism and religious discrimination does not limit the attack against any one people or any one creed." It ended with an appeal to the secretary of state to break off relations, not with the German people, "but with the band of Nazi slaughterers who are controlling Germany."[81]

Over the next few weeks, various organizations and political leaders appealed to the government to take the Nazis to task. For example, the Mizrachi Organization of Baltimore, which represented Orthodox Jews, sent a message to Hull pleading that he "take immediate steps" to "prevent the reversion to barbarism." The protests were not limited to Jews. On March 21, 1933, the president of the International Catholic Truth Society asked the U.S. government to "assume leadership in a worldwide humanitarian protest and demand that the Hitler regime . . . cease its inhuman and unnationalistic [sic] furies." In May, Senator Royal S. Copeland, a conservative Democrat representing New York, asked Hull for "details of the latest information you have on the situation in Germany with regard to the Jewish people."[82]

Generally, the State Department or the president's subordinates answered the appeals with letters that expressed sympathy for the persecuted, but beyond that they tended to be noncommittal. Occasionally, if the protests came from especially influential or prominent citizens, State Department officials were more forthcoming. Thus, when Charles H. Strong together with nine other lawyers protested the Nazi dismissal of Jewish judges and the imposition of severe restrictions on Jewish lawyers in practicing their profession, Phillips replied that although normally the State Department avoided transmitting private messages to foreign governments, in this case the department had forwarded the lawyers' protest to the German ambassador in Washington with the added statement that it "indicated the widespread feeling which is aroused in this country by measures of religious discrimination wherever they may be applied."[83] Hull seems to have been unsure of his stance on this sensitive issue; hence, he asked Chargé d'Affaires Gordon in Berlin for his advice and for proposals on how to respond to the demands by prominent Jews that he publicly chastise the German government.

Surprisingly, Gordon, who had demonstrated an acute understanding of Nazism, agreed "entirely" with Hull that "outside intercession" would be counterproductive. On March 25, 1933, he warned that protests from the United States and other Western countries would be regarded as further evidence that groups hostile to Germany were conducting "atrocity propaganda" against the country, a persistent complaint by Nazi officials. Even some leading Jews in Germany, the chargé d'affaires noted, opposed "outside intercession" for fear that it would only enrage the Nazis. But Gordon believed that foreign leaders could take a step toward calming the tense situation in Germany. He urged them to issue a statement expressing "confidence in Hitler's determination to restore peaceful and normal conditions emphasizing what a great place he will achieve in the estimation of the world if he is able to bring it about." Moreover, Gordon thought that such a statement could aid the forces of moderation within the Nazi Party, and that Hitler himself would welcome any move to "strengthen his hand."[84]

Three days after voicing these views, Gordon had second thoughts about the government's policies regarding Jews. His sudden change of mind occurred because the authorities had announced that a boycott of Jewish businesses would begin on April 1. To Gordon, this was an "extraordinary action . . . a manifestation of the same mentality as dictated the most ruthless war-time measures"; he feared it would have "evil consequences." The Nazi radicals, it seemed to him, were bent on seizing the "present opportunity to crush the Jews in Germany." Gordon still believed that the Nazi Party was divided between radicals and moderates (led by Hitler), even though he acknowledged that there was evidence that the Führer supported the boycott with the proviso that it be implemented without violence. Gordon now conceded that the hotheads were the dominant force in the Nazi movement.[85]

Although the boycott was not a success and ended after only one day, American diplomats were profoundly moved by the German government's action, and from this moment until their departure from Germany in 1941, they focused on every aspect of Nazi anti-Semitism. They frequently sent dispatches that dealt only with the Jews, and some of them were so detailed that they ran to several long pages, and at least one of them could pass for an accomplished scholarly paper. Neither the British nor the French diplomats in Germany came close to covering this subject so systematically.

Hull was also very troubled by the boycott and now expressed "deep concern" over the mistreatment of Jews; he asked Gordon to convey to Foreign Minister Neurath the secretary of state's view that the "friendship of the two countries might not remain unaffected" if Germany's policy of persecution continued.[86] The first dispatches on the Nazi persecution of Jews reached Washington at a time when both the president and the secretary of state were already angry at the Nazi leadership for their refusal to honor their war debts to the United States. The reparations imposed on Germany in 1919 for the damage and expenses caused by World War I had been substantially reduced twice (in 1924 and 1929), yet the Nazi leaders resorted to various deceptions to avoid payments. Roosevelt was so put out that he instructed Hull to snub Hjalmar Schacht, the minister of economics, when he arrived at the State Department in May 1933 to discuss the reparations issue. The president directed Hull not to pay attention to the minister when he appeared in his office by pretending to be studying papers on his desk.[87]

Schacht may have been offended, but the slight did not induce him to change his policy regarding the payment of reparations. Nor did Hull's expression of concern over the plight of the Jews prompt the Nazis to moderate their anti-Semitic policies. In fact, early in July the State Department received a dispatch from Gordon sharply critical of the German government for contemplating a law to deprive Jews of German citizenship. The purpose of such a law, he wrote, "would be to reduce the German Jews to the position of ignominy to which they were subjected during the Middle Ages. Nazi leaders have repeatedly boasted in the past that one of the first acts of a Nazi regime would be to set up ghettoes in Germany." And he could not see any sign that the government intended to "let up on these discriminatory measures."[88]

The evidence on the persecution of the Jews that American diplomats sent to Washington could leave no doubt in any reader's mind that Germany was being engulfed by a wave of sadism and that the Jews were living under a state of siege. Often the dispatches included details of anti-Semitic incidents in smaller towns, where the prejudice was more virulent than elsewhere, especially in the early years of Nazi rule. Thus, the State Department learned that in 1934 local National Socialist newspapers in several towns in Franconia and Hessen had stationed photographers in front of Jewish stores to take pictures of people entering to make purchases. In towns in other parts of the country, the local press published lists of Jewish stores with calls to Aryans not to patronize them. In still other towns, officials displayed pillories on which the names of Aryans who had made purchases in Jewish stores or had visited Jewish doctors were inscribed. Interestingly, ordinary Catholics often ignored the Nazis and defiantly made "purchases from Jewish stores in a veritable spirit of bravado." But in numerous rural regions, the impact of the anti-Semitic campaign was so effective that communal leaders urged Jews to move to larger cities or at least to acquire cars or trucks so that they would be able to leave quickly in the event of physical attacks on them. Some local newspapers warned Jews that pogroms were likely.[89]

Ambassador Dodd became fully aware of the depth and irrationality of Hitler's loathing of the Jews during a "personal and confidential" meeting with the Führer on March 7, 1934. Prior to the meeting, two "very prominent people" in the German government had urged the ambassador to speak freely on such issues as "propaganda and also the necessity of better international relations." Dodd therefore decided to ask Hitler about a recently published brochure that had called on Germans in foreign countries "to think of themselves always as Germans and owing moral, if not political, allegiance to the fatherland." Hitler immediately shot back that Jews "almost certainly" had disseminated such untrue charges. Then he continued to talk with "great emotion about the Jews, claiming that they were responsible for substantially all of the ill feeling in the United States toward Germany."

Still under the illusion that he could influence Hitler to adopt a more moderate political stance, Dodd suggested to the Führer that there were two "procedure[s]" for dealing with the Jewish issue, both of which avoided the extreme measures taken by the Nazis. He made the suggestion, Dodd stressed, without "ever giving pointed advice." Dodd also told Hitler that James McDonald, an American diplomat and the League of Nations high commissioner for refugees, was forming an organization in Lausanne with the "assistance" of the United States Senate to help Jews emigrate from countries where they were unwelcome. McDonald had "at his command some millions of dollars" and intended to support the departure of Jews "without too much suffering." He hoped that in "eight or ten years" the Jewish "problem" might thus "be solved in a humane way."

The ambassador then offered Hitler some additional information on how the Jewish problem might be solved; he explained that in the United States a way had been found to handle the issue of the "over-activity of Jews in university or official life" whenever that threatened to cause "trouble." Senior administrators "managed to redistribute the offices in such a way as not to give great offense." Even "wealthy Jews" supported the practice of limiting the number of Jews in "high positions."

Clearly, Dodd did not understand the nature of Hitler's anti-Semitism, which was rooted in racial doctrines that did not allow for toleration of people such as the Jews, who were considered degenerate and ruthlessly ambitious. To the ambassador's surprise, the Führer "came back [to his suggestion] with a still more vigorous reply"; he claimed that Jews "occupied 59% of all public positions in Russia and that they had ruined the country." Taken aback, Dodd could not think of anything to say except that Nazi policies toward the Jews were causing "embarrassments" in the United States. But this comment did not deter Hitler from continuing his harangue. When Dodd tried to change the subject by asking if Hitler favored the convocation of a disarmament conference, "he waived an answer and turned once again to attacking the Jews as being responsible for the feeling that Germany wants to go to war."[90]

Despite all we now know about the atrocities of the Nazis, some details about the depth of their hatred for Jews still seem incredible. On April 1, 1935, Ambassador Dodd passed on to Washington a particularly incendiary comment made by Julius Streicher, editor of *Der Stürmer*, the leading organ of anti-Semitic venom: "To those who argue that Christ was a Jew, I would say, 'Were I to call Christ a Jew, I would be calling him a criminal.'"[91] Perhaps even more noteworthy in light of subsequent developments was the circumspection with which Nazi leaders touched on the possibility of exterminating the Jews. Dodd reported, also on April 1, 1935, that the "fanatical Julius Streicher lately published a warning against 'certain irresponsible elements who have spread rumors that the Jews were planning an attack upon the Führer's life and that consequently they must be exterminated.'" Streicher made it clear that he insisted on "the utmost discipline in his district" and that he had therefore dismissed a local leader "for undue rashness." The implication of the last two words requires no comment. Dodd also reported that a journalist known by American diplomats had told someone at the embassy that Goebbels had "made the significant statement that the 'Jewish question will soon be liquidated' but denied permission that publicity be given to his remark."[92] After publication of the

Nuremberg Laws in late September 1935, which, among other things, deprived Jews of civic and political rights and formally defined the category of "non-Aryan," Dodd predicted that the "last word" on anti-Jewish measures had not yet been said.[93]

Virtually all of the numerous reports on the Jewish question contained interesting and little-known details, but there was one that stood out for its intellectual depth and sweep. It was a dispatch written in August 1935 by Samuel W. Honaker, the consul general in Stuttgart. In the Foreign Service for over twenty years, Honaker was an experienced diplomat, but he also had a scholarly bent. His report, entitled "The Jewish Problem in the Stuttgart Consular District: A Political Survey of the Social, Economic, and General Cultural Situation," ran to twenty-four pages and focused on the plight of the Jews in the city of Stuttgart and in the states of Württemberg and Baden, both of which formed the consular district served by the American consulate in Stuttgart. But it also paid considerable attention to the history and sociology of the Jewish communities in those localities. Honaker intended to counteract the "recent propaganda concerning the menace presented by Jews in criminal matters," and he therefore included a "Supplement" listing forty-eight different types of crime reported in Germany in 1913 that demonstrated that the charge was baseless. For instance, 35 people were convicted of high treason and only 1 of them was a Jew; 4,987 had committed offenses against conscription laws and only 50 of them were Jews; 801 were convicted of involuntary manslaughter and 3 of them were Jews. All told, 414,301 crimes were committed that year, and of these only 2,833, roughly 0.5 percent, were ascribed to Jews.

These statistics supported the larger point that Honaker was making, that the Jews made up a respected group of communities with their own religious and welfare institutions, and that, on the whole, relations between Jews and Gentiles in Württemberg and Baden had been reasonably friendly. The communities were small, 10,823 people out of a total of 2,713,150 in Württemberg and 20,619 out of 2,429,977 in Baden, and before 1933 they had not generally been looked upon as in any way a threat. The Jews made their living in many different economic fields, but were notably successful in the professions and fine arts. In Baden, they virtually monopolized medicine and the law and played a prominent role in banking. But because of their small number, they occupied very few positions in "public life."

Honaker found that since the advent of National Socialism, relations between the religious groups had changed, but not as much as might have been expected under the stressful circumstances. Catholics and Jews had turned more antagonistic toward each other, but in the Protestant regions relations between the Christians and Jews had deteriorated only "in the slightest degree." In Stuttgart, for example, streets still carried the names of "Jewish philanthropists," and there were still a few societies and clubs that "welcome Jews, a situation almost inconceivable in the state of Baden."

Honaker described in considerable detail the restrictions—economic and cultural—that the Nazis had imposed on Jews, most of which have already been mentioned in this study.[94] But there were two restrictions that especially hurt Jews in Württemberg and Baden, the prohibitions against their buying agricultural land and against their membership in any organization of farmers. Determined to be precise on the subject of Jewish persecution, Honaker noted that thus far, that is, until the summer of 1935, the authorities had not prevented Jews from practicing their religion, although he indicated that a few synagogues in smaller towns had been damaged and sacred objects such as "Bible rolls" (Torah scrolls) had been "polluted."

The tone of Honaker's dispatch was dispassionate, but no reader could fail to notice the message he sought to convey. In a separate dispatch of August 23, he reiterated that "many responsible people in the Stuttgart area" opposed the "anti-Jewish agitation," but in the last sentence he warned that the "situation" was nevertheless "likely to develop along dangerous lines." And in the foreword to the report itself, he stressed that the "Jewish question . . . affects the foreign and domestic policies of Germany" and "inspires the attitude of a large group of foreigners towards Germany." He warned that "out of the complications arising from these [anti-Semitic] policies and attitudes much unhappiness and distress and even bitterness is springing up, with an ever increasing tendency to envelop more and more people." In what can only be interpreted as advice to his superiors in Washington to react to these developments in a forceful way, he insisted that the "United States must be reckoned as one of the countries interested in this dire trend."[95]

~

Ironically, despite Hitler's crudeness and cruelty, he evinced a high degree of sensitivity to any perceived slight. He could not tolerate criticism and invariably blamed the Jews for any unkind words about him. When in early 1934 the American Jewish Committee and the American Federation of Labor announced that on March 7 a mock trial of Hitler would be held in Madison Square Garden in New York City, the news drove German diplomats into a frenzy of activity. On at least seven occasions, the German foreign minister, the German ambassador to the United States, or the counselor to the German embassy in Washington (Dr. Leitner) appealed to senior American officials to stop the trial. Dodd reminded the foreign minister that Americans were indeed shocked by "many things" in Germany and that the American government did not have the authority, even if it was so inclined, to stop the trial. When John Hickerson, the assistant chief of the Division of Western European Affairs, made a similar point to Dr. Leitner, the latter said that if "circumstances were reversed, the German Government would certainly find a way of stopping such a proceeding." In polite diplomatic language, Hickerson replied, "it is my understanding that the German Government is not so limited in the action it can take in such matters as is the American Government." Secretary of State Hull told the German ambassador that his assistants had "ransacked" all the law books and had found no legal ground for stopping the trial.[96] The proceeding took place as planned in front of twenty thousand people, including Governor Alfred Smith and Mayor Fiorello La Guardia. Officially called the "Case of Civilization against Hitler," it found the Nazis guilty of "high crimes against civilization." The press gave the trial extensive publicity; the *New York Times*, for example, carried a front-page article on March 8, 1934, that described the event in considerable detail.[97]

Nazi leaders leveled a barrage of protests against criticisms from abroad, and when that failed they resorted to ridicule. In August 1935, Goebbels derided the foreign press by declaring, "when one looks askance at a Jew on Kurfürstendamm, then there arises a cry to be heard from London to Peking." He advised the press to turn its attention to other, more important events, such as the war in Abyssinia and the plans for world revolution being hatched in Moscow.[98]

Germany's complaints did not deter American diplomats from continuing to monitor the Nazi persecution of Jews, and they often reported on developments not widely known at the time outside of Germany. For example, on April 23, 1937, Ambassador Dodd informed the State Department that the secret police had suppressed all eighty lodges of the B'nai B'rith, an organization devoted to humanitarian and charitable work. In addition, the police had confiscated 1.5 million marks in cash and real estate worth two million marks from the Jews, losses that, according to Dodd, would "hurt the poorer members of the Jewish community." Leaders of that community were informed that these measures had been taken in retaliation against "foreign anti-Nazi agitation."[99]

In August 1938, the Nazis announced several measures that, according to the American ambassador, were designed simply to insult and annoy Jews. He could not resist ridiculing one of them: "The procedure of annoying Jews, the thoroughness of which reflects creditably upon German inventiveness and attention to detail, has been carried in Berlin to the point of withdrawing low license numbers from Jewish automobile owners who are now being given plates higher than the number IA 300,000." It was considerably milder than the law proposed by Streicher, who called for the cancellation of all licenses held by Jews.[100]

Repressive measures against Jews were often enacted on the initiative of local officials, which, the embassy noted, demonstrated the intensity of anti-Semitic feelings among lower-level officials. The *Völkischer Beobachter* of August 19, 1937, "gleefully" reported that a judge at the local court in Remscheid, a city in North Rhine–Westphalia, had ruled that the debts incurred by a woman in Jewish stores were not the legal responsibility of her husband. The ruling was intended to discourage women from patronizing such stores and thus to reduce "marital strife" in the family when the husband tended to be more scrupulous than his wife in following the Nazi Party line against dealing with Jews.[101]

A MISSTEP

Among the hundreds of dispatches sent to Washington by diplomats throughout Germany during the 1930s, some differences in emphasis can be detected, but what is much more striking is the degree of agreement about the undemocratic and barbaric nature of Nazism. One diplomat, however, struck a discordant note, and his report merits discussion precisely because it was so atypical. The experience of this diplomat, Vice Consul Ware Adams, took an ironic twist that may have eventually raised doubts in his mind about the soundness of his favorable assessment of Nazism.

Adams was a young Foreign Service officer whose assignment to Berlin was probably his first, which may account for his naïveté. In the fall of 1936, he joined a group of representatives from Holland, Portugal, and Switzerland that the Nazis took on an inspection of a penal colony at Papenburg in the Ems-Moorland, an area close to the Dutch border. The group spent three days, always in the company of German officials, on a tour of the colony, which consisted of six prison camps that housed about fifty-five hundred men. Of these, thirty-five hundred were serving "penitentiary sentences" for serious offenses, and about two thousand were serving "ordinary prison sentences." In his report, Adams claimed that none of them were "persons in protective custody" for alleged political offenses, although he acknowledged that until May 1934 one of the camps had been a concentration camp. The inmates worked on a project designed to reclaim the "Moorland" and to make it arable. Once the land had been transformed, it was expected to yield a "variety of good crops" of potatoes, beans, sweet lupine, tomatoes, cabbage, cucumbers, and cauliflower.

Adams described the barracks as rather comfortable: the prisoners had access to a dispensary, laundry, kitchen, and shower room, all of them "furnished with modern equipment." The camp seemed to Adams to be "remarkably clean and comfortable for temporary quarters. The barracks are all well aired and lighted, with high ceilings and many windows, even the confinement barracks having a window of about 1 1/2 by 2 feet in each cell." The prisoners were permitted to visit a "hall where lectures were given and religious services held." The medical facilities were impressive, as were the possibilities for entertainment: the Nazi band of "60 pieces" regularly offered concerts. Sports facilities, including a large swimming pool, were abundant. All in all, the inmates "appeared to be well-nourished, healthy and clean." Most of them were skilled workers, and all were paid for their work; they could buy goods from the camp canteen, including tobacco, but they were not allowed to smoke in the barracks.

The visit, Adams continued, had been arranged at the request of several foreign delegates who had remained in Berlin after a recently concluded meeting of the International Penal and Penitentiary Congress. The senior officials at the German Ministry of Justice were initially split on whether to permit foreigners into the penal colony, probably because a section of it had been "a concentration camp for persons in protective custody." The older officials in the ministry feared that the camp would make an unfavorable impression on foreigners, but Undersecretary Roland Freisler—who a few years later was the notorious judge in the trials of men accused of planning to assassinate Hitler—argued that it would be "an opportunity to make a favorable impression abroad." And, as Adams pointed out, Freisler proved to be correct.[102]

How this report passed muster at the American embassy is a mystery. It was approved by Douglas Jenkins, the American consul general, who was an experienced diplomat and by 1936 should have known better than to be taken in by Adams's account. It is also puzzling that Adams did not realize that he had been shown a "Potemkin village"; he himself reported that the fifty-five hundred prisoners were guarded by no fewer than 770 men in SA uniforms. True, he conceded that the worst institutions would not have been shown to foreigners, and yet he wrote a laudatory report on the camp. He was not known to be sympathetic to appeasement, let alone Nazism. The best explanation is that he was simply very unsophisticated.[103]

It is likely that he changed his mind about the Nazi regime a year and a half later, when his wife had an "unpleasant experience" that was more revealing of Nazi attitudes than those displayed to foreigners at the Moorland Penal Colony. On June 28, 1938, Mrs. Adams did some shopping at Rosenhain's, a store on the fashionable Kurfürstendamm, and when she approached the exit with her purchases she learned that a small group of Nazis was picketing the store because it was owned by Jews. They blocked the exit and would not allow shoppers to leave the store. Every time Mrs. Adams made an effort to go into the street, the Nazis "forcefully pushed [her] back." She showed her diplomatic identity card to the young Nazi in charge of the crowd, and he replied, "This only makes it worse." And when she told him that she could not believe that he would want to "cause unfriendliness with America," he replied, "Why not?" The Nazis now made some "derisive remarks," putting her in a "very humiliating" situation. Finally, the director of the store persuaded the crowd to let her leave, and even then she had to "force [her] way through." Mrs. Adams reported the incident to two policemen, who took some notes and recorded her name as well as that of the leader of the Nazi crowd. The American ambassador forwarded Mrs. Adams's account of the incident to Washington and noted that the chief of the American Section at the German Foreign Office expressed "regrets" for the unpleasant experience. The ambassador did not indicate how Mr. Adams reacted to the incident.[104]

THE DEPARTURE OF DODD

By this time, Dodd had retired from his post. Intensely disliked by Nazi officials for his unconcealed hatred of Hitlerism, out of favor with the State Department, and, according to Messersmith, no longer mentally capable of performing his duties effectively, Dodd had begun to think of retiring in mid-1937, although he hoped to remain on the job until March 1938. In August 1937, he left for a prolonged stay in the United States, and it became clear to him that President Roosevelt did not intend to send him back to Berlin.[105] His replacement, Hugh R. Wilson, who arrived in January 1938, was in many ways quite different from Dodd. A career Foreign Service officer with twenty-seven years of experience in the State Department, he was well regarded in Washington and was expected to be more "diplomatic" than his predecessor; he would follow protocol and send all his reports only to the State Department rather than mailing some of them to President Roosevelt. Wilson also would be less offensive to the German government; he belonged to the school of "realists" who favored negotiations with the Nazis rather than confrontation, and his demeanor was much more amiable than Dodd's.

Wilson has even been depicted as "inordinately impressed by Hitlerite Germany. Nazism appealed to this ardent anti-Communist." But this characterization seems to be a bit too harsh. True, in his meeting with Hitler early in March 1938 he complimented the Führer rather effusively "as a man who had pulled his people from moral and economic despair into the state of pride and evident prosperity which they now enjoyed."[106] This comment, it should be kept in mind, was made in response to Hitler's introductory remarks, in which he complimented Wilson for his knowledge of German and his ability, therefore, to understand the German people. It was the first meeting between the two, and both were doing their utmost to start their relationship on a friendly footing.

It is also true that in an unsent letter to Secretary of State Hull, Wilson sharply criticized the "Jewish controlled press" in the United States for its "hymn of hatred" directed at Germany.[107] Moreover, Wilson thought that Germany had some legitimate claims with regard to the Sudetenland and he urged the State Department to advise the Czechs to make concessions to the Germans.[108] And, finally, in a partly autobiographical book, published after the outbreak of World War II, he still expressed admiration—as did several other Western diplomats—for some of the Nazi social programs such as Kraft durch Freude (Strength through Joy), which he thought was "going to be beneficial to the world at large." The program, he thought, had enriched the lives of ordinary workers by making art, music, and the "beauties of the landscape" available to them.[109]

THE ROAD TO KRISTALLNACHT

Nevertheless, there is no evidence that Wilson approved of the overall political program of the Nazis. In fact, within weeks of his arrival in Berlin he sent dispatches to Washington that differed from Dodd's more in tone than in substance. On March 23, 1938, Wilson met Goebbels, the minister of propaganda, who voiced regret over the poor "press relations" between the two countries, for which he blamed American journalists. Some criticism by foreigners was to be expected, but what most troubled him were "the willful misstatements of fact, and [the] slander and libel against the person of the Reich Chancellor and those immediately around him." This treatment infuriated many people, because the Führer was "venerated by every German"; Goebbels then indicated that he would use a word that he knew would "astonish" Wilson: "to the Germans there was something 'heilig' [sacred] about the Führer. Therefore the Germans deeply resented the personal attacks on him." Politely but firmly, Wilson told Goebbels that he had spoken at length with American journalists in Germany and had concluded that most were serious professionals trying to tell the truth, although he granted that they viewed developments in Germany "through American eyes" and from an American background. But Wilson added that the "most pressing thing that stood between any betterment of our Press relationship was the Jewish question," a point he reiterated toward the end of the interview.[110]

Over the next seven months, Ambassador Wilson, his staff in Berlin, and the officials in the consular offices sent no fewer than forty-eight dispatches to Washington on the persecution of the Jews, and their thrust was similar to that of previous reports on this topic. These diplomatic messages are noteworthy, not only because they reflect the continuing interest of American diplomats in the issue but also because they demonstrate that the Nazis were stepping up their campaign against the Jews throughout 1938. The violence during Kristallnacht, the Night of Broken Crystal (November 9–10), did not signal the adoption of a new policy; nor was it a reaction to the murder of a German diplomat in Paris by a Jewish refugee from Germany. It was the high point of a long series of increasingly harsh measures taken to impoverish and humiliate the Jews.

Some of the dispatches touched on such relatively minor restrictions on Jews as the refusal to issue them passports for temporary travel abroad, but most dealt with decrees that imposed heavy burdens on them. One dispatch written by the ambassador himself described the Decree of April 26, which required all Jews—that is, all those defined as non-Aryans by the Reich Citizenship Law of November 14, 1935—to itemize their assets held in Germany and abroad, a measure designed to provide information to the government for the imposition of new, severe taxes on Jews. If Rudolf Brinkmann, the state secretary of the German Ministry of the National Economy, was to be believed, Jewish wealth in Germany and Austria amounted to seven billion marks.[111] In another report, Wilson noted that Hitler had insisted that Austrian, not German, Nazis take charge of running the recently annexed country because Austrian Nazis were more anxious "to work . . . off old hatreds and [desirous of] taking revenge" against political enemies and persecuting Jews, whose assets they coveted.[112] The State Department was especially concerned that the Nazis might force American Jews living in Germany to declare their assets, and on June 2, 1938, Wilson sent a note directly to President Roosevelt urging him to "consider some form of retaliation."[113]

In mid-June, the ambassador's reports became much more alarming. He had learned that "a fairly large scale series of arrests" of Jews had taken place in Berlin and other cities. The police had rounded up people whose names were on their records for minuscule violations of the law that had actually been settled some time earlier. The prisoners underwent physical examinations before the police decided whether they should be sent to a concentration camp or forced to do manual labor. Jewish community leaders assumed that the purpose of this action was to stoke emigration, which Wilson considered a plausible explanation. He mentioned a recent report in the press that had indicated that if emigration was not accelerated, it would take thirty years for Germany to be rid of all its Jews.[114]

Six days later, Wilson informed Washington of yet another campaign against Jews, which, he said, "outstrips in thoroughness anything of the kind since early 1933, extending beyond a mere summer exuberance of the Party such as made itself manifest in 1935." The major immediate cause of the new campaign seems to have been Nazi anger over the influx into Berlin of Jews from Austria, where the Nazis were even more brutal than their brethren in Germany. "Is it not altogether outrageous," Goebbels fumed, "and does it not bring a blush of rage to one's face, that in the last month no less than three thousand Jews have emigrated to Berlin? What do they want here?" In the new campaign small groups of civilians marched from one store to another to paint the word *Jude* on the windows in large red letters accompanied by the Star of David and caricatures of Jews. A previous decree ordering Jews to write their names in large white letters facilitated the work of the gangs. Wilson toured the city and saw a "sorry spectacle particularly in those districts inhabited by Jews, where practically the only persons to be seen were policemen patrolling the vacant and besmirched streets." At least four foreign correspondents who took photographs of the stores that had been defaced were arrested, but once they pointed out that they were foreigners and had done nothing illegal, they were released.[115]

In one series of reports, Ambassador Wilson focused on the racial underpinnings of Nazi anti-Semitism. A government decree issued in August 1938 stated that as of January 1, 1939, all male Jews would have to use the given name "Israel" and all female Jews the name "Sara." Those who failed to register the new names with authorities or to use them at all times would face at least one month's imprisonment.[116] Early in November, the U.S. embassy called an official at the Reichsärztekammer (Reich Physicians' Chamber) to inquire whether a visiting American, who was not Jewish, could be treated by a Jewish doctor. The official hastened to point out that the Law of July 26, 1938, prohibited Jewish doctors from treating any "non-Jewish persons, irrespective of whether they were of German or foreign nationality, and that no exception would be made." To emphasize the seriousness of the restriction, the German official sent "copies of the law" to the embassy.[117]

Immediately after Kristallnacht, during which the Nazis unleashed the bloodiest and most far-reaching campaign of violence against Jews to date, American diplomats diligently reported on the rampage of Nazi hooligans throughout the country: on their destruction of the windows of Jewish shops before looting them; their desecration of synagogues, many of which were then burned to the ground; and, finally, their arrest of about thirty thousand Jewish men between the ages of eighteen and eighty, all of whom were sent to one of three concentration camps.[118] The American diplomats made it clear that they lent no credence to Goebbels's claim that the attacks were a spontaneous response of the German people to the assassination by a Jew of Ernst vom Rath, an official of the German embassy in Paris.

Some of the most dramatic and detailed accounts of Nazi bestiality came from consuls in cities other than Berlin. On November 21, 1938, David H. Buffum, the American consul in Leipzig, wrote a report on the "anti-Semitic onslaught," as he called it, that revealed both the sadism of the Nazis and their fascination with bizarre rituals. This report also sheds much light on the mindset of National Socialism, and it provides additional evidence in support of the now generally accepted view that the attack on Jews throughout Germany on Kristallnacht and the following few days was well orchestrated.

Several hours before the attacks started, local Nazis in Leipzig staged an elaborate ritual in a square known as the Altermarkt. Nazi officials had exhumed the remains of the bodies of some of their comrades "who had been considered rowdyish violators of law and order" by the authorities and had been killed at least five years earlier. Now they were considered martyrs to the Nazi cause. Their remains were placed in "extravagant coffins; arranged around a colossal, flaming urn on the *Altermarkt* for purposes of display, and ultimately conveyed amid marching troops, flaring torches and funeral music to the 'Ehrenhain,'" Leipzig's National Socialist burial plot. For this propagandistic ceremony the entire marketplace had been surrounded "with wooden lattice work about ten yards high. This was covered with white cloth to form the background for black swastikas at least five yards high and broad. Flame-spurting urns and gigantic banners completed a Wagnerian ensemble as to pomposity of stage-setting." The only reassuring aspect of the ritual was the indifference of many Leipzig citizens, who seemed to be distressed by the waste of materials and the expense, but for "obvious reasons" no one openly protested. Many Leipzigers were "much more perturbed" the next morning, when they became aware "of the most violent debacle the city had probably ever witnessed."

The devastation had begun at 3 a.m. on November 10, and it constituted "a barrage of ferocity as had had no equal hitherto in Germany, or very likely anywhere else in the world since savagery, if ever." In addition to the widespread destruction of Jewish property and the theft of valuables of every kind, the Nazis manhandled human beings. "In one of the Jewish sections an eighteen year old boy was hurled from a three story window to land with both legs broken on a street littered with burning beds and other household furniture and effects from his family's and other apartments." The Nazi ruffians made special efforts to locate and seize valuables in the homes and offices of affluent Jews. The "main streets of the city were a positive litter of shattered plate glass." The fury of the Nazis reached beyond Jewish businesses. Three of the city's synagogues "were fired simultaneously by incendiary bombs and all sacred objects and records desecrated or destroyed, in most instances hurled through the windows and burned in the streets. No attempts were made to quench the fires, function[aries] of the fire brigade having been confined to . . . [pouring] water on adjoining buildings." To add insult to injury, the Nazis pulled the owners of one clothing store from their beds at six in the morning and imprisoned them for allegedly having set fire to their own business.

Consul Buffum described in some detail what he dubbed a particularly "ghoulish" form of violence in the Jewish cemetery. The Nazi marauders torched the temple, as well as the building where the caretakers lived, and then uprooted and desecrated tombstones and graves. Ten corpses remained "unburied" for an entire week because all the workers at the cemetery had been arrested. Elsewhere many male Jews were taken into custody and shipped to concentration camps. But in Leipzig the "insatiably sadistic perpetrators" committed an additional abhorrent crime. After destroying the dwellings of Jewish families and throwing their "movable effects" into the streets, they threw many Jewish men, women, and children "into a small stream that flows through the Zoological Park, commanding horrified spectators to spit at them, defile them with mud and jeer at their plight." Even the "slightest manifestation of sympathy" for the Jews by bystanders "evoked a positive fury on the part of the perpetrators." Several Jews were reliably reported to have been beaten to death. All these "tactics were carried out the entire morning of November 10th without police intervention." At the end of the dispatch, Buffum reported that three professors at the University of Jena who voiced disapproval of this "insidious drive against mankind" had been sent to concentration camps. The stamps on the cover of this document indicate that it reached the desk of George Messersmith, now an assistant secretary of state.[119]

Several reports from other parts of Germany that were similar to Buffum's reached the Department of State, and a few of them included references to an ultimate solution of the Jewish question, which is of special interest because they touch on an ongoing controversy among historians over the date when the Nazi leadership decided on the most drastic measure against the Jews.* The policy of extermination was not put into effect until 1941–42, and there is no evidence that a decision on such a policy had been reached before then; but, as already noted, occasional hints had emerged that some Nazis were contemplating such a course. In a dispatch of November 23, 1938, Prentiss Gilbert, then the chargé d'affaires at the Berlin embassy, called attention to another reference to the possible physical elimination of the German Jews. That article, which Gilbert characterized as one "of unusual vulgarity and cynical ruthlessness," appeared in the SS newspaper *Schwarze Korps*. The author mocked the "super-democrats" in the United States who criticized Germany's Jewish policies: "Neither Mr. Roosevelt nor an English archbishop nor any other prominent super-democrat would put their young daughter in the bed of a greasy Eastern Jew. However, when it is a question of Germany they suddenly are ignorant of any Jewish question but only see the 'persecution of innocent people for their faith'—as if we ever were interested in what a Jew did or did not believe." The author went on to boast that Germany had now built up its military strength to such a level that no country "can hinder" it from "undert[aking] a total solution of the Jewish question, which signifies not

*For more details on this controversy, see below, pp. 204–5.

only the elimination of Jews from economic life but driving them from German dwellings and putting them in a section by themselves." Jews, the article predicted, would grow poorer and would then "constitute a breeding ground for Bolshevism and crime." At that point, Germany would be faced with the necessity of "exterminating the Jewish underworld in the same way we in our orderly state are wont to exterminate criminals, i.e., with fire and sword. The result would be the actual and definite end of Jewry in Germany and its complete extermination." The only alternative to this outcome would be for the democracies, especially the United States and Britain, to admit large numbers of Jews into their countries. Elsewhere in the dispatch, Gilbert quoted an editorial of November 23 in the *Völkischer Beobachter* to the effect that the "German people have now embarked upon the 'final and unalterably uncompromising solution' of the problem of the Jews in Germany."[120]

The events during the night of November 9–10 were so horrendous that Messersmith pleaded for more than disapproval by the United States. "When a country which vaunts its civilization as superior," he wrote to Hull on November 14, "commits in cold blood and with deliberation acts worse than those we have in the past dealt with vigorously, the time has come, I believe, when it is necessary to take action beyond mere condemnation." It was a "mad act" by the German leaders, made all the more reprehensible by their threat to take "further action" if foreign countries "should even pass censure." Messersmith urged Hull to recommend to the president that Ambassador Wilson be ordered to return to Washington immediately "for consultation." Messersmith acknowledged that such a step would not stop Nazi persecution of the Jews, but at least it would encourage "right-thinking people" in Germany and would give the authorities there "food for thought." Moreover, in France and England, as well as throughout Europe, such a step would certainly be welcome.[121]

On the very day that Hull received this memorandum, he discussed it with President Roosevelt and other members of the administration. Some officials thought that Wilson should remain in Germany at this critical time to keep an eye on events, while others feared that his removal from Berlin would be seen as a defeat for the "realists," who still favored negotiations with the Nazi regime. Roosevelt agreed with Messersmith, who also received support from Hull. On November 15, the president announced that Wilson had been summoned to Washington for "consultations" and issued a statement condemning the violence in Germany, which had "deeply shocked public opinion in the United States."[122] Americans, the president declared, would react similarly to news of such violence from anywhere in the world, an observation designed to make it clear that Americans were not criticizing events in Germany only because the victims were Jews. "I myself," Roosevelt concluded, "could scarcely believe that such things could occur in a 20th century civilization."[123] The president was the only world leader publicly to condemn the November pogrom.

At the same time, Secretary of State Hull informed Wilson that "the situation in Germany . . . has so shocked the American Government and American public opinion that the President desires you to report to him in person." Wilson was ordered to return to the United States for consultation as soon as possible and was asked to make only a short statement to the German Foreign Office in explaining his sudden departure.[124] When the German ambassador in Washington visited Hull to inform him that he, in turn, had been recalled to Berlin, clearly in retaliation for the American action, Hull greeted him coolly. "I felt no spirit of cordiality and naturally acted accordingly." It was a brief encounter, and the German official left after Hull "personally wished him a safe voyage and health."[125] No other country followed the example of the United States.

The American action was unlikely to prod the Nazis into moderating their policies toward the Jews, but at least it made them aware of foreign disapproval. And, as already noted, Hitler and his subordinates viscerally resented criticism from abroad. When Harold Ickes, the secretary of the interior, delivered a speech in Cleveland in late December 1939 that criticized Nazi attacks on Jews, the Deutsches Nachrichtenbüro (German News Agency) denounced him as driven by "blind hatred" for the German people. Various German publications disparaged the Roosevelt administration as a "tool of the Jews" and claimed that the president was "backed by Jewish influence seeking to profit from a colossal rearmament."[126]

For three years before the rupture of all diplomatic relations between the two countries on December 11, 1941, the American ambassadorship in Germany remained unoccupied, as did the German one in Washington. But the diplomats in charge of embassy affairs in Berlin (first Prentiss Gilbert, followed by Raymond H. Geist and Alexander Kirk) continued to report on developments in Germany, although their dispatches were not as detailed or frequent as before, no doubt out of suspicion that they would be scrutinized by Nazi officials. A central theme of the reports was the steady deterioration of conditions for Jews. On December 9, 1938, Gilbert sent the Department of State a detailed account of the aryanization (in effect, seizure) of Jewish properties, businesses, and other assets. To justify the massive theft, the *Völkischer Beobachter* claimed that "half of the big cities, even half of Berlin, belongs to Jews of German or foreign nationality."[127] Six weeks later, Gilbert informed the secretary of state that a new "ordinance" issued by the government decreed that German lawyers who were members of the National Socialist Party were henceforth forbidden to represent Jews or to give advice to Jewish firms, although some "exceptions might be made for German lawyers to represent Jews with foreign passports."[128]

At about the same time, the government issued a decree ordering German Jews to surrender "all objects of gold, platinum or silver . . . as well as precious stones and pearls" in their possession to the authorities within two weeks. The authorities promised to issue regulations on how the objects would be evaluated and what "indemnity" would be paid to the owners. A statute issued early in May ordered Jews to vacate apartments in buildings in which some Aryans were also tenants.[129] A few weeks later, the government announced detailed regulations on the visits of Jews to "German health and bathing resorts."[130] This is not a complete list of the restrictions imposed on Jews after Kristallnacht and before the decision to exterminate them, but they suffice to indicate the direction in which the Nazi government was moving. Gilbert concluded in early December 1938 that the Nazis had not exhausted their program of persecution. He wrote the following prophetic words to the secretary of state: "With reference to recent decrees affecting Jews in Germany which I have reported, I regret to state that it is my painful impression that a series of still more drastic measures respecting the status of Jews in this country may be forthcoming and that the general trend is for the lot of Jews in Germany to grow progressively worse."[131]

WASHINGTON'S RESPONSE TO ITS DIPLOMATS

Overall, in the years from 1930 to 1941, the dispatches composed by American diplomats in Germany accurately depicted the political crisis that tore apart the Weimar Republic and the fundamental political change—actually a revolution—that the Nazis carried out within a matter of weeks. They also described in impressive detail the barbaric methods employed by the authorities in imposing their will on a nation of sixty million people.[132] The American diplomats dwelled particularly on the persecution of the Jews, in part because they found the anti-Semitic policies repugnant but also because those policies seemed, even as early as the first months of the Nazi regime, to epitomize the bestiality of Hitler's rule. The existence in the United States of a large Jewish community that frequently expressed its horror at Nazi persecutions of co-religionists and called on the Roosevelt administration to protest Nazi policies no doubt played a role in stimulating the diplomats to focus on the mistreatment of Jews. But their concentration on this subject also suggests that the diplomats realized that they were describing a regime unique in the twentieth century. Their perspicacity would become fully evident only a few years after they left Germany, when the Nazi assault on the Jews turned into what is now known as the Holocaust.

The American diplomats were less comprehensive and less insightful in their reporting on Hitler's foreign political goals. They paid less attention than their British and French colleagues to the significance of Hitler's withdrawal from the League of Nations, his program of rapid rearmament, his march into the Rhineland, his annexations of Austria, and even his march into Czechoslovakia. This is not to say that the American diplomats entirely ignored these matters or that they expressed no apprehension about the Nazis' expansionist ambitions. As noted, Ambassador Dodd pointed to some dangerous signs of bellicosity in Nazi policies and statements. And in a letter of June 9, 1934, Raymond Geist, who was outraged by Nazi domestic policies, wrote a letter to Jay Pierrepont Moffat, the chief of the Division of Western European Affairs in the Department of State, warning that Germany "would certainly rearm and definitely prepare to wage a war against Europe in general, which would change the course of history, if not of civilization beyond what we even dream, if their supreme effort would be successful."[133] But these were relatively isolated comments.

This stance of American diplomats no doubt reflected the prevailing views in the upper circles of the government and of large sectors of public opinion. During the first five years of the Third Reich, from 1933 to 1938, President Roosevelt tended to downplay the danger of Nazism. He disparaged its ideology and privately referred to Hitler as a "madman" who would never be able to revive the German economy. When he was presented with a copy of *Mein Kampf* in 1933, he read it in English although he knew German, and concluded that the translation was so shoddy that it could not be considered an accurate rendering of Hitler's views; the "original would make a very different story." The president believed that Hitler only wanted to persuade the West to agree to strike out the clauses in the Treaty of Versailles that Germany found most objectionable, which could be achieved, in Roosevelt's view, by negotiation. Only in the fall of 1938, when Hitler made demands on Czechoslovakia for territorial concessions, did Roosevelt decide that negotiations between the West and the Führer were pointless.[134] The president was now convinced that Hitler's policies threatened to unleash a military conflict and that measures should be taken to resist him. But he could not come up with any specific steps that Western powers should undertake.[135]

The authorities in Washington received pleas from citizens all over the country, often from people respected in the professions or in their community, to avoid any measures that could result in America's being drawn into war. The two following letters may be taken as samples of the thousands that reached the capital. On November 18, 1938, when many people in the political class in Europe had concluded that war was inevitable, J. Anton De Haas, the William Ziegler Professor of International Relations at Harvard and the author of five well-regarded books, sent President Roosevelt a plea for "positive, constructive action" to prevent military conflict. De Haas complimented Roosevelt for having condemned Germany for its recent "barbarism" in attacking the Jews, but he warned that this "negative action" would not be effective. The professor asserted that the German people were not united in supporting Hitler. In fact, the "outrages" against the Jews and Catholics had disaffected many of them, and they yearned for a viable alternative to Nazism. The United States, the professor claimed, could help bring about regime change. "We can offer a trade treaty and financial aid in the rebuilding of Germany on condition that the nation returns to the republican form of government, guarantees fair treatment of minority groups, and is prepared to join in a world conference for limitation of arms." Even at this "crucial time," De Haas contended, such an offer could "strengthen the cause of decent Germans sufficiently to bring about a collapse of Hitlerism."[136] The letter can only be described as a fanciful dream, but the desperate desire to avoid war generated many such dreams.

Another letter, this one sent to Under Secretary of State Sumner Welles in early January 1939 by Wallace H. Strowd from Nashville, Tennessee, was less visionary but probably more representative of American thinking on foreign policy. Strowd's missive amounted to a passionate plea against American intervention in the "domestic affairs of a friendly power" on behalf of persecuted Jews. Strowd warned that such intervention "may lead to war, and if it does, would lead to the killing of more American boys and probably women and children than there are Jews in Germany, and at a cost exceeding the entire holdings of German Jews." He declared his sympathy for the plight of the Jews, but he insisted that the United States could not possibly settle "the affairs of the world." He knew many people, none of them "Jew haters" or "Jew baiters," who agreed with him, and he was confident that most Americans also agreed with him. Strowd ended his letter on a patriotic note: he would be willing to have his son "give his life if necessary in defense of our country but not to protect alien property in a foreign country."

The under secretary passed the letter on to Moffat, who found it so compelling—he referred to it as "the only one that appears to be reasoned and not violently anti-Semitic"—that he thought it important for Welles to send more than a formal reply. He did just that and assured Strowd that although the United States abhorred the repressive policies of the German government and had made that clear, it had no intention of interfering in the domestic affairs of Germany or any other country.[137]

As indicated at the beginning of this chapter, many Americans among the elite and the general public shared this isolationist point of view. Not only conservatives took up that cause. In 1936, the platform of the Democratic Party contained the following plank: "We shall continue to observe a true neutrality in the disputes of others." During the presidential campaign that year, Roosevelt declared, "We shun political commitments which might entangle us in foreign wars; we avoid connection with the political activities of the League of Nations."[138]

It should also be noted that anti-Semitism had "increased dramatically" during the 1920s and 1930s, and often the isolationists propagated that prejudice most vigorously.[139] Various cultural and political currents proved to be fertile ground for movements hostile to the Jews: the fear of Bolshevism, a political ideology that many considered a Jewish invention; the broad interest in racial doctrines that attributed cultural and moral inferiority to Jews; and widespread apprehension that Jewish immigrants would replace Americans in the labor markets and also in the corporate world then dominated by Protestants. Even a diplomat as hostile to Nazism as Messersmith opposed easing restrictions on Jewish immigration into the United States because he feared that an influx of Jews would increase unemployment.

During the initial period of the Hitler regime there was also considerable skepticism, among the public and even among some journalists, about the reports of mistreatment of Jews and the ruthlessness of the Nazi regime in general.[140] Consequently, the U.S. government, despite its abhorrence of the anti-Jewish violence and the frequent appeals for help by the Jewish community, failed to file an official protest with the German government until the events of Kristallnacht in November 1938, and even then the protest was not especially strong. In part, the government's inaction also reflected Hull's belief that foreign intervention would only evoke resentment among Germany's leaders, who would then inflict even more cruel measures on the Jews.

But there may have been another reason, not acknowledged publicly, for the restraint of the American government's condemnation of the Nazis' treatment of Jews. In a memorandum written on January 19, 1934, Assistant Secretary of State Walton Moore questioned the advisability of a resolution that Senator Millard E. Tydings and some of his colleagues were thinking of sponsoring; it would call on President Roosevelt to issue a formal protest to the German government over the mistreatment of Jews. Moore granted that the Senate had the right to pass such a resolution, but he warned that it would place the president in a dilemma. If he failed to protest, he would be heavily criticized in the United States. If he complied with the resolution, he "would not only incur the resentment of the German Government, but might be involved in a very acrimonious discussion with that Government which conceivably might, for example, ask him to explain why the negroes of this country do not fully enjoy the right of suffrage; why the lynching of negroes in Senator Tydings' State and other States is not prevented or severely punished; and how the anti-Semitic feeling in the United States, which unfortunately seems to be growing, is not checked."[141] In my examination of government documents of the 1930s, I have not come across any other reference to domestic considerations of this kind as a factor in the formulation of American foreign policy during those years, but one cannot help wondering whether it was an unspoken concern of several senior officials in the State Department.

It soon turned out that Moore's fears were not groundless. Not long after he issued his warning, a leading Nazi referred to the treatment of Negroes (as they were then generally called) in the United States. On August 15, 1935, Streicher delivered a two-and-a-half-hour tirade at the Sportspalast in Berlin in which he touched on the "Negro question." He began by denouncing the foreign press for getting "excited" about the persecution of Jews in Germany and questioned why journalists from abroad should be concerned "if we have a house-cleaning." Just as Germans do not meddle in American affairs, so Americans should stay out of other countries' affairs, he argued: "To the Americans I would say: we read almost every week that in America a Negro is hanged who has raped some white woman or other. Here in Germany we say that if the Negro really committed the rape, it served him right. We do not bother about the execution of Negroes, and they should not bother if we in Germany lead racial violators through the streets"—a reference to public humiliations of Jews and Christians who engaged in sexual relations with each other.[142] About three weeks after Streicher made these comments, *Der Führer*, the official organ of the state of Baden and its leading newspaper, carried an article with the following title: "Race Hatred in the United States. Torturing of Negroes and Lynch Justice Which Are Called Persecutions in Germany." The article then dwelled on one theme, that "race hatred in the United States is now an unwritten law" everywhere. Even in New York, the article stated, no Negro would dare visit a "medium-class restaurant for fear of being beaten . . . a stranger would be rebuked for exchanging friendly words with a Negro."[143]

Cordell Hull's reluctance to issue a formal protest to Germany over the Jewish question may also have been motivated by a very personal consideration. He was certainly not known to be in any way hostile to Jews. In fact, his wife was apparently of Jewish descent, which was not widely known at the time. One historian has speculated that Hull "feared that the Jewish connection made him vulnerable to attacks from anti-Semites, who would argue that his wife had forced him to support Jewish causes, and that therefore he had succumbed to un-American influences." Moreover, if he was suspected of being a philo-Semite, his chances of ever running for the White House, apparently one of his ambitions, would have been slight.[144]

America's aloofness from European affairs cannot simply be dismissed as irrational, and it can be argued that economic and political conditions within the country would have made any other course by the administration politically unwise. But in the end the policy proved to be very costly. Had the administration drawn the right conclusions from the dispatches by American diplomats in Germany, it would have realized that it was in the interest of the United States to take a firm stand against the Nazi dictatorship, a stand that might have strengthened the hand of the European statesmen who understood the nature of Nazism and favored a policy designed to rein in Hitler's Germany. America's European policy in the 1930s is yet another example of the costliness of the failure of statesmen not only to gauge the intentions of foreign leaders accurately but also to implement sound policies when those intentions pose a serious threat.

Conclusion

Even today, sixty-five years after the defeat of Hitler, at a time when vast amounts of archival documents on the 1930s and early 1940s as well as autobiographies of statesmen and generals who participated in the major events of those years are available, questions are still being raised about the true nature of Nazism. Were the diplomats examined in this study still alive, they might well be amazed to discover that despite all their reports on almost every aspect of social and political developments in Germany during the 1930s, scholars still cannot agree on Hitler's aims, the sources of his ideology, or the overall historical significance of Nazism's destructive policies. It would seem to them that, despite their best efforts, they had failed to solve the question posed by Sir Maurice Hankey in October 1933, when he declared that Hitler was a riddle whose goals and conduct could not be divined.

In an issue of the *American Historical Review* published in 2010, the scholar A. Dirk Moses indicated just how divided professional historians still are on the subject of National Socialism. Moses lauded a new school of interpretation of Nazism that considers it a mistake "to insist upon the centrality of antisemitism in the Nazi project" and believes it should be acknowledged that the Holocaust "is not that defining an experience after all." Instead, Nazism should be viewed as a political movement whose "real transgression" was not "genocide per se" but, rather, "the importation into Europe of brutal colonial rule over non-Europeans."[1] This interpretation amounts to a partial revival of the thesis advanced by Hannah Arendt in 1951 in her influential book *The Origins of Totalitarianism*, where she argued that imperialism was one of the main sources of totalitarian movements in

Germany and the Soviet Union. But Arendt also insisted that anti-Semitism and nationalism were crucial intellectual and historical sources of Hitler's movement. Professor Moses grants that anti-Semitism was an ingredient of Nazi ideology, but in placing primary emphasis on imperialism and relegating the Jewish issue in Nazism to a secondary level of importance, he offers an interpretation of Nazism that differs from the consensus that had prevailed among the leading scholars of the movement.

The British, French, and American diplomats who were eyewitnesses to Nazism and are the focus of this study did not consider anti-Semitism to be a secondary influence on Nazi leaders. True, in their reports they also stressed the importance of expansionism and the desire to dominate Europe as driving forces in the thinking of National Socialist leaders. But in depicting the brutality of the Nazis in the 1930s they invariably emphasized the persecution of political opponents and, above all, the sadistic treatment of the Jews, neither one of which would seem to have been directly related to Hitler's determination to act like the imperial powers by conquering vast stretches of Europe in colonialist style. Moreover, most of the Western diplomats who interviewed Hitler made a point of the Führer's fanatical hatred of Jews. Once the subject of Jews came up in conversation, Hitler found it impossible to control his emotions. His outbursts, all his interlocutors agreed, were not feigned; they were authentic expressions of his feelings, which undoubtedly affected many of his political decisions.

One report on the intemperate behavior of Hitler at the mere mention of Jews would be amusing if it did not touch on a subject so fraught with horrible events. In April 1937, George Lansbury, a leader of the Labour Party and a fervent pacifist, visited Hitler to persuade him to support a world conference that would focus on the prevention of war. Toward the end of the interview, Lansbury raised "one further question": could Hitler say a few words promising to let up on the persecution of the Jews that Lansbury could then pass on to his Jewish constituents in Bow and Bromley in London? According to a person who heard Lansbury relate the Führer's reaction, the response was instantaneous. As soon as the translator "came to the word 'Jude,' Hitler jumped to his feet and, giving the Nazi salute, poured out a torrent of words, whereupon George said [to the translator]: 'You need not trouble to translate the rest—I know what the answer means.'" Nevertheless, Lansbury considered the meeting "a triumph" and told a fellow socialist and pacifist that Hitler "will not go to war, unless pushed into it by others." The Führer, he believed, "was a distressed and lonely man."[2]

The Führer was not the only Nazi obsessed with a fanatical hatred of the Jews. Streicher, the editor of the virulently anti-Semitic *Stürmer*, was equally obsessed with the Jewish threat to Germany; Goebbels, the Nazi Party's chief propagandist, never tired of denouncing the Jews as the source of all evil; and Heinrich Himmler, the head of the Gestapo, devoted much of his working day to the same issue. During the early Nazi period, R. P. F. Edwards, the commercial secretary to the British embassy in Berlin, expressed dismay at the fervor with which senior Nazi officials spoke of the Jewish danger. On April 5, 1933, he wrote a personal letter to Sir Edward Crowe on a meeting with Göring and Goebbels, both of whom seemed "only comparable [in their fanaticism] with those distinguished students from Oxford, who have decided not to fight for King and country under any circumstances. Their one topic of conversation is the destruction of the Jews. Apart from that I do not think that they have any ideas at all, but unfortunately they have been exciting the population and their own followers for the last five or six years and promising that the Jews should be exterminated."[3] But officials below the top level in the Nazi movement also toed the line on anti-Semitism. "No leading Nazi could prosper," Christopher R. Browning rightly noted, if he did not "appear to take the Jewish question as seriously as Hitler himself did."[4]

The diplomats' accounts of Germany's persecution of the Jews, especially those composed by British and American officials, were often so detailed that they brought to light facts not widely known. The most startling revelation was that although Nazi leaders did not decide on genocide until sometime in 1941, the subject was bruited about throughout the 1930s. On no fewer than nine occasions—beginning in 1933 and ending early in 1939—the subject of the physical elimination of the Jewish community was touched upon in diplomatic dispatches. The most revealing consideration of this sensitive subject took place in April 1935, when Streicher warned Nazis not to spread rumors that Jews must be exterminated for allegedly planning to assassinate the Führer. Streicher actually dismissed one local official who had violated the rule of silence on the ground that he had been guilty of "undue rashness." Streicher did not deny that the elimination of the Jews was a possibility, but he considered it unwise and premature to bring the subject into the open.

Several references by Western diplomats to the likelihood that the Nazis would resort to mass murder of the Jews were based on their perception of Nazi intentions, not on specific pronouncements by Hitler or his subordinates. The diplomats sensed that the Nazis' hatred of the minority was so deep-seated and irrational that the persecution would continue to intensify to the point that they would see no alternative but to eliminate the Jews altogether. It is well known that in his speech of January 31, 1939, Hitler actually warned that if war broke out he would "annihilate the Jewish race in Europe." Even more specific and detailed was an article that appeared in the weekly newspaper of the SS, *Das Schwarze Korps*, in November 1938; it predicted that the Nazi government would initiate a series of actions that would lead to the "actual and definite end of Jewry in Germany and its complete extermination." This paper was printed in runs ranging from 500,000 to 750,000.

These various references to the physical extermination of the Jews are of special interest because they touch on a long-standing controversy among scholars on the origins of the Holocaust. Two major interpretations have emerged, although it should be kept in mind that different shadings are found within each. On the one hand, the so-called intentionalists insist that Hitler planned all along to implement what the Nazis called the "final solution" of the Jewish question. On the other hand, the "functionalists" argue that the origins of the mass murder are to be sought not in any ideological predispositions of Hitler or other leading Nazis but in the "cumulative radicalization" that resulted from bureaucratic chaos during the early months of the invasion of the Soviet Union, which was launched on June 22, 1941. Until 1940, the functionalists point out, the Hitler government sought a "territorial" solution to the Jewish problem, that is, the settlement of the Jews somewhere outside Europe; Madagascar was a favored place. But when it became clear by 1941 that such a transfer of population was infeasible, local bureaucrats in eastern Europe faced severe problems for which there were no easy solutions. They had to find housing for Germans moving east and they needed provisions for a population whose economy had stagnated. According to some estimates at the time, the economy of Poland could be revived only if the population were reduced by 25 percent.[5] Then, when the campaign in Russia began to falter late in 1941 and early in 1942, Nazi fury at the Jews reached a high pitch. In their anger, Nazis sought revenge by slaughtering Jews.[6]

Without doubt, until 1941–42 no concrete plan for the implementation of the final solution had been devised. At the same time, it hardly seems credible that the eight years of anti-Semitic effusions had no effect in preparing the way for the Holocaust. Nor does it seem plausible that in a regime where the Führer was virtually deified, a decision so important as the one to carry out the mass murder of millions could have been made without his approval. Browning, who considers himself a "moderate functionalist," put it well: "Hitler had not decided on the Final Solution as the culmination of any long-held or predetermined plan, but . . . he had made a series of key decisions in 1941 that ordained the mass murder of European Jews."[7]

Yet it is striking that Western diplomats—British, French, and American—were so prescient. Their warnings, close to predictions, do not mean that the Holocaust was inevitable. But for the student of history, they are very significant because they help to explain the widespread, although far from universal, indifference of Germans to the murders in the East. The policy of extermination was not an altogether novel idea. It had been "in the air," so to speak, for some time.

Certainly, most of the Western diplomats in Germany in the 1930s could not have been surprised by the Nazis' final solution of the Jewish question. They had pointed out that in Hitler's mind the Jews represented a menace not only to the German economy and culture, but to all of Western civilization. He saw himself (together with Mussolini), as he said in one of his more delusional moments, as the most effective defender of the West. Today, this extreme animus of Hitler may seem surreal and utterly absurd, but it is worth emphasizing that Western diplomats early on raised questions about the Führer's mental state, and they were troubled that a man with such a psychological makeup was exercising dictatorial power in a major country. On more than one occasion they warned their governments that the absolute ruler of Germany was unhinged and therefore a great danger to their countries. The first such warning was issued in June 1933 by Sir Horace Rumbold, when he wrote to London that many diplomats in Berlin felt that they were "living in a lunatic asylum." His successor, Sir Eric Phipps, did not use these words to describe the atmosphere in Berlin, but in several dispatches he indicated that the Führer's behavior was strikingly abnormal for a national leader. Phipps also depicted Göring, the second most powerful man in Germany, as consumed to an irrational degree with his own importance. Perhaps most interesting, even the third British ambassador to Hitler's Germany, Sir Nevile Henderson, who saw much good in National Socialism and was an ardent proponent of appeasement, at one point, in September 1938, also suggested that Hitler was deranged, that he had "crossed the border-line of insanity." The French ambassador, André François-Poncet, was less consistent than his European colleagues in his assessments of the Führer, but even he sent several dispatches to Paris that depicted the dictator as abnormal. This aspect of Hitler's personality was not mentioned by the American diplomats, but their descriptions of Hitler's and the Nazis' sadism could not leave any reader in Washington in doubt that the German leader was capable of pursuing policies that could easily set Europe afire. In fact, the American ambassador, William Dodd, found the Führer so abhorrent that he could not bear to be in his presence.

The diplomats who referred to Hitler as deranged did not claim to be passing a medical judgment about the Führer's state of mind. No evidence suggests that they considered him to be clinically insane, incapable of rational analysis of political and military issues and therefore unable to make calculated decisions on them. On the contrary, they realized that he was a clever and cunning politician who knew very well how to manipulate people, especially when he addressed mass audiences. The diplomats used the terms "insane" and "unbalanced" in a colloquial sense to explain his sudden changes of mood during conversations and public speeches, as well as his proclivity to take positions that were so extreme and far-fetched—and often untrue—as to be preposterous. More important, soon after assuming the office of chancellor, Hitler initiated policies in foreign affairs that struck most Western diplomats as unprincipled and reckless. In domestic affairs, he transformed the country from a democracy to a dictatorship whose brutality the diplomats considered shameful and unwarranted.

The question of Hitler's sanity has attracted considerable attention, with some arguing that only a madman could have ordered the murder of millions of innocent civilians and sanctioned the sadism that prevailed in the ghettos of eastern Europe and the concentration camps scattered through the Third Reich and the Nazi empire. The weakness of this line of reasoning is that it can serve as an excuse for Hitler and for many Germans who participated in the murders or simply stood by and approved of them. The most authoritative study of Hitler's state of mind, written by Fritz Redlich, a professor of psychiatry at Yale University, reached conclusions that provide helpful guidance for interpreting the diplomats' depiction of the Führer's character. Redlich argued that although Hitler suffered from numerous neuroses, some of which could be considered "symptoms of mental disorder," on the whole his "personality functioned more than adequately." As a leader, he often made calculated decisions—political as well as military—against the advice of his subordinates and proved to be right, a major reason why so many people followed him blindly. And as Redlich points out, hours before he committed suicide, at a time when everything he had dreamed of was crumbling before his eyes, he managed to compose his political and personal will, in which he indicated how his belongings were to be distributed and reiterated his political ideology. The document is "clear evidence of his mental competence."[8] He "knew what he was doing and he chose to do it with pride and enthusiasm."[9] Hitler's crimes and errors were not caused by illness, and he bears full responsibility for his actions.

In any case, the warnings of great danger to Europe frequently issued by foreign diplomats did not depend only on assessments of Hitler's personality. Time and again, British and French officials in Germany sent comprehensive reports to their governments on the country's remilitarization. They supplied their superiors in Paris and London with detailed accounts on the number of troops in Hitler's army and the sophisticated weapons under production, and at various times they also reported highly secret information on the military plans of Hitler and his generals. The claim of government leaders in the West that Hitler was a riddle and that it was therefore impossible to devise a firm policy to restrain him hardly seems credible. True, the diplomatic reports were not always consistent and the diplomats were loath to make clear-cut policy recommendations, which, in any case, was not their main function. Too often they allowed themselves to be deceived by signs of discontent within the Nazi Party or sharp differences within the leadership of the movement, which, they believed, could signify a tendency toward the adoption of a more moderate course by the Nazis. No doubt their single most serious mistake was to assume—as did the French ambassador François-Poncet on several occasions—that Hitler either was a moderate or would be swayed by moderates in the Nazi Party to steer away from radical and provocative policies.

Such speculation was unconvincing, all the more so since it contradicted the diplomats' descriptions of Hitler's persona. As several envoys frequently pointed out, Hitler was determined to root out the influence of Jews in Germany's economy and cultural affairs and to restore the country to a dominant position in Europe. He had formulated these ideas in the 1920s in *Mein Kampf* and he never intended to deviate from them. One of the first and greatest mistakes of the political class in the leading Western democracies was to ignore Hitler's outpourings in that book. They found it highly improbable that anyone could really mean all the vile things he had written. Although theirs was a commendably civilized attitude, it failed to address the troubling question why an aspiring political leader would utter such extremist views if he did not take them seriously.

Still, when all is said and done, the primary task of diplomats in Germany was to provide their superiors with as full a picture as possible of what Nazi rule signified, politically and militarily. That task they performed with distinction, and the real riddle is not the one posed by Hankey in

1933 about the difficulty of understanding Hitler and his aims. The real riddle is one that historians must try to solve: why did the leaders of the three major democracies fail to take action against a dictator that their own diplomats warned was a menace to world order? The answer may be less complicated than one might think: in each of the three democracies, the public mood was uncongenial to a firm response to Germany's threatening moves against Europe. The Great Depression of 1929 diverted attention from international affairs and sharply reduced the funding available to governments for rebuilding their military capacities. And the heavy casualties incurred by France and Great Britain in the years from 1914 to 1918 had invigorated the peace—or pacifist—movements in both countries, making it difficult for statesmen to pursue a robust foreign policy that would have led to estrangement from Germany and, as many people feared, to war. In fact, until late 1936, Germany was militarily too weak to resist foreign pressure to halt its rearmament, and the failure of the political leadership of these two democracies to impress this weakness upon their countrymen may be regarded as their most grievous error in judgment. Ironically, the peace movement unwittingly helped make war inevitable.

In the United States, it was not so much pacifism as isolationism that inhibited the government from playing a significant role in European affairs. President Franklin D. Roosevelt gradually came to recognize that Hitler posed a threat, but within his administration some senior officials saw the world differently. In November 1937, Jay Pierrepont Moffat, who a few months earlier had been appointed chief of the newly created Division of European Affairs in the State Department, declared, "My personal preoccupation is to prevent at any cost the involvement of the United States in hostilities anywhere, and to that end to discourage any formation of a common front of the democratic powers."[10]

Ultimately, one is bound to agree with Winston Churchill, who in 1948 referred to World War II as the "unnecessary war." He did not mean that Hitler should not have been resisted by force in 1939. Rather, he meant, "never was a war more easy to stop than that which has just wrecked what was left of the world from the previous struggle."[11]

REFERENCE MATTER

Notes

The following abbreviations are used in the Notes. Complete authors' names, titles, and publication data are given in the Bibliography:

BDFA British Documents on Foreign Affairs: Reports and Papers from the Foreign Office. Confidential Print. Series F. Europe 1919–1939. General Editors: Kenneth Bourne and D. Cameron Watt. University Publications of America, n.p., 1993.

CAC   Churchill Archives, Churchill Archives Centre, Cambridge, UK.

CADN   Centre des Archives diplomatiques de Nantes.

DDF   Documents Diplomatiques Français, 1re Série (1932–1935) 12 vols.; 2e Série (1936–1939), 12 vols. Paris, 1963–1969.

FRUS   Foreign Relations of the United States; Diplomatic Papers/Department of State, Washington, 1930–1941.

NA   National Archives, Hyattsville, Md., USA.

TNA   The National Archives, London, UK.

INTRODUCTION

1. Shirer, *Berlin Diary*, pp. 84–87; Self, *Neville Chamberlain*, p. 396.

2. The article is reprinted in Remak, *The Nazi Years*, pp. 80–82. On Lloyd George, see the biography by K. Morgan, *Lloyd George*.

3. Norman Ebbutt, "Germany To-Day: Herr Hitler's Foreign Policy," *The Times* of London, April 21, 1933.

4. Quoted in Gilbert, *Winston S. Churchill*, vol. V, p. 407.

5. Gilbert, *Churchill: A Life*, pp. 506–7.

6. Langworth, *Churchill by Himself*, p. 254.

7. The quotation is from Olson, *Troublesome Young Men*, p. 76.

8. Wheeler-Bennett, *Munich—Prologue to Tragedy*, pp. 206–7.

9. Wächter, *Von Stresemann zu Hitler*, p. 41.

10. Williamson, *Stanley Baldwin*, p. 301.

11. Quoted in Kershaw, *Making Friends with Hitler*, p. 36.

12. Wright, *France*, p. 498.

13. Bullock, *Hitler*, p. 293. The words in quotation marks are from one of Hitler's speeches in May 1933.

14. Quoted in Granzow, *Mirror*, pp. 220–21.

15. Quoted in Robbins, *Present and Past*, p. 36.

16. Kershaw, *Making Friends with Hitler*, pp. 25–26.

17. Clemens, *Herr Hitler*, pp. 439–47; Johnson, "Sir Eric Phipps, the British Government"; Kershaw, *Making Friends with Hitler*, pp. 44–45.

18. Peter Jackson, "French Intelligence," p. 705.

19. BDFA, Series F, vol. 49, Part II, p. 376.

20. See, for example, Craig and Gilbert, *The Diplomats*; Evans, *The Coming of the Third Reich*; Namier, *Diplomatic Prelude*; Offner, *American Appeasement*; Steiner, *The Lights That Failed*; Taylor, *The Origins*; Weinberg, *Hitler's Foreign Policy*; Wheeler-Bennett, *Munich*.

CHAPTER ONE

1. Gilbert, *Sir Horace Rumbold*, pp. 49, 51–52, 61; Wächter, *Von Stresemann zu Hitler*, pp. 30, 35.

2. Gilbert, *Sir Horace Rumbold*, p. 319; Wächter, *Von Stresemann zu Hitler*, pp. 30, 36–37.

3. Gilbert, *Sir Horace Rumbold*, p. 336.

4. Clemens, *Herr Hitler*, p. 45.

5. Ibid., pp. 48–50.

6. TNA, FO 371/15945, pp. 317–18.

7. Wächter, *Von Stresemann zu Hitler*, p. 195.

8. TNA, FO 371/15945, pp. 129–30.

9. Ford, "Three Observers in Berlin," pp. 444–45.

10. BDFA, Series F, vol. 44, p. 11. Erwin Planck was the son of the eminent theoretical physicist Max Planck and was a staunch anti-Nazi. He participated in the plot of July 20, 1944, to assassinate Hitler. He was arrested three days after the attempt, found guilty, and quickly executed.

11. TNA, FO 371/15945, p. 12.

12. Ibid., p. 194.

13. CAC, VNST, 2/5, p. 10.

14. TNA, FO 371/15943, pp. 270–79. For more information on Christie, see the account in Clemens, *Herr Hitler*, pp. 213–16, 224.

15. TNA, FO 371/15943, p. 46 (reverse side of the page).

16. Elias, *Reflections on a Life*, p. 43; Kershaw, *Hitler, 1889–1936*, p. 368.

17. See Clark, *Fall of the German Republic*.

18. Benz, *Die Juden in Deutschland*, pp. 286–92; Craig, *Germany, 1866–1945*, p. 572; BDFA, Series F, vol. 44, pp. 44, 65–66.

19. Barkai, *From Boycott to Annihilation*, p. 22.

20. BDFA, Series F, vol. 44, p. 24.

21. Ibid., p. 28.

22. Ibid., p. 32.

23. Ibid., p. 65.

24. Ibid., p. 66.

25. Ibid., pp. 108–9, 120–22.

26. TNA, FO 371/16721, p. 179.

27. BDFA, Series F, vol. 44, p. 143.

28. Ibid., p. 139. The words within single quotation marks are from *Mein Kampf.* Recent research by Götz Aly and Timothy Snyder has borne out the accuracy of Rumbold's prophecy of the nexus between Nazi racism and Nazi expansionism.

29. BDFA, Series F, vol. 44, pp. 140, 142.

30. Ibid., p. 172.

31. Ibid., p. 173.

32. Ibid., p. 142; Gilbert, *Sir Horace Rumbold*, p. 383.

33. BDFA, Series F, vol. 44, pp. 216–18. See also p. 177 for Rumbold's comment on the "strain of hooliganism."

34. Johnson, *Our Man in Berlin*, p. 10.

35. BDFA, Series F, vol. 44, p. xix.

36. For a discussion of Phipps's flirtation with appeasement, see Kershaw, *Making Friends*, pp. 44–46; and Johnson, *Sir Eric Phipps, the British Government*. To be precise, Johnson argues that Phipps was not an anti-appeaser. For more details on Phipps's biography prior to his arrival in Berlin, see Jaroch, *Too Much Wit?* pp. 25–37.

37. BDFA, Series F, vol. 44, p. 406.

38. Johnson, *Our Man in Berlin*, p. 64.

39. BDFA, Series F, vol. 44, pp. 345–46.

40. TNA, FO 371/16712, pp. 45–46.

41. BDFA, Series F, vol. 45, pp. 378, 380, 385.

42. BDFA, Series F, vol. 46, pp. 395, 398.

43. Ibid., p. 403.

44. BDFA, Series F, vol. 45, pp. 177–78.

45. Ibid., pp. 197, 226–28, 235.

46. See, for example, Barkai, *From Boycott to Annihilation*, p. 54; Benz, *Die Juden in Deutschland*, p. 292.

47. BDFA, Series F, vol. 46, pp. 150–51.

48. Ibid., p. 276.

49. Ibid., p. 246.

50. Ibid., p. 249.

51. The measures applicable to the Jews drew a distinction between citizens who were "entitled to full political and civic rights" and subjects, most notably Jews, who were not. In addition, the Law for the Defense of German Blood and Honor prohibited sexual contact (including marriage) between Aryans and Jews. Finally, Jews were prohibited from employing any Aryan woman under the age of forty-five as a domestic servant. See Friedländer, *Nazi Germany*, vol. I, pp. 142–44.

52. BDFA, Series F, vol. 46, p. 325.

53. Ibid., p. 273.

54. BDFA, Series F, vol. 47, p. 385.

55. Ibid., p. 252.

56. On Foley's career, see Smith, *Foley*, and Paldiel, *Diplomat Heroes*.

57. TNA, FO 371/18861, pp. 169–76.

58. TNA, FO 371/19919, pp. 83–86.

59. Ibid.

60. MacMillan, *Paris 1919*, pp. 166–79.

61. Klein, *Germany's Economic Preparations for War*, passim.

62. On these estimates, see the dispatch by Newton to Simon, September 6, 1933, BDFA, Series F, vol. 46, p. 296.

63. See Thorne's entire report in BDFA, vol. 44, pp. 297–306.

64. BDFA, Series F, vol. 45, pp. 213–21; for the entire report, see pp. 223–41.

65. BDFA, Series F, vol. 46, pp. 84–90.

66. Ibid., p. 113.

67. Ibid., p. 341.

68. TNA, FO 371/1885, pp. 33–35.

69. Self, *Neville Chamberlain*, vol. 4, p. 23.

70. BDFA, Series F, vol. 46, p. 165.

71. BDFA, Series F, vol. 47, p. 377.

72. Churchill, *The Gathering Storm*, pp. 192–99.

73. Quoted in Weinberg, *Hitler's Foreign Policy*, p. 253. See pp. 240–95 for a full discussion of the Rhineland question.

74. The quotations are from Kershaw, *Hitler, 1889–1936*, p. 188.

75. Quoted in Jaroch, *Too Much Wit?* p. 241.

76. TNA, FO 371/19893, p. 145.

77. Jaroch, *Too Much Wit?* p. 244.

78. BDFA, Series F, vol. 47, pp. 170–71.

79. See especially Johnson, *Our Man in Berlin*, pp. 4–5; Johnson, "Sir Eric Phipps," pp. 651–69; Neville, "The Foreign Office," p. 114; Kershaw, *Making Friends*, pp. 44–45. For a comprehensive and perceptive analysis of Phipps's seemingly conflicting or divergent views on Hitler and Nazism, see Jaroch (*Too Much Wit?*), who concluded that especially after 1935 the ambassador sent dispatches to London that agreed with those in Britain who favored "a critical attitude toward National Socialism and its representatives" (p. 336).

80. Herman, *The Paris Embassy of Sir Eric Phipps*, p. 101.

81. Ibid., pp. 112–13.

82. For details, see ibid., p. 113.

83. Johnson, *Our Man in Berlin*, p. 35. See also the dispatch of January 30, 1936, by François-Poncet, in which the French ambassador pointed out that Phipps was "very opposed" to making any concessions to Germany regarding the return of colonies. It was also clear to François-Poncet that Phipps detested Hitler's regime. See DDF, 2ᵉ série (1936–1939), vol. I, p. 162.

84. BDFA, Series F, vol. 47, p. 326.

85. BDFA, Series F, vol. 45, p. 43.

86. Ibid., pp. 43–45, 208.

87. TNA, FO 371/19893, p. 200.

88. Jaroch, *Too Much Wit?* pp. 119, 275–77.

89. BDFA, Series F, vol. 48, pp. 101, 103.

90. Ibid., pp. 97, 100.

91. Ibid., p. 99.

92. Ibid., pp. 103–4.

93. Marquand, *Ramsay MacDonald*, p. 751. For a discussion of MacDonald on Nazism, see pp. 748–51.

94. On Baldwin's foreign policy, see Williamson, *Stanley Baldwin*, pp. 11, 47–48, 294, 301–2, 316–17; and Havighurst, *Twentieth Century Great Britain*, pp. 221–31, 241–42, 244.

95. See Marquand, *Ramsay MacDonald*; Williamson, *Stanley Baldwin*; Dutton, *Sir John Simon*; Dutton, *Anthony Eden*.

96. Dutton, *Sir John Simon*, pp. 1–14.

97. Ibid., p. 39.

98. Ibid., p. 171.

99. Eden, *Memoirs: Facing the Dictators*, p. 25.

100. Dutton, *Sir John Simon*, pp. 200, 237, 240.

101. TNA, CAB/24/241.

102. Dutton, *Sir John Simon*, p. 170.

103. Gilbert, *Sir Horace Rumbold*, p. 379; see also Clemens, *Herr Hitler*, pp. 285–89, for a thorough discussion of the reaction to Rumbold's dispatch.

104. CAC, VNST, 1/10.

105. Kershaw, *Making Friends with Hitler*, p. 42.

106. The information in this paragraph is based on documents in TNA, FO 371/16721.

107. Lukowitz, "British Pacifists," p. 116. For a biography of Sheppard, see Scott, *Dick Sheppard*.

108. Lukowitz, "British Pacifists," p. 121.

109. For a detailed and nuanced analysis of the National Peace Ballot, see Ceadel, "The First British Referendum."

110. Dutton, *Sir John Simon*, p. 201; Weinberg, *Hitler's Foreign Policy*, p. 213.

111. TNA, CAB/24/242.

112. Quotations are from Dutton, *Anthony Eden*, p. 35.

113. On Eden's first visit to Hitler, see Eden, *Memoirs: Facing the Dictators*, pp. 68–80.

114. Ibid., p. 139.

115. Ibid., pp. 156, 158–59.

116. Simon, *Retrospect*, p. 203.

117. For an excellent study of a leading member of the third group, Lord Londonderry, see Kershaw, *Making Friends with Hitler*. On English Fascism, see Pugh, *Hurrah for the Blackshirts*.

118. TNA, FO 371/21665, pp. 56–57.

119. Vansittart, *The Mist Procession*, p. 360.

120. Birkenhead, *Halifax*, p. 358.

121. Neville, *Appeasing Hitler*, p. 20.

122. Ibid., p. 9; Strang, "Two Unequal Tempers," p. 109; on Henderson's unpleasant character, see also Watt, "Chamberlain's Ambassadors," p. 169. For more details on Henderson's career before his appointment to Berlin, as well as on his family background, see Strauch, *Sir Nevile Henderson*, pp. 13–26.

123. Henderson, *Failure of a Mission*, p. 13.

124. Neville, *Appeasing Hitler*, pp. 6, 8; Watt, "Chamberlain's Ambassadors," p. 154.

125. Henderson, *Failure of a Mission*, p. vii.

126. Ibid., p. 7.

127. TNA, PREM 1/334, p. 70.

128. Neville, *Appeasing Hitler*, p. xi; Gilbert and Gott, *The Appeasers*, p. 64.

129. Watt, "Chamberlain's Ambassadors," p. 146.

130. Mosley, *On Borrowed Time*, pp. 15, 56.

131. *Documents on British Foreign Policy, 1919–1939*, Second Series, vol. XVIII, p. 842.

132. Henderson, *Failure of a Mission*, pp. 17, 19.

133. TNA, FO 794/10, pp. 29–30. The speech is reprinted in *Documents on British Foreign Policy, 1919–1939*, Second Series, vol. XVIII, pp. 840–42.

134. TNA, FO 794/10, pp. 32–34.

135. Ibid., pp. 60–61, 64–65, 70–71.

136. Ibid., pp. 79–80.

137. BDFA, Series F, vol. 48, pp. 246–48.

138. Ibid., p. 278.

139. TNA, FO 794/10, pp. 46–48, 50–53.

140. BDFA, Series F, vol. 49, Part II, p. 59.

141. Ibid., p. 266.

142. Ibid., pp. 265–66.

143. Ibid., pp. 56–58. See also Neville, "The Foreign Office," pp. 111–29, esp. 125.

144. BDFA, Series F, vol. 49, Part II, p. 8.

145. Strang, "Two Unequal Tempers," pp. 2–14; Noakes, introduction to BDFA, vol. 49, Part II, p. xxii.

146. BDFA, Series F, vol. 49, Part II, pp. 374–75.

147. TNA, FO 371/21636, p. 114.

148. BDFA, Series F, vol. 49, Part, II, p. 351.

149. Ibid., p. 376.

150. BDFA, Series F, vol. 50, p. 45.

151. Strang, "Two Unequal Tempers," p. 118.

152. BDFA, Series F, vol. 50, p. 43, for the last quotation; on Hitler's regrets about the Munich agreements, see BDFA, Series F, vol. 49, Part II, p. 353.

153. BDFA, Series F, vol. 49, Part II, p. 1.

154. BDFA, Series F, vol. 50, pp. 8–9.

155. Strang, "Two Unequal Tempers," pp. 127–28.

156. BDFA, Series F, vol. 50, p. 118. For Henderson's entire dispatch, see pp. 108–32.

157. Ibid., p. 127.

158. Ibid., pp. 128–29.

159. Ibid., pp. 150, 152, 153.

160. Ibid., p. 156.

161. Ibid., pp. 237–38.

162. TNA, FO 794/10, p. 99.

163. Ibid., pp. 113, 122, 124.

164. Dutton, *Neville Chamberlain*, p. 93; McKercher, "Old Diplomacy and New," p. 102; Self, *Chamberlain Diary Letters*, vol. 4, p. 5; Self, *Neville Chamberlain*, pp. 271–72.

165. Birkenhead, *Halifax*, pp. 422–23.

166. Ibid., pp. 418–20.

167. BDFA, Series F, vol. 48, Part II, p. 364. For more details on Halifax's meeting with Hitler, see Schwoerer, "Lord Halifax's Visit."

168. Stacey, *A Very Double Life*, pp. 35–48, 160–63.

169. TNA, PREM 1/334, pp. 70–71.

170. Ibid., pp. 59–63, 68.

171. Ibid., pp. 69, 62.

172. Ibid., pp. 29–36.

173. On Lothian's early career, see Butler, *Lord Lothian*, pp. 1–85.

174. Ibid., pp. 114–21.

175. Quoted in ibid., p. 203; for Lothian's report on the meeting, see pp. 330–45.

176. Ibid., p. 206.

177. TNA, PREM 1/215, pp. 1–15.

178. Butler, *Lord Lothian*, pp. 222–24.

179. Ibid., p. 227.

180. See Kershaw, *Making Friends with Hitler*, p. 243.

181. Self, *Chamberlain Diary Letters*, vol. 4, p. 456.

182. Ibid., pp. 466–67.

183. Ibid., p. 458.

184. On the militarization of the Rhineland, see Weinberg, *Hitler's Foreign Policy*, pp. 240–63.

CHAPTER TWO

1. Édouard Daladier, a member of the Radical Party, was prime minister from January 31, 1933, until October 26, 1933, and again for a few weeks in 1934 and for two years beginning in April 1938. Bertrand de Jouvenel was a distinguished philosopher and political economist who in 1934 abandoned the Radical Party and became an advocate of right-wing politics. Joseph Paul-Boncour was a socialist who served as foreign minister on three occasions, December 1932–January 1934, January–June 1936, and in March 1938.

2. The two letters may be found in Ministère des Affaires Étrangères: Hamburg Consulat, série B, boîte 139 (à Nantes), CADN.

3. Bury, *France*, p. 254; Duroselle, *France and the Nazi Threat*, pp. xxvii–xxix.

4. Hitler, *Mein Kampf*, pp. 619, 674–75.

5. Adamthwaite, *France and the Coming of the Second World War*, p. 284.

6. Ibid., pp. 283–84; Vaïse, "Against Appeasement," p. 227.

7. Ascher, *A Community under Siege*, pp. 65–66.

8. I have relied for this information on François-Poncet's early life on Messemer, "André François-Poncet und Deutschland," pp. 506–8; Craig and Gilbert, *The Diplomats*, pp. 460–64; and Schäfer, *André François-Poncet als Botschafter*, pp. 25–39.

9. See Messemer, "André François-Poncet und Deutschland," pp. 509–11.

10. François-Poncet, *The Fateful Years*, pp. 50, 62, 257–58.

11. Cameron, *Prologue to Appeasement*, p. 177, quoted in Ford, "Three Observers," p. 464.

12. Ford, "Three Observers," p. 470.

13. Picker, *Hitlers Tischgespräche*, p. 106.

14. Ibid., pp. 105–6.

15. DDF, 1re série, tome I, pp. 125, 131; Messemer, "André François-Poncet und Deutschland," p. 520.

16. DDF, 1re série, tome I, p. 217.

17. DDF, 1re série, tome II, pp. 689–90.

18. Ibid., pp. 264–66.

19. Ibid., pp. 526–29.

20. Ibid., p. 539.

21. Ibid., p. 543.

22. Ibid., pp. 580–85.

23. Ibid., pp. 744–45.

24. DDF, 1re série, tome III, pp. 156–61.

25. Ibid., pp. 189–91.

26. Ibid., pp. 255–56; 1re série, tome IV, p. 275.

27. DDF, 1re série, tome IV, pp. 42–43. For a biographical sketch of Schmitt, see Evans, *The Third Reich in Power*, pp. 352–55.

28. DDF, 1re série, tome III, pp. 459–60.

29. François-Poncet developed this argument in the dispatch in ibid., pp. 459–63.

30. Ibid., p. 343.

31. DDF, 1re série, tome V, pp. 12–19, 102.

32. The two preceding paragraphs are based on dispatches in DDF, 1re série, tome V, pp. 104–7, 122–23, 203, 244–47. On the SA, see François-Poncet's dispatch of December 14, 1933, in DDF, 1re série, tome V, pp. 259–63.

33. See DDF, 1re série, tome V, pp. 393, 728–29.

34. François-Poncet, *The Fateful Years*, pp. 123, 127–28.

35. DDF, 1re série, tome VI, p. 562.

36. François-Poncet, *The Fateful Years*, pp. 125–26; Duroselle, *France and the Nazi Threat*, pp. 28, 61.

37. For more details on the Night of the Long Knives, see the comprehensive account in Kershaw, *Hitler, 1889–1936*, pp. 502 ff.

38. DDF, 1re série, tome VI, pp. 890–91.

39. Ibid., p. 863.

40. Ibid., pp. 853, 856, 873.

41. Ibid., p. 857.

42. On this point, see Kershaw, *Hitler, 1889–1936*, p. 503.

43. DDF, 1re série, tome VI, p. 886.

44. Ibid., p. 999.

45. Ibid., p. 998.

46. Kershaw, *Hitler, 1889–1936*, p. 526.

47. DDF, 1re série, tome VII, pp. 75–76.

48. Ibid., pp. 125–26.
49. Ibid., pp. 364–66.
50. Ibid., pp. 768–70.
51. Ibid., pp. 854–56.
52. Ibid., p. 855.
53. DDF, 1ʳᵉ série, tome IX, pp. 38, 40–41.
54. Ibid., p. 579.
55. DDF, 1ʳᵉ série, tome X, p. 69.
56. Ibid., pp. 69, 102.
57. DDF, 1ʳᵉ série, tome XI, pp. 275–77.
58. François-Poncet, *The Fateful Years*, pp. 196–97.
59. DDF, 1ʳᵉ série, tome XI, pp. 238–41.
60. Kershaw, *Hitler, 1889–1936*, pp. 563–64.
61. DDF, 1ʳᵉ série, tome XII, pp. 350–55. For additional reports on Nazi persecution of the Jews, see unpublished documents scattered in diplomatic reports from Germany located in CADN.
62. DDF, 1ʳᵉ série, tome XIII, pp. 384–85, 402–3.
63. Ibid., pp. 423–28.
64. For more on Phipps's meeting with Hitler, see above, p. 33.
65. DDF, 1ʳᵉ série, tome XIII, pp. 603–4.
66. DDF, 2ᵉ série, tome I, pp. 399, 462.
67. Ibid., pp. 462–67, 660.
68. Ibid., pp. 578–80.
69. See ibid., pp. 593–600, for the entire dispatch.
70. DDF, 2ᵉ série, tome II, pp. 170–71.
71. Ibid., pp. 262–63.
72. Ibid., pp. 279, 478.
73. DDF, 2ᵉ série, tome III, pp. 277–78, 290–97.
74. Ibid., pp. 496–500.
75. DDF, 2ᵉ série, tome V, pp. 363–65.
76. Ibid., pp. 532–34.
77. Kershaw, *Hitler, 1936–1945*, p. 53. For a thorough account of the two events of early 1938, see pp. 51–60.
78. DDF, 2ᵉ série, tome VIII, pp. 211–12; see also Kershaw, *Hitler, 1936–1945*, p. 57.
79. See DDF, 2ᵉ série, tome VIII, pp. 274–91, for the entire dispatch in which François-Poncet makes this argument.
80. Ibid., p. 358.
81. See ibid., pp. 493–506, for the entire dispatch.
82. Ibid., pp. 782–83.
83. DDF, 2ᵉ série, tome X, pp. 92–93.
84. *The Economist*, Feb. 3, 1938, p. 279.
85. DDF, 2ᵉ série, tome X, pp. 159–60.
86. DDF, 2ᵉ série, tome XI, p. 368.
87. Ibid., pp. 589, 591, 646–49.
88. DDF, 2ᵉ série, tome XII, p. 34.

89. DDF, 2ᵉ série, tome VI, pp. 883–92.

90. On François-Poncet's move to Italy and his activities there, see Messemer, "André François-Poncet und Deutschland," p. 533.

91. Ibid., p. 505.

92. Craig and Gilbert, *The Diplomats*, p. 555.

93. On Coulondre and Nazism, see Adamthwaite, *France and the Coming of the Second World War*, p. 153.

94. DDF, 2ᵉ série, tome XII, pp. 732–33, 752–53.

95. Ibid., pp. 853–54; tome XIII, pp. 210–12.

96. Goebbels had fallen in love with an exotic actress and wanted to make her part of his family by establishing a ménage à trois, which would also include his five children. When Hitler heard of this plan, he was "deeply shaken." Under no circumstances did he want another scandal in the top echelon of the Nazi Party. He summoned Goebbels and ordered him to end the relationship. See Reuth, *Goebbels*, p. 226, and Kershaw, *Hitler, 1936–1945*, p. 145.

97. DDF, 2ᵉ série, tome XII, pp. 569–73.

98. DDF, 2ᵉ série, tome XIII, p. 252.

99. Ibid., p. 629.

100. See ibid., pp. 281–84, for the entire dispatch.

101. DDF, 2ᵉ série, tome XIV, pp. 210–15.

102. Ibid., pp. 104–5.

103. DDF, 2ᵉ série, tome XV, pp. 17–18.

104. This paragraph is based on information in Duroselle, *France and the Nazi Threat*, pp. xxxi–xxxiii, and Wright, *France in Modern Times*, p. 494.

105. Jackson, *Politics of Depression*, p. 2.

106. Bury, *France*, p. 258.

107. On French pacifism, see Ingram, *The Politics of Dissent*.

108. Wright, *France in Modern Times*, pp. 473–75. On the Stavisky affair, see Jankowski, *Stavisky*.

109. Quoted in Colton, *Léon Blum*, p. 203. On Blum's foreign policy, see also Jackson, *The Popular Front*, pp. 189–214.

110. This paragraph is based largely on Colton, *Léon Blum*, pp. 84–85, 117–22, 177. See also Duroselle, *France and the Nazi Threat*, p. 235.

111. Wright, *France in Modern Times*, p. 472.

112. Colton, *Léon Blum*, p. 199.

113. Ibid.

114. Steiner, *Triumph of the Dark*, p. 612.

CHAPTER THREE

1. Quoted in Offner, *American Appeasement*, p. 216.

2. Breitman and Kraut, *American Refugee Policy*, pp. 64–65.

3. Weinberg, *Hitler's Foreign Policy*, p. 352.

4. FRUS, 1930, vol. III, pp. 90–91.

5. Ibid., p. 89.

6. Burke, *Ambassador Frederick Sackett*, pp. 73–74.

7. Ibid., pp. 185–87.

8. FRUS, 1930, vol. III, pp. 77–79.

9. Ibid., pp. 85–86.

10. On Schickedanz, see Kellogg, *The Roots of Nazism*, pp. 42, 82, 83, 90, 128, 203, 211, 214, 252. On Rosenberg, see Kershaw, *Hitler, 1889–1936*, p. 298.

11. FRUS, 1930, vol. III, p. 81; the account of the conversation with Schickedanz may be found on pages 79–83.

12. Ibid., p. 83.

13. FRUS, 1932, vol. III, pp. 276–77.

14. Ibid., pp. 278–81.

15. The letter by John Wiley can be found in FRUS, 1932, vol. II, pp. 281–86.

16. Ibid., pp. 295, 296.

17. Ibid., p. 299.

18. Ibid., p. 297.

19. Ibid., p. 303.

20. Ibid., pp. 303, 306–9.

21. Ibid., pp. 309–13.

22. Craig, *Germany, 1866–1945*, p. 568.

23. FRUS, 1933, vol. II, pp. 183–87.

24. Ibid., pp. 198–91, 199.

25. Ibid., pp. 193–98.

26. Ibid., p. 216.

27. Ibid., p. 209.

28. Ibid., pp. 210–13.

29. Ibid., pp. 236–39.

30. Ibid., p. 223.

31. Ibid., p. 286. For Dodd's use of the term, see p. 277.

32. Ibid., pp. 313–21.

33. Ibid., pp. 236–39.

34. Ibid., pp. 239–40.

35. Ibid., p. 245. On the conflict between the Evangelical Church and the Nazis, see below, pp. 162–68.

36. Ibid., pp. 244, 245.

37. Ibid., p. 397.

38. On Dodd, see the fine biography by Dallek, *Democrat and Diplomat*.

39. FRUS, 1933, vol. II, pp. 251–54.

40. Ibid., p. 256.

41. Ibid., pp. 256–59.

42. The information and quotations in the preceding two paragraphs may be found in ibid., pp. 261–68.

43. Ibid., pp. 292–94, 300–301.

44. Ibid., pp. 303, 308.

45. Ibid., p. 307; 1934, vol. II, pp. 272–73.

46. FRUS, 1934, vol. II, p. 267.

47. FRUS, 1933, vol. II, p. 311. For historical treatments of the Nazi conflicts with the churches, see Bergen, *Twisted Cross*; Evans, *The Third Reich in Power, 1993–*

1939, esp. pp. 220–60: Lewy, *The Catholic Church and Nazi Germany*; and Scholder, *Churches of the Third Reich*.

48. FRUS, 1934, vol. II, p. 275.

49. FRUS, 1933, vol. II, pp. 310–11.

50. Ibid., pp. 298–99.

51. FRUS, 1934, vol. II, pp. 265–66.

52. On Barth, see FRUS, 1935, vol. II, pp. 349–50.

53. FRUS, 1934, vol. II, pp. 265–69.

54. FRUS, 1935, vol. II, pp. 349–50.

55. Ibid., pp. 358–60.

56. Ibid., p. 361.

57. Ibid., p. 372.

58. Ibid., p. 375.

59. Lewy, *The Catholic Church and Nazi Germany*, pp. 130–32. See also Scholder, *Churches of the Third Reich*; and Conway, *Nazi Persecution of the Churches*.

60. FRUS, 1933, vol. II, p. 322.

61. Ibid., p. 329.

62. On this point, see Kershaw, *Hitler, 1889–1936*, pp. 471–72.

63. FRUS, 1933, vol. II, pp. 323, 329.

64. NA, RG59, 862.4016/615.

65. Ford, "Three Observers," p. 460; Stiller, *George S. Messersmith*, p. 40.

66. On Messersmith's biography, see Stiller, *George S. Messersmith*, pp. 1–13.

67. Ibid., p. 35.

68. FRUS, 1933, vol. III, p. 325.

69. NA, RG59, 862.4016/496.

70. Ibid., 862.4016/1103.

71. Ibid., 862.4016/496.

72. Moss, "George S. Messersmith and Nazi Germany," p. 116.

73. FRUS, 1933, vol. II, pp. 360–65. On the Nazi seizure of Jewish assets, see Aly, *Hitler's Beneficiaries*.

74. Moss, "George S. Messersmith and Nazi Germany," pp. 117–18; Stiller, *George S. Messersmith*, pp. 61, 92.

75. Stiller, *George S. Messersmith*, pp. 59, 118.

76. FRUS, 1937, vol. I, pp. 140–45; Stiller, *George S. Messersmith*, pp. 117–19.

77. FRUS, 1933, vol. II, p. 327.

78. Ibid., pp. 327–28.

79. The most sophisticated discussion of this issue is in Arad, *America, Its Jews and the Rise of Nazism*.

80. On Hull's reaction to Wise's visit, see NA, RG59, 862.4016, 155A. In late 1936, Wise met with President Roosevelt in an attempt to convince him of the precarious situation of German Jewry, but the president thought the reports on Nazi brutality were exaggerated. See Friedländer, *Nazi Germany*, vol. I, pp. 180–81.

81. NA, RG59, 862.4016/328. The appeals and petitions are located in several boxes under NA, RG59.

82. The messages are in NA, RG59, 862.4016/328, RG59, 862.4010/1066, RG59, 862.4016/53, RG59, 862.4016/71, and RG59, 862.4016/939.

83. NA, RG59, 862.4016/1010.

84. FRUS, 1933, vol. II, pp. 330–34, 359.

85. Ibid., pp. 334–35.

86. Ibid., p. 337.

87. Fischer, *Hitler & America*, p. 55.

88. FRUS, 1933, vol. II, p. 356.

89. FRUS, 1934, vol. II, pp. 297–300.

90. Ibid., pp. 218–21. See also Larson, *In the Garden of Beasts*, pp. 235–36.

91. FRUS, 1935, vol. II, p. 392.

92. Ibid., p. 395.

93. Ibid., p. 279.

94. See above, pp. 23–24, 36–38, 39–41, 76, 114, 122–23, 163, 178.

95. For Honaker's report, see NA, RG59, 862.4016/1516; the dispatch of August 23 can be found in NA, RG59, 862.4016/1543.

96. FRUS, 1934, vol. II, pp. 510–12.

97. On the trial, see Anthes, "Publicity Delivers Drama."

98. NA, RG59, 862.4015/1515 GDG.

99. FRUS, 1937, vol. II, pp. 320–22.

100. FRUS, 1938, vol. II, pp. 389–90.

101. FRUS, 1937, vol. II, p. 324.

102. Adams's report may be found in NA, RG59, 862.6112/5.

103. On Adams's account of his visit to the camp, see also the interesting article "Observing a Dictatorship" by Strupp, especially pp. 90–91.

104. NA, RG59, 123 Adams, Ware/107.

105. See Dallek, *Democrat and Diplomat*, pp. 294–97; Stiller, *George S. Messersmith*, p. 93.

106. See Stiller, *George S. Messersmith*, p. 129.

107. Ibid.

108. Ibid.

109. Wilson, *Career Diplomat*, p. 65. See also Offner, *American Appeasement*, pp. 214–15.

110. FRUS, 1938, vol. II, pp. 435–37.

111. Ibid., pp. 365–67.

112. Ibid., pp. 367–68. On "popular sentiment" in Austria during the Nazi era, see the excellent study by Bukey, *Hitler's Austria*.

113. FRUS, 1938, vol. II, pp. 374–75.

114. Ibid., pp. 376–77.

115. Ibid., pp. 380–82.

116. Ibid., pp. 389–90.

117. Ibid., p. 395.

118. Reports on Kristallnacht and subsequent repressive measures by the German government can be found in ibid., pp. 395–97, 399–418. For a recent, comprehensive account of Kristallnacht, see Steinweis, *Kristallnacht*.

119. For the entire dispatch, see NA, RG59, 862.4016/2019.

120. NA, RG59, 862.4016/1893.

121. FRUS, 1938, vol. II, pp. 396–98.

122. Stiller, *George S. Messersmith*, p. 131.

123. Freidel, *Franklin Roosevelt*, p. 314.

124. FRUS, 1938, vol. II, p. 399.

125. Ibid., p. 405.

126. Ibid., pp. 456–57.

127. For more details, see ibid., pp. 408–9.

128. FRUS, 1939, vol. II, pp. 582–83.

129. Ibid., pp. 584–86.

130. Ibid., pp. 588–89.

131. NA, RG59, 862.4016/1975.

132. The different figures for Germany's population cited in this study reflect the unavailability of precise numbers.

133. Quoted in Weinberg, *Hitler's Foreign Policy*, p. 155.

134. Kennedy, *Freedom from Fear*, p. 158; Casey, *Cautious Crusade*, pp. 4–8; Fischer, *Hitler & America*, p. 280.

135. Fischer, *Hitler & America*, p. 131.

136. The letter is in NA, RG59, Central Decimal File 1930–39, 862.4016/1882, Box 6789.

137. The exchange of letters may be found in NA, F.W. 862.4016/2074.

138. Quotations are from Fischer, *Hitler & America*, pp. 57–58.

139. Dinnerstein, *Anti-Semitism*, pp. 78–127; Arad, *America, Its Jews and the Rise of Nazism*, p. 106; Hamerow, *Why We Watched*, pp. 130–31.

140. Hamerow, *Why We Watched*, p. 137.

141. FRUS, 1934, vol. II, p. 293.

142. NA, RG59, 862.4016/1538.

143. Ibid., 862.4016/1532.

144. Gellman, *Secret Affairs*, p. 98.

CONCLUSION

1. A. Dirk Moses, review of *Hitler's Empire* by Mark Mazower, *American Historical Review*, vol. 115, no. 3, June 2010, pp. 885–86.

2. Shepherd, *George Lansbury*, p. 340. For a more detailed discussion of Lansbury's interview with Hitler, see Lukowitz, "George Lansbury's Peace Mission."

3. TNA, FO 371/16721, p. 118.

4. Browning and Matthaus, *Origins of the Final Solution*, p. 425.

5. See Aly, *Architects of Annihilation*.

6. Browning, "Beyond 'Intentionalism.'"

7. Ibid., p. 88.

8. Redlich, *Hitler*, p. 338.

9. Ibid., p. 359.

10. Casey, *Cautious Crusade*, p. 4; Hooker, *Moffat Papers*, p. 183.

11. Churchill, *Gathering Storm*, p. iv.

Bibliography

Adamthwaite, Antony. *France and the Coming of the Second World War, 1936–1939.* London, 1977.

——. "France and the Coming of War." In Wolfgang Mommsen and Lothar Kettbacker, eds. *The Fascist Challenge and the Policy of Appeasement*, pp. 245–56. London, 1983.

Adler, Selig. *The Isolationist Impulse: Its Twentieth Century Reaction.* London, 1957.

Aly, Götz, and Suzanne Heim. *Architects of Annihilation: Auschwitz and the Logic of Destruction.* Tr. A. G. Blunden. Princeton, N.J., 2002.

——. *Hitler's Beneficiaries: Plunder, Racial War, and the Nazi Welfare State.* Tr. Jefferson Chace. New York, 2006.

——. *Warum die Deutschen? Warum die Juden? Gleichheit, Neid und Rassenhass–1899 bis 1933.* Frankfurt, 2011.

Anderson, Brian C. "Bertrand de Jouvenel's Liberalism," *Public Interest* (Spring 2001): 87–104.

Anderson, Mosa. *Noel Buston: A Life.* London, 1952.

Anthes, Louis. "Publicity Delivers Drama: The 1934 Mock Trial of Adolf Hitler for Crimes against Civilization," *American Journal of Legal History*, vol. II (October 1934): 391–40.

Arad, Gulie Ne'eman. *America, Its Jews and the Rise of Nazism.* Bloomington, Ind., 2000.

Aronson, Shlomo. *Hitler, the Allies, and the Jews.* Cambridge, UK, 2005.

Ascher, Abraham. *A Community under Siege: The Jews of Breslau under Nazism.* Stanford, Calif., 2007.

——. "Was Hitler a Riddle?," *Journal of Historical Studies*, vol. IX, no. 1 (March 2009): 1–21.

Aster, Sidney, ed. *Appeasement and All Souls: A Portrait with Documents, 1937–1939.* London, 2004.

Bajohr, Frank. *"Aryanization" in Hamburg: The Economic Exclusion of Jews and the Confiscation of Their Property in Nazi Germany.* New York, 2002.

———, and Dieter Pohl. *Der Holocaust als offenes Geheimnis: Die Deutschen, die NS-Führung und die Allierten*. Munich, 2006.

Bankier, David, ed. *Probing the Depths of German Antisemitism: German Society and the Persecution of the Jews*. New York, 1999.

Barkai, Avraham. *From Boycott to Annihilation: The Economic Struggle of German Jews*. Tr. William Templer. London, 1989.

Beevor, Antony. *The Battle for Spain: The Spanish Civil War*. New York, 2006.

Bell, P. M. H. *The Origins of the Second World War in Europe*. Third edition. London, 2007.

Benz, Wolfgang. *Die Juden in Deutschland 1933–1945. Leben unter nationalsozialistische Herrschaft*. Munich, 1996.

Bergen, Doris L. *Twisted Cross: The German Christian Movement in the Third Reich*. Chapel Hill, N.C., 1996.

Birkenhead, Frederick W. F. S. *Halifax: The Life of Lord Halifax*. Boston, 1966.

Bracher, Karl Dietrich. *The German Dictatorship: Origins, Structure, and Consequences of National Socialism*. Harlow, Essex, UK, 1991.

Breitman, Richard. "American Diplomatic Records Regarding German Public Opinion during the Nazi Regime." In Bankier, ed., *Probing the Depths of German Antisemitism*, pp. 501–10.

———. *The Architect of Genocide: Himmler and the Final Solution*. Waltham, Mass., 1992.

———. *Official Secrets: What the Nazis Planned, What the British and Americans Knew*. Waltham, Mass., 1999.

Breitman, Richard, and Alan M. Kraut. *American Refugee Policy and European Jewry, 1933–1945*. Bloomington, Ind., 1987.

Breitman, Richard, Barbara McDonald, and Severin Hochberg, eds. *Advocate for the Doomed: The Diaries and Papers of James McDonald*. Bloomington, Ind., 2007.

Browning, Christopher R. "Beyond 'Intentionalism' and 'Functionalism': The Decision for the Final Solution Reconsidered." In Christopher R. Browning, *The Path to Genocide: Essays on Launching the Final Solution*, pp. 86–124. New York, 1992.

Browning, Christopher R., and Jürgen Matthaus. *The Origins of the Final Solution: The Evolution of Nazi Jewish Policy, September 1939–March 1942*. Lincoln, Neb., 2004.

Bukey, Evan Burr. *Hitler's Austria: Popular Sentiment in the Nazi Era*. Chapel Hill, N.C., 2000.

Bullock, Alan. "Hitler and the Origins of the Second World War." In E. M. Robertson, ed., *The Origins of the Second World War*, pp. 189–224. London, 1971.

———. *Hitler: A Study of Tyranny*. New York, 1960.

Burke, Bernard V. *Ambassador Frederick Sackett and the Collapse of the Weimar Republic, 1930–1933*. Cambridge, UK, 2003.

Bury, J. P. T. *France, 1814–1940*. Philadelphia, 1949.

Butler, J. R. M. *Lord Lothian (Philip Kerr) 1882–1940*. New York, 1960.

Butterworth, Susan B. "Daladier and the Munich Crisis: A Reappraisal," *Journal of Contemporary History*, no. 9 (July 1974): 191–216.

Cameron, Elizabeth R. *Prologue to Appeasement. A Study of French Foreign Policy, 1933–36*. Washington, D.C., 1942.

Carlton, David. *Anthony Eden: A Biography*. London, 1981.

Carr, E. H. *Britain: A Study of Foreign Policy from the Versailles Treaty to the Outbreak of War*. New York, 1939.

Carsten, Francis Ludwig. *Britain and the Weimar Republic: The British Documents*. London, 1984.

Casey, Steven. *Cautious Crusade: FDR, American Public Opinion and the War against Nazi Germany*. New York, 2009.

Ceadel, Martin. "The First British Referendum: The Peace Ballot, 1934–5," *English Historical Review*, vol. 95 (1980): 810–39.

Challener, Richard D. *From Isolation to Containment: Three Decades of American Foreign Policy from Harding to Truman (Documents of Modern History)*. New York, 1970.

Chamberlain, Neville. *The Neville Chamberlain Diary Letters*. Vol. 4. Ed. Robert C. Self. London, 2005.

Charmley, J. *Chamberlain and the Lost Peace*. London, 1989.

Churchill, Winston S. *The Gathering Storm*. Boston, 1948.

Clark, Robert T. *The Fall of the German Republic*. London, 1935.

Clemens, Detlev. *Herr Hitler in Germany. Wahrnehmung und Deutung des National-sozialismus in Grossbritannien 1920 bis 1939*. Göttingen and Zürich, 1966.

Colton, Joel. *Leon Blum, Humanist in Politics*. Cambridge, Mass., 1966.

Colvin, Ian Goodhope. *The Chamberlain Cabinet: How the Meetings in 10 Downing Street, 1937–39, Led to the Second World War, Told for the First Time from Cabinet Papers*. London, 1971.

———. *Vansittart in Office*. London, 1945.

Combs, William L. *The Voice of the SS: A History of the SS Journal 'Das Schwarze Korps.'* New York, 1986.

Conradi, Peter. *Hitler's Piano Player: The Rise and Fall of Ernst Hanfstaengl: Confidant of Hitler, Ally of Roosevelt*. New York, 2004.

Conway, J. S. *The Nazi Persecution of the Churches*. London, 1968.

Conwell-Evans, T. P. *None so Bland*. London, 1947.

Conze, Eckart, Norbert Frey, Peter Hayes, Moshe Zimmerman. *Das Amt und die Vergangenheit: Deutsche Diplomaten im Dritten Reich und der Bundesrepublik*. Munich, 2010.

Coulondre, Robert. *De Staline à Hitler: souvenirs de deux ambassades, 1936–1939*. Paris, 1950.

Cowling, Robert. *The Impact of Hitler: British Policy and British Politics 1933–1940*. Chicago, 1977.

Craig, Gordon A. "The British Foreign Office from Grey to Austen Chamberlain." In Craig and Gilbert, eds., *The Diplomats, 1919–1939*, pp. 15–48.

———. *Germany 1866–1945*. New York, 1978.

———. "High Tide of Appeasement: The Road to Munich, 1937–1938," *Political Science Quarterly*, vol. 65 (1950): 20–37.

Craig, Gordon A., and Felix Gilbert, eds. *The Diplomats, 1919–1939*. Princeton, 1994.

Cross, J. A. *Sir Samuel Hoare: A Political Biography*. London, 1977.

Dallek, Robert. "Beyond Tradition: The Diplomatic Career of William E. Dodd and George S. Messersmith, 1933–1938," *South Atlantic Quarterly* (Spring, 1967): 233–44.

———. *Democrat and Diplomat: The Life of William E. Dodd.* New York, 1968.

———. *Franklin D. Roosevelt and American Foreign Policy, 1932–1945.* New York, 1995.

Dawson, Robert MacGregor. *William Lyon Mackenzie King, a Political Biography.* Toronto, 1958.

Dinnerstein, Leonard. *Anti-Semitism in America.* New York, 1994.

Dockrill, Michael, and Brian McKercher, eds. *Diplomacy and World Power: Studies in British Foreign Policy, 1890–1950.* Cambridge, UK, 1996.

Documents on British Foreign Policy, 1919–1939. Second Series. London, 1946– .

Dodd, Martha. *Through Embassy Eyes.* New York, 1939.

Dodd, William E., and Martha Dodd, eds. *Ambassador Dodd's Diary, 1933–1938.* New York, 1941.

Duroselle, Jean-Baptiste. *France and the Nazi Threat: The Collapse of French Diplomacy, 1932–1939.* Translation of *La Décadence 1932–1939* by Catherine E. Dop and Robert I. Miller. New York, 2004.

Dutton, David. *Anthony Eden: A Life and Reputation.* London, 1997.

———. *Neville Chamberlain.* New York, 2001.

———. *A Political Biography of Sir John Simon.* London, 1992.

Eden, Anthony. *The Memoirs of Anthony Eden: Facing the Dictators.* Cambridge, Mass., 1962.

Elias, Norbert. *Reflections on a Life.* Tr. Edmund Jephcott. Cambridge, UK, 1994.

Evans, Richard J. *The Coming of the Third Reich.* New York, 2004.

———. *The Third Reich at War.* New York, 2009.

———. *The Third Reich in Power, 1933–1939.* New York, 2005.

Feiling, Sir Keith. *The Life of Neville Chamberlain.* London, 1946.

Feingold, Henry. *Did American Jews Do Enough during the Holocaust?* Syracuse, N.Y., 1985.

———. *The Politics of Rescue: The Roosevelt Administration and the Holocaust.* New Brunswick, N.J., 1970.

Ferguson, Niall. *The War of the World: Twentieth-Century Conflict and the Descent of the West.* London, 2006.

Fischer, Klaus P. *Hitler & America.* Philadelphia, 2011.

Ford, Franklin L. "Three Observers in Berlin: Rumbold, Dodd, and François-Poncet." In Craig and Gilbert, eds., *The Diplomats,* pp. 437–76.

Ford, Franklin L., and Carl E. Schorske. "The Voice in the Wilderness: Robert Coulondre." In Craig and Gilbert, eds., *The Diplomats,* pp. 555–78.

François-Poncet, André. *The Fateful Years.* London, 1949.

Freidel, Frank. *Franklin Roosevelt: A Rendezvous with Destiny.* Boston, 1990.

Friedländer, Saul. *Nazi Germany and the Jews.* Volume I: *The Years of Persecution, 1933–1939.* New York, 1997. Volume II: *The Years of Extermination.* New York, 2007.

Fromm, Bella. *Blood and Banquets: A Berlin Diary.* New York, 1942.

Fuchser, Larry William. *Neville Chamberlain and Appeasement: A Study in the Politics of History.* New York, 1982.

Gannon, Franklin Reid. *The British Press and Germany, 1936–1939.* Oxford, UK, 1971.

Gellman, Irwin F. *Secret Affairs: FDR, Cordell Hull and Sumner Welles.* Baltimore and London, 1995.

Gilbert, Felix. "Two German Ambassadors: Perth and Henderson." In Craig and Gilbert, *The Diplomats*, pp. 537–54.

Gilbert, Martin. *Churchill: A Life*. London, 1991.

———. *Sir Horace Rumbold: Portrait of a Diplomat, 1859–1941*. London, 1973.

———. *Winston S. Churchill*. Volume V: *1922–1939*. London, 1979.

Gilbert, Martin, and Richard Gott. *The Appeasers*. Boston, 1963.

Goldman, Aaron. "Two Views of Germany: Nevile Henderson versus Vansittart and the Foreign Office," *British Journal of International Studies*, no. 6 (1980): 247–77.

Granzow, Brigitte. *A Mirror of Nazism: British Opinion and the Emergence of Hitler, 1929–1933*. London, 1964.

Gross, G. A. *Sir Samuel Hoare: A Political Biography*. London, 1977.

Halifax, Eduard Frederick Lindley Wood, Earl of. *Fullness of Days*. London, 1957.

Hamerow, Theodore S. *Why We Watched: Europe, America, and the Holocaust*. New York, 2008.

Hauser, Oswald. "Der Botschafter François-Poncet und Deutschland." In Albert Barrera-Vidal, ed., *Lebendige Romania: Festschrift für Hans-Wilhelm Klein*, pp. 125–42. Göppingen, Germany, 1976.

Havighurst, Alfred F. *Twentieth Century Britain*. Second Edition. New York, 1962.

Henderson, Sir Nevile. *Failure of a Mission: Berlin 1937–1939*. New York, 1940.

———. "Final Report by the Right Honorable Sir Nevile Henderson, G.C.M.G., on the Circumstances Leading to the Termination of His Mission to Berlin, September 20, 1939." London, 1939.

Herman, John. *The Paris Embassy of Sir Eric Phipps, Anglo-French Relations and the Foreign Office 1937–1939*. Brighton, Sussex, UK, 1998.

Herzstein, Robert Edwin. *Roosevelt and Hitler: Prelude to War*. New York, 1989.

Hinton, Harold B. *Cordell Hull—A Biography*. New York, 1942.

Hitler, Adolf. *Mein Kampf*. Tr. Ralph Manheim. Boston, 1971.

Hooker, Nancy Harrison, ed. *The Moffat Papers. Selections from the Diplomatic Journals of Jay Pierrepont Moffat, 1919–1943*. Cambridge, Mass., 1956.

Hörling, Hans. "L'Opinion française face à l'avènement d'Hitler au pouvoir," *Francia*, 2 (1975): 584–641.

Howard, Michael. *The Lessons of History*. New Haven, Conn., 1991.

Howard, Peter, Frank Owen, and Michael Foot. *Guilty Men*. London, 1940.

Hull, Cordell. *The Memoirs of Cordell Hull*. 2 vols. London, 1948.

Hurd, Douglas. *Choose Your Weapons: The British Foreign Secretary, 200 Years of Argument, Success and Failure*. London, 2010.

Ingram, Norman. *The Politics of Dissent: Pacifism in France, 1919–1939*. Oxford, UK, 1991.

Jackson, Julian. *The Politics of Depression in France, 1932–1936*. New York, 1985.

———. *The Popular Front in France: Defending Democracy, 1934–38*. Cambridge, UK, 1990.

Jackson, Peter. *France and the Nazi Menace: Intelligence and Policy Making 1933–1939*. Oxford, UK, 2001.

———. "French Intelligence and Hitler's Rise to Power," *Historical Journal*, vol. 4 (Sept. 1981): 795–824.

James, Robert Rhodes. *Churchill: A Study in Failure, 1900–1939.* London, 1940.

Jankowski, Paul E. *Stavisky: A Confidence Man in the Republic of Virtue.* Ithaca, N.Y., 2002.

Jaroch, Matthias. *Too Much Wit and Not Enough Warning? Sir Eric Phipps als Britischer Botschafter in Berlin von 1933 bis 1937.* Frankfurt am Main, 1999.

Johnson, Gaynor. *The Berlin Embassy of Lord D'Abernon, 1920–1926.* New York, 2002.

———. "Sir Eric Phipps, the British Government and the Appeasement of Germany, 1933–1937," *Diplomacy and Statecraft,* vol. 16 (no. 4): 651–69.

———, ed. *The Foreign Office and British Diplomacy in the Twentieth Century.* London, 2005.

———. *Our Man in Berlin: The Diary of Sir Eric Phipps, 1933–1937.* Chippenham and Eastbourne, UK, 2008.

Jones, Kenneth Paul. *United States Diplomats in Europe, 1919–41.* Santa Barbara, Calif., 1981.

Jones, Thomas. *A Diary with Letters, 1931–50.* London, 1954.

Kaufmann, William W. "Two American Ambassadors: Bullitt and Kennedy." In Craig and Gilbert, eds., *The Diplomats,* pp. 649–81.

Kellogg, Michael. *The Roots of Nazism: White Emigrés and the Making of National Socialism, 1917–1945.* Cambridge, UK, 2005.

Kennedy, David M. *Freedom from Fear: The American People in Depression and War, 1929–1945.* New York, 1999.

Kershaw, Ian. *Hitler, 1889–1936: Hubris.* New York, 1999.

———. *Hitler, 1936–45: Nemesis.* London, 2001.

———. *Making Friends with Hitler: Lord Londonderry, the Nazis and the Road to World War II.* New York, 2004.

Kirkpatrick, Sir Ivone. *The Inner Circle: The Memoirs of Ivone Kirkpatrick.* London, 1959.

Kimmel, Adolf. *Der Aufstieg des Nationalsozialismus im Spiegel der französischen Presse, 1930–1933.* Bonn, 1969.

Klein, Burton H. *Germany's Economic Preparations for War.* Cambridge, Mass., 1959.

Langworth, Richard, ed. *Churchill by Himself: The Definitive Collection of Quotations.* New York, 2008.

Lansbury, George. *My Quest for Peace.* London, 1938.

Larson, Erik. *In the Garden of Beasts: Love, Terror, and an American Family in Hitler's Berlin.* New York, 2011.

Lear, Lina J. *Harold L. Ickes: The Aggressive Progressive, 1874–1933.* New York, 1981.

Leff, Laurel. *Buried by the Times: The Holocaust and America's Most Important Newspaper.* New York, 2005.

Lewy, Guenter. *The Catholic Church and Nazi Germany.* New York, 1964.

Lipstadt, Deborah. *Beyond Belief: The American Press and the Coming of the Holocaust, 1933–1945.* New York, 1986.

Loewenheim, Francis L. *Peace or Appeasement? Hitler, Chamberlain, and the Munich Crisis.* Boston, 1965.

London, Louise. *Whitehall and the Jews, 1933–1948.* Cambridge, UK, 2002.

Lukasz, John R. *Blood, Toil, and Sweat: The Dire Warning.* New York, 2009.

——. *The Hitler of History*. New York, 1997.

Lukowitz, David C. "British Pacifists and Appeasement: The Peace Pledge Union," *Journal of Contemporary History*, vol. 9, no. 1 (Jan. 1994): 115–27.

——. "George Lansbury's Peace Mission to Hitler and Mussolini in 1937," *Canadian Journal of History*, vol. 15 (1980): 67–82.

Macklin, Graham. *Chamberlain (20th Century PM)*. London, 2006.

MacMillan, Margaret. *Paris 1919: Six Months That Changed the World*. New York, 2002.

Marquand, David. *Ramsay MacDonald*. London, 1977.

May, Ernest R. *Strange Victory: Hitler's Conquest of France*. New York, 2000.

McKercher, Brian. "Old Diplomacy and New: The Foreign Office and Foreign Policy, 1919–1939." In Dockrill and McKercher, eds., *Diplomacy and World Power*, pp. 79–114.

Medlicott, William Norton. *Britain and Germany: The Search for Agreement, 1930–1937*. London, 1969.

Messemer, Annette. "André François-Poncet und Deutschland: Die Jahre zwischen den Kriegen," *Vierteljahreshefte für Zeitgeschichte*, vol. 39 (1991): 505–34.

Middlemas, Keith. *Diplomacy of Illusion: The British Government and Germany, 1937–1939*. London, 1972.

Middlemas, Keith, and John Barnes. *Baldwin: A Biography*. London, 1969.

Miller, Philip Douglas. *You Can't Do Business with Hitler*. New York, 1941.

Morgan, Kenneth. *Lloyd George*. Worthing, UK, 1974.

Morgan, Ted. *FDR: A Biography*. New York, 1985.

Morris, Benny. *The Roots of Appeasement: The British Weekly Press and Nazi Germany during the 1930s*. London, 1991.

Mosley, Leonard. *On Borrowed Time: How World War II Began*. New York, 1969.

Moss, Kenneth. "George S. Messersmith and Nazi Germany: The Diplomacy of Limits in Central Europe," *Delaware History*, vol. 7 (Fall 1977): 236–49.

Mowat, C. L. "Baldwin Restored?," *Journal of Modern History*, vol. 27 (June 1955): 169–74.

Mühle, Robert W. *Frankreich und Hitler, 1933–1935*. Paderborn, Germany, 1995.

Nagorski, Andrew. *Hitlerland: American Eyewitnesses to the Nazi Rise to Power*. New York, 2012.

Namier, L. B. *Diplomatic Prelude 1938–1939*. London, 1948.

Neville, Peter. *Appeasing Hitler: The Diplomacy of Sir Nevile Henderson, 1937–39*. New York, 2000.

——. "The Appointment of Sir Nevile Henderson, 1937: Design or Blunder?," *Journal of Contemporary History*. vol. 38 (1998): 609–19.

——. "The Foreign Office and Britain's Ambassadors to Berlin 1933–1939," *Contemporary British History*, vol. 18 (2004): 110–29.

——. "A Prophet Scorned? Ralph Wigram, the Foreign Office and the German Threat, 1933–36," *Journal of Contemporary History*, vol. 40 (2005): 41–54.

Newman, Michael. *Harold Laski: A Political Biography*. London, 1993.

Nicolson, Harold George, Sir. *In the Dedication of Diplomacy*. London, 1939.

Offner, Arnold A. *American Appeasement: United States Foreign Policy and Germany*. Cambridge, Mass., 1969.

——. "Appeasement Revisited: The United States, Great Britain, and Germany, 1933–1940," *Journal of American History*, vol. 64 (September, 1977): 373–93.

——. "William E. Dodd. "Romantic Historian and Diplomatic Cassandra," *The Historian*, vol. 34 (1962): 451–69.

Olson, Lynne. *Troublesome Young Men: The Rebels Who Brought Churchill to Power and Helped Save England*. New York, 2007.

Ott, Johann. *Botschafter Sir Eric Phipps und die deutsch-englischen Beziehungen: Studien zur britischen Aussenpolitik gegenüber dem Dritten Reich*. Erlangen, Germany, 1968.

Ovendale, Ritchie. *"Appeasement" and the English Speaking World: Britain, the United States, the Dominions and the Policy of "Appeasement" 1937–1939*. Cardiff, Wales, 1975.

Owen, Frank. *Tempestuous Journey: Lloyd George, His Life and Times*. New York, 1955.

Paldiel, Mordecai. *Diplomat Heroes of the Holocaust*. Jersey City, N.J., 2007.

Pappenheim, Friedrich-Carl von. *Erinnerungen des Soldaten und Diplomaten 1914–1955*. Osnabrück, Germany, 1987.

Parker, R. A. C. *Chamberlain and Appeasement: British Policy and the Coming of the Second World War*. Houndmills, UK, 1993.

Paul-Boncour, Joseph. *Entre Deux Guerres. Souvenirs sur la IIIe République: Sur les Chemins de la Défaite 1935–1940*. Paris, 1946.

Paxton, Robert O. *Vichy France: Old Guard and New Order, 1940–1944*. New York, 1972.

Payne, Stanley G. *France and Hitler: Spain, Germany, and World War II*. New Haven, Conn., 2008.

Pertinaux (André Géraud). *The Gravediggers of France*. Garden City, N.Y., 1944.

Picker, Henry. *Hitlers Tischgespräche im Führerhauptquartier*. Stuttgart, Germany, 1976.

Postgate, Raymond William. *The Life of George Lansbury*. Toronto, 1951.

Pugh, Martin. *Hurrah for the Blackshirts: Fascists and Fascism in Britain between the Wars*. London, 2005.

Redlich, Fritz. *Hitler: Diagnosis of a Destructive Prophet*. New York, 1998.

Remak, Joachim. *The Nazi Years: A Documentary History*. Longrove, Ill., 1990.

Reuth, Ralf Georg. *Goebbels*. Tr. Krishna Winston. New York, 1993.

Robbins, Keith. *Appeasement*. Oxford, UK, 2001.

——. *Present and Past: British Images of Germany in the First Half of the Twentieth Century and Their Historical Legacy*. Göttingen, Germany, 1999.

Roberts, Andrew. *The Holy Fox: The Life of Lord Halifax*. London, 1987.

Roberts, Stephen Henry. *The House That Hitler Built*. London, 1937.

Robertson, Esmonde M., ed. *The Origins of the Second World War: Historical Interpretations*. London, 1971.

Rock, William R. *British Appeasement in the 1930s*. New York, 1977.

Rose, N. *Vansittart: Study of a Diplomat*. London, 1978.

Rosen, Robert N. *Saving the Jews: Franklin Roosevelt and the Holocaust*. New York, 2006.

Russell, William. *Berlin Diary*. New York, 1962.

Salvemini, Gaetano. *Prelude to World War II*. Garden City, N.Y., 1954.

Schäfer, Claus W. *André François-Poncet als Botschafter in Berlin (1931–1938)*. Munich, 2004.

Schmitz, David F., and Richard Challener, eds. *Appeasement in Europe: A Reassessment of U.S. Policies (Contributions to the Study of World History)*. New York, 1990.

Scholder, Klaus. *The Churches of the Third Reich*. 2 vols. London, 1987–88.

Schroeder, Paul W. "Munich and the British Tradition," *Historical Journal*, vol. 19 (Jan. 1976): 223–43.

Schwoerer, Lois G. "Lord Halifax's Visit to Germany, November 1937," *The Historian*, vol. 32 (May 1970): 353–75.

Scott, Carolyn. *Dick Sheppard: A Biography*. London, 1977.

Scott, Robert E. "Neville Chamberlain and Munich: Two Aspects of Power." In L. Krieger and F. Stern, eds. *The Responsibility of Power: Historical Essays in Honor of Hajo Holborn*, pp. 381–99. Garden City, N.Y., 1969.

Self, Robert C. *Neville Chamberlain: A Biography*. Aldershot, UK, 2006.

———, ed. *The Neville Chamberlain Diary Letters*. Aldershot, UK, 2000.

Sencourt, Robert C. "The Foreign Policy of Neville Chamberlain," *Quarterly Review*, vol. 62 (April 1964): 145–55.

———. "How Neville Chamberlain Fought Hitler," *Quarterly Review*, vol. 52 (Oct. 1954): 413–25.

Shamir, Haim. "Die Kristallnacht, die Notlage der deutschen Juden und die Haltung Englands," *Jahrbuch des Instituts für Deutsche Geschichte*, vol. 1 (1972): 171–214.

Sharf, Andrew. *The British Press and Jews under Nazi Rule*. Oxford, UK, 1964.

Shed, Alan, and Chris Cook, eds. *Crisis and Controversy: Essays in Honor of A. J. P. Taylor*. London, 1976.

Shepherd, John. *George Lansbury: At the Heart of Old Labour*. Oxford, UK, 2007.

Shirer, William L. *Berlin Diary. The Journal of a Foreign Correspondent, 1934–1941*. Baltimore and London, 2002.

———. *The Collapse of the Third Republic: An Inquiry into the Fall of France*. New York, 1969.

Simon, John Allesbrook. *Retrospect: The Memoirs of the Rt. Hon. Viscount Simon*. London, 1952.

Smart, Nick. *Neville Chamberlain*. London, 2010.

Smith, Howard K. *Last Train from Berlin: An Eye-Witness Account of Germany at War*. New York, 1942.

Smith, Michael. *Foley, the Spy Who Saved 10,000 Jews*. London, 1999.

Snyder, Timothy. *Bloodlands: Europe between Hitler and Stalin*. New York, 2010.

Solo, Roselyn. "André François-Poncet as Ambassador of France." Ph.D. dissertation, Michigan State University, 1978.

Sontag, Raymond J. "The Origins of the Second World War," *Review of Politics*, vol. 35 (Oct. 1963): 497–508.

Soucy, Robert. *French Fascism: The Second Wave, 1933–1939*. New Haven, Conn., 1995.

———. "The Nature of Fascism in France," *Journal of Contemporary History*, vol. 1 (1966): 27–55.

Später, Jörg. *Vansittart: Britische Debatten über Deutsche und Nazis, 1902–1945*. Göttingen, Germany, 2003.

Stacey, Charles Percy. *A Very Double Life: The Private World of Mackenzie King*. Toronto, 1976.

———. *Mackenzie King and the Atlantic Triangle*. Toronto, 1976.

Steiner, Zara. *The Lights That Failed: European International History 1919–1933*. Oxford, 2005.

———. *The Triumph of the Dark: European International History, 1933–1939*. Oxford, 2011.

Steinweis, Alan E. *Kristallnacht*. Cambridge, Mass., 2009.

Sternhell, Zeev, and David Maisel. *Neither Right nor Left: Fascist Ideology in France*. Princeton, N.J., 1995.

Stiller, Jesse H. *George S. Messersmith, Diplomat of Democracy*. Chapel Hill, N.C., 1987.

Strang, B. "Two Unequal Tempers: Sir George Ogilvie-Forbes, Sir Nevile Henderson and British Foreign Policy," *Diplomacy and Statecraft*, vol. 5 (March 1994): 107–37.

Strauch, Rudi. *Sir Nevile Henderson, British Botschafter in Berlin, 1937 bis 1939*. Bonn, Germany, 1959.

Strupp, Christoph. "Observing a Dictatorship: American Consular Reporting on Germany, 1933–1941," *German Historical Institute Bulletin*, no. 39 (Fall 2006): 79–98.

Taylor, A. J. P. *The Origins of the Second World War*. New Edition. New York, 1996.

Thompson, Neville. *The Anti-Appeasers: Conservative Opposition in the 1930s*. Oxford, UK, 1971.

Tietze, Hans. *Die Juden Wiens: Geschichte—Wirtschaft—Kultur*. Vienna, 1987.

Tooze, Adam. *The Wages of Destruction*. New York, 2007.

Vaïse, Maurice. "Against Appeasement: French Advocates of Firmness, 1933–1938." In Wolfgang Mommsen and Lothar Kettenacker, eds., *The Fascist Challenge and the Policy of Appeasement*, pp. 227–35. London, 1983.

Vansittart, Robert. *Lessons of My Life*. London, 1943.

———. *The Mist Procession: The Autobiography of Lord Vansittart*. London, 1958.

Wächter, Detlef. *Von Stresemann zu Hitler: Deutschland 1928 bis 1933 in Spiegel der Berichte des englischen Botschafter Sir Horace Rumbold*. Frankfurt am Main, 1997.

Wala, Michael. *Weimar und Amerika: Botschafter Friedrich von Prittwitz und Gaffron und die deutsch-amerikanischen Beziehungen von 1927 bis 1933*. Stuttgart, Germany, 2001.

Wark, Wesley K. "Three Military Attachés at Berlin in the 1930s: Soldier-Statesmen and the Limits of Ambiguity," *International History Review*, vol. IX, no. 4 (1987): 586–610.

Watt, Donald Cameron. "Appeasement: The Rise of a Revisionist School?," *Political Quarterly* (April–June, 1965): 191–213.

———. "Chamberlain's Ambassadors." In M. Dockrill and R. McKercher, eds., *Diplomacy and World War*, pp. 136–70.

———. "The German Diplomats and the Nazi Leaders 1933–1939," *Journal of Central European Affairs*, vol. XV (1955): 148–60.

———. "The Historiography of Appeasement." In Alan Shed and Chris Cook, eds., *Crisis and Controversy*, pp. 10–29.

————. *Personality and Policies: Studies in the Formulation of British Foreign Policy in the Twentieth Century.* London, 1965.

Webster, A. "The Transnational Dream: Politicians, Diplomats and Soldiers in the League of Nations," *Contemporary European History*, vol. 14 (2005): 493–518.

Webster, Sir Charles. "Munich Reconsidered: A Survey of British Policy," *International Affairs* (April 1961): 137–53.

Weinberg, Gerhard L. *Hitler's Foreign Policy.* New York, 2005.

————. "Hitler's Image in the United States," *American Historical Review*, vol. 69 (July 1964): 1006–21.

Wheeler-Bennett, Sir John. *Munich—Prologue to Tragedy.* London, 1948.

Williamson, Philip. *Stanley Baldwin: Conservative Leadership and National Values.* Cambridge, UK, 1999.

Wilson, Hugh Robert. *A Career Diplomat, the Third Chapter: The Third Reich.* New York, 1961.

————. *Diplomat between Wars.* New York, 1941.

Wohl, Robert. "French Fascism: Both Right and Left Reflections on the Sternhell Controversy," *Journal of Modern History*, vol. 63 (March 1991): 91–98.

Wright, Gordon. *France in Modern Times: 1760 to the Present.* Chicago, 1960.

Young, Robert J. *France and the Origins of the Second World War.* New York, 1996.

————. *In Command of France: French Foreign Policy and Military Planning, 1933–1940.* Cambridge, Mass., 1978.

Zeck, Mario. *Das Schwarze Korps.* Tübingen, Germany, 2002.

Zucker, Bet-Am. *In Search of Refuge: Jews and U.S. Consuls in Nazi Germany.* London, 2001.

Index